The MAILBOX

SUPERBOOK

Kindergarten

Everything You Need for a Successful Year!

- **Literacy**
- **Math**
- **Science and Health**
- **Social Studies**
- **Centers**

- **Circle Time and Games**
- **Differentiation Tips**
- **Classroom Management**
- **Bulletin Boards**
- **Arts and Crafts**

And Much More!

Revised and Updated!

Managing Editor: Sharon Murphy

Editorial Team: Becky S. Andrews, Kimberley Bruck, Diane Badden, Thad H. McLaurin, Kimberly Brugger-Murphy, Lynn Drolet, Gerri Primak, Kelly Robertson, Karen A. Brudnak, Juli Docimo Blair, Hope Rodgers, Dorothy C. McKinney

Production Team: Lori Z. Henry, Pam Crane, Rebecca Saunders, Jennifer Tipton Cappoen, Chris Curry, Sarah Foreman, Theresa Lewis Goode, Greg D. Rieves, Eliseo De Jesus Santos II, Barry Slate, Donna K. Teal, Zane Williard, Tazmen Carlisle, Kathy Coop, Marsha Heim, Lynette Dickerson, Mark Rainey, Amy Kirtley-Hill, Ben Wooster

www.themailbox.com

Manufactured in the United States
10 9 8 7 6 5 4 3 2 1

TABLE OF CONTENTS

TABLE OF CONTENTS

Arts and Crafts

Holidays and Seasonal

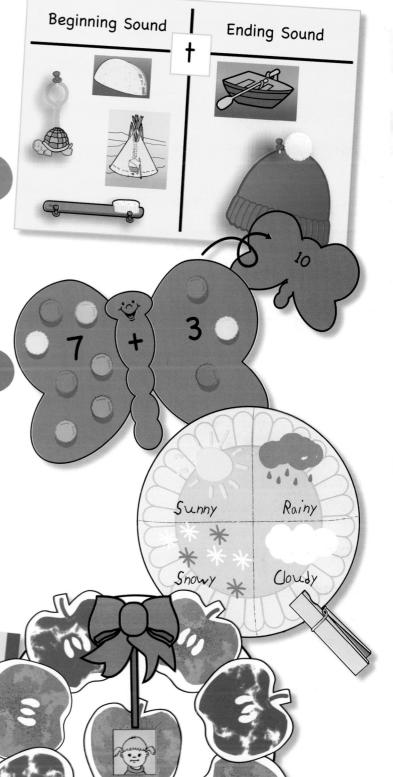

Welcome to School

Common Concerns

Kindergarten parents have many common concerns. Address them quickly and efficiently with this idea. Before school begins, send a welcome letter to each family. In the letter, invite parents to anonymously express any concerns or ask questions regarding the class, school, schedule, or any other school-related matter. Then, with each letter, enclose a self-addressed, stamped postcard for parents to use for their responses. After you receive the postcards, list each question with an appropriate response on chart paper. Display the list during your meet-the-teacher event. Parents will appreciate the attention you've shown to their concerns.

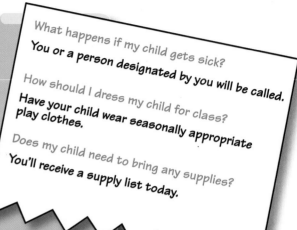

What happens if my child gets sick?
You or a person designated by you will be called.

How should I dress my child for class?
Have your child wear seasonally appropriate play clothes.

Does my child need to bring any supplies?
You'll receive a supply list today.

First-Day Folders

Important Kindergarten Information

Use these special folders to handle your kindergarten families' first-of-school anxieties. For each student's family, prepare a folder to include a parent handbook, a school calendar, transportation details, important school phone numbers, child safety information, PTA information, a class schedule, a list of suggested children's books, and a personal welcome letter from yourself and the principal. Enclose all the materials in a folder; then send the folder home with students on the first day of school. Families are sure to appreciate all this information in one handy folder.

Welcome to Kindergarten

(sung to the tune of "Deck the Halls")

Welcome to our kindergarten.
We will learn a lot of things today.
Here we are in kindergarten.
We will have a lot of time to play.
We will learn the alphabet and
We will learn how to write numbers too.
We'll have fun in kindergarten,
'Cause there are so many things to do!

First-Day Postcards

Your kindergarten families will cherish these official reminders of their little ones' first day of kindergarten. For each child, convert a plain 4" x 6" blank notecard into a postcard by printing his home address and the return address (your school's) on one side of the card. Before the end of the first day, invite each child to illustrate one of his first-day activities and then dictate a statement about his drawing. Have each child affix a stamp to the addressed side of his postcard. After class, rush the postcards to the post office for a special delivery to each youngster's home.

Pictorial Scavenger Hunt

Here's a first-day activity to put anxious students at ease right away. Make a copy of page 8 for each child. Have each youngster search to find each of the pictured items and then mark the box next to each found item as shown. This scavenger hunt is a great way to familiarize youngsters with their new classroom.

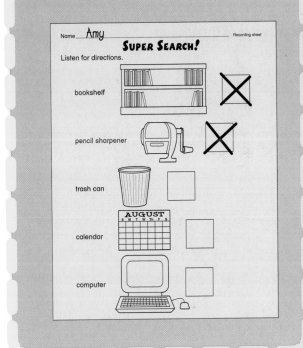

Photo Puppets

Duplicate a photograph of each child; then enlarge it onto tagboard. Cut out the child's picture and glue a craft stick to the back. Hold up one child's puppet as you lead students in singing this song to the tune of "Skip to My Lou." Then have the youngster respond to the final question in the song. Continue in the same way with each remaining child.

Hello, [child's name], how are you?
Hello, [child's name], how are you?
Hello, [child's name], how are you?
How are you this morning?

Class Directory

Help students get to know their classmates with this informative idea. At the beginning of the school year, take a photo of each child. Next, assist each child in completing a copy of the biography sheet on page 9. Glue each child's picture to his biography sheet and then laminate all the sheets. Finally, place the sheets in a three-ring binder. Have each child, in turn, take the finished directory home to share with his family. Parents will appreciate the chance to get to know their child's classmates too!

Let Me Introduce Myself

My name is _Brian Scott_

I am __6__ years old.

I have __1__ brother(s) and __1__ sister(s).

My favorite activity is

riding my bike

My favorite food is _pizza_

My favorite book is _Where the Wild Things Are_

Ms. Waterford's
Kindergarten Picture

Kindergarten of Long Ago

Show your youngsters that you were once a kid too! Display photographs of yourself when you were in kindergarten. Then share some of your favorites from that time, such as your favorite game, TV show, and book. Students will be thrilled at the chance to get the inside scoop on their teacher!

A Marvelous Mascot

Make routine activities more exciting by including a class mascot. Have the mascot help you with your morning greeting, attendance, or lunch count. Make construction paper cutouts of the mascot to use as nametags, desktags, or center signs. Have the mascot host special class events such as birthday parties or holiday celebrations. No matter where the mascot appears, he's sure to make the activity more enjoyable for your students!

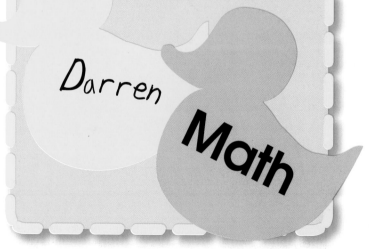

Darren

Math

Make It and Take It...Home!

Encourage students to create open house invitations to present to their families. Make one copy of the invitation on page 10; then fill in the date and time of your open house in the blank spaces on the copy. For each student, duplicate the schoolhouse pattern on red construction paper and the programmed text box on white copy paper. Have each child cut out the schoolhouse and the text box and then cut along the dotted lines. Help her glue the text box to the back of her schoolhouse so the information shows through the doors when they are folded back. Have students complete the invitations by brushing glue over the bell and then sprinkling gold glitter over the glue.

Come On In!

We're getting ready—
There's so much to do!
We're eager for guests;
We're waiting for you!
Please come
to our Open House
on _Sept. 19, 2007_
at _7:00 p.m_

Do the students have P.E. every day?
Mrs. Clements

Do the kindergartners attend computer lab?
Mr. Piru

Hope this is a great year!
Mr. Walsh

I work for a printing company. Let me know if you want some scrap paper for the classroom.
Mrs. Lewiston

Graffiti Board

Find out what's on parents' minds with this handy idea. Cover a bulletin board or tabletop with bulletin board paper. Provide markers, and invite parents to jot down any advice, good wishes, comments, or questions they have. Be sure to answer any questions either during open house or in a future issue of your class newsletter.

Parent Portraits

Surprise parents at open house with student-drawn portraits. Have each child draw a picture of his parent, parents, or guardian. Then assist students in writing short descriptions of these special people. Mount the portraits on a bulletin board or classroom wall for parents to view on the big night.

SUPER SEARCH!

Listen for directions.

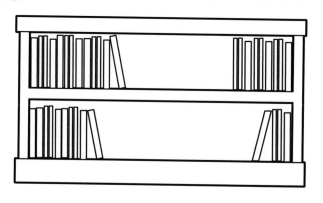

bookshelf

pencil sharpener

trash can

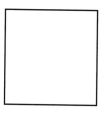

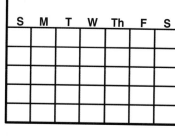

calendar

computer

Note to the teacher: Use with "Pictorial Scavenger Hunt" on page 5.

Let Me Introduce Myself

Glue student's
picture here.

My name is _____.

I am _____ years old.

I have _____ brother(s) and _____ sister(s).

My favorite activity is

_____.

My favorite food is _____.

My favorite book is _____.

Note to the teacher: Use with "Class Directory" on page 6.

Open House Invitation

Use with "Make It and Take It…Home!" on page 7.

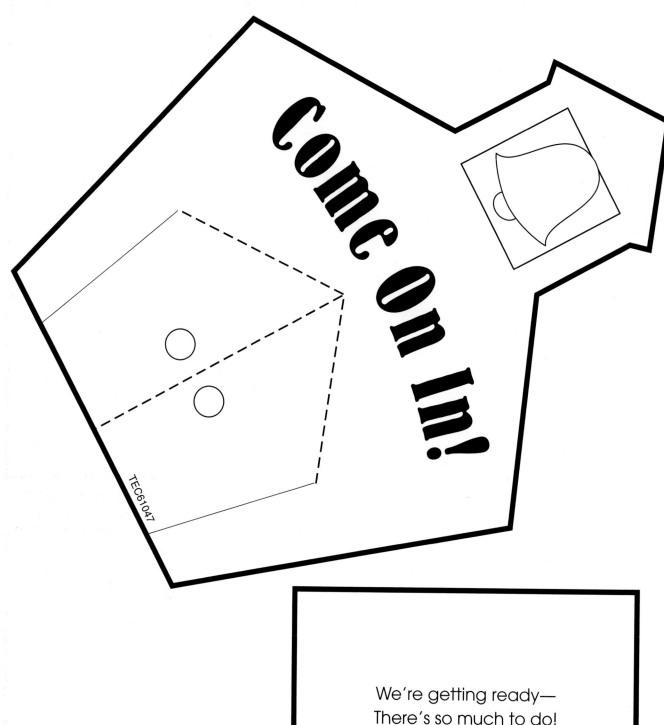

Come On In!

TEC61047

We're getting ready—
There's so much to do!
We're eager for guests;
We're waiting for you!
Please come
to our open house

on _____

at _____

Student Information Card

Student no.

First name _____ Last name _____

Address _____

Student's birthdate _____

City _____ State _____ Zip _____

Mother's name _____

Mother's phone _____

Mother's email _____

Father's name _____

Father's phone _____

Father's email _____

Comments: _____
_____

Emergency contact _____

Medical concerns: _____
_____

Emergency phone _____

Transportation to and from school: _____ walks _____ rides bus (#_____) _____ other

©The Mailbox® • Superbook® • TEC61047

HOORAY!

_____

had a great first day in kindergarten.

_____
teacher signature

_____
date

©The Mailbox® • Superbook® • TEC61047

CONCEPTS OF PRINT

Craft Stick Names

Little ones will be eager to arrange these craft sticks to make their names! Write the letters in each child's name on separate jumbo craft sticks. Place each youngster's set of sticks in a resealable plastic bag. Have each child remove her sticks and place them in a row to spell her name. When youngsters are successful with this activity, program sticks with each youngster's last name and add them to the bags. **Writes own name**

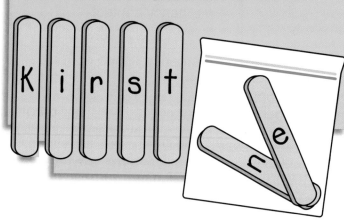

Cute Little Caterpillars

Have each youngster write the letters in her name on different construction paper circles. Then encourage her to glue the circles in the appropriate order onto a sheet of green construction paper. Invite her to add details to the circles to resemble a caterpillar and then cut it out. Display these completed name projects on a supersize leaf cutout. **Writes own name**

Personal Pocket Chart

Give students daily practice in identifying their names. Write each student's first and last names on a sentence strip. Make a puzzle-like cut between the first and last names of each child. Hang a large pocket chart where students can reach it. Place the first names in a column down the left side of the chart. Place the last names on a tabletop nearby. Each morning, have each student find her last name and place it next to her first name. She'll know she's done it correctly if the puzzle pieces fit. Once students can easily match their first and last names, change the puzzle cards to have students match their names with addresses, phone numbers, or birthdates. **Name recognition**

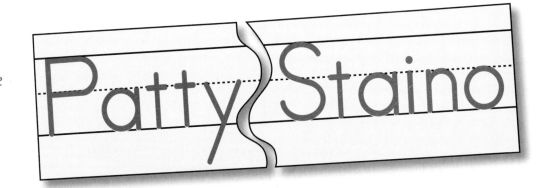

The Spaces Are Missing!

What's wrong with this morning message? No doubt your little ones will be eager to tell you! In advance, write your morning message on a sheet of chart paper, omitting the spaces between the words. Post the sheet on your wall. When students arrive for the day, explain to them that something is wrong with the morning message and it's very difficult to read. Lead students to conclude that the spaces are missing from between the words. Next, have youngsters help you rewrite the message correctly on a clean sheet of chart paper. Now that looks better! **Concept of space between words**

Goodmorningclass!
TodayisTuesday.Wehave
gymthisafternoon.
It'sgoingtobeagreatday!

Left to Right

Make tracking text a fun game with this adorable monster! In advance, color and cut out a copy of the monster and cookie patterns on page 15. Transform the monster into a stick puppet and add Sticky-Tac to the back of the cookie. Open a big book youngsters are familiar with and attach the cookie after the final word on the first page. Explain to youngsters that the monster has to follow the words in the right direction to get to the cookie. Have a volunteer move the monster along the words as you read them out loud. When the monster reaches the cookie, encourage all the youngsters to make crunching and slurping noises as if they were monsters devouring the cookie. Continue in the same way, moving the cookie to another page and choosing a different student volunteer. **Left-to-right progression**

Printing Periods

Help youngsters understand that sentences end with punctuation. Have youngsters share their thoughts on a topic related to your current theme; write each sentence on a sheet of chart paper, omitting the periods. Provide access to a pencil with an unused eraser and an ink pad. Read the first sentence; then tell students that there is a special mark called a period needed at the end of the sentence so the reader knows the sentence is finished. Invite a child to press the pencil eraser on the ink pad and then use it to make a period at the end of the sentence. Continue in the same way for each remaining sentence. *Periods*

I like it when it rains ●
I like to jump in puddles ●
The sky gets all dark ●
Sometimes there are
    worms on the sidewalk
Storms are scary

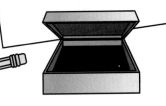

Clip It!

Help youngsters identify different parts of a book with these handy clothespins. On each of several spring-style clothespins write a different part of a book you would like youngsters to identify, such as the front cover, back cover, title page, last page, first letter, and spine. Place the clothespins in a container. After storytime, invite a youngster to choose a clothespin and then find the corresponding part of the book. Finally, have her clip the clothespin to the edge of the container. When all of the clothespins have been chosen, place them back in the container for use during your next storytime. **Book awareness**

Choose a Card

In advance, cut out a copy of the cards on page 17; then place them in a decorative gift bag. Give each child a book. After a volunteer chooses a card, read the card out loud and encourage youngsters to follow the direction given. Continue in the same way for several rounds. Youngsters are sure to know their books inside and out! **Book awareness**

Authors and Illustrators

Students identify the author and illustrator of a book with this catchy song! In advance, cut out a copy of the paintbrush and pencil patterns on page 16. Introduce a book selection; then lead students in singing the first verse of the song below, changing the pronouns as appropriate. Have youngsters help you write the book's author on the pencil cutout. Then repeat the process with the second verse below, writing the book's illustrator on the paintbrush. Display the cutouts on a board. Repeat the process before each storytime, adding the cutouts to the display. Book awareness

(sung to the tune of "Are You Sleeping?")

Who's the author? Who's the author?
What's her name? What's her name?
She wrote all the words to
Make this story for you.
What's her name? What's her name?

Who's the illustrator? Who's the illustrator?
What's her name? What's her name?
She drew pictures to view
As the story's read through.
What's her name? What's her name?

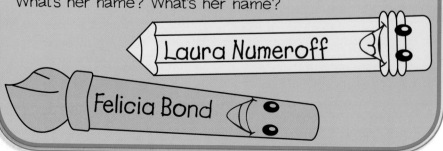

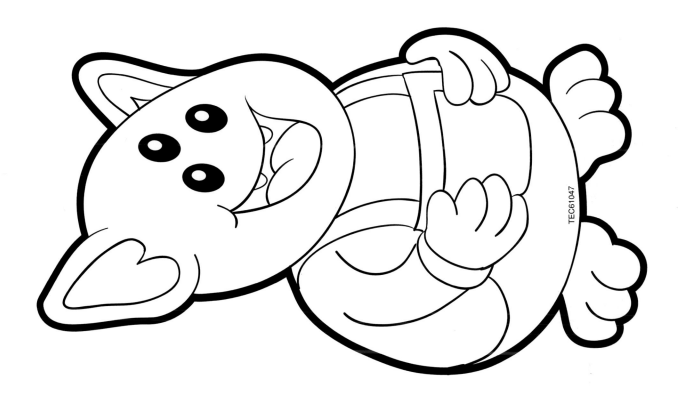

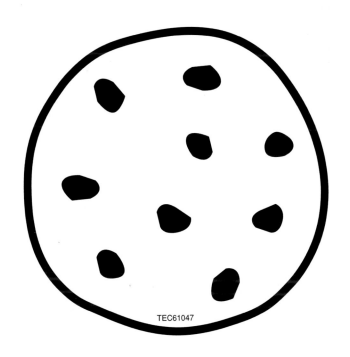

Paintbrush and Pencil Patterns

Use with "Authors and Illustrators" on page 14.

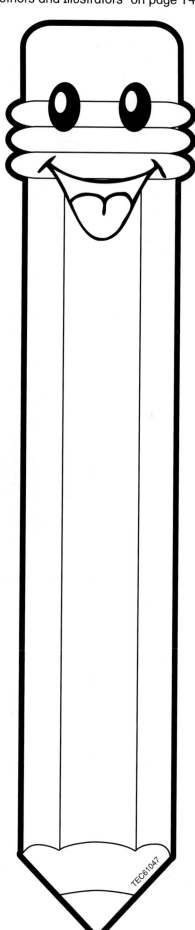

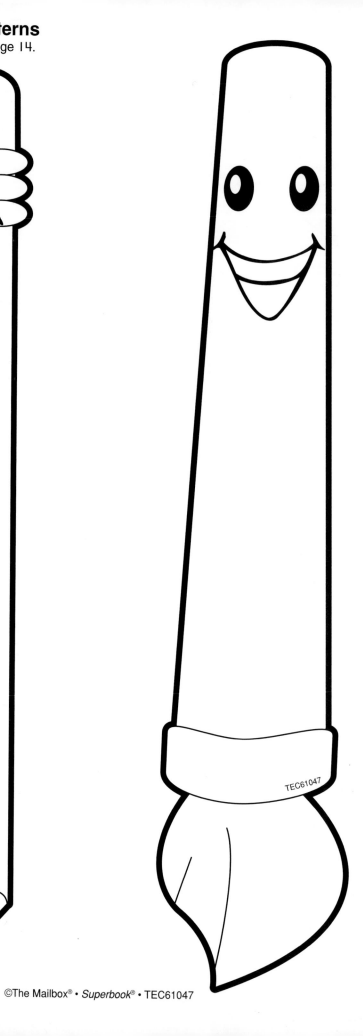

Point to the front cover.

TEC61047

Point to the back cover.

TEC61047

Point to the title of the book.

TEC61047

Point to the first page of the story.

TEC61047

Point to the last page of the story.

TEC61047

Pretend to read the book. Follow the words with your finger.

TEC61047

Point to a picture.

TEC61047

Point to the title page.

TEC61047

Point to the author's and illustrator's names on the front cover.

TEC61047

Letter Boards

Your little ones will be eager to get their hands on this letter activity. Create a letter board by tracing a chosen letter onto several materials of different textures. Cut them out; then glue the letters in a row onto a strip of tagboard. Next, cut out the chosen letter, plus several different letters, from tagboard. Place the letter cutouts in a bag; then store the bag with the letter board. To use the board, encourage a child to use her finger to touch and trace each textured letter several times. Then challenge her to close her eyes and find the matching letter in the bag. **Letter recognition**

On the Road Again

Shift letter learning into high gear with this activity! Cut large letters from sheets of black tagboard and paint yellow road stripes on each letter. Place the resulting letter roads and a supply of tiny cars and trucks in a center. Encourage students to work together to create an alphabet highway by laying the letter roads on the floor. Have a child name each letter as she "drives" a car along the letter-learning highway. Letter identification

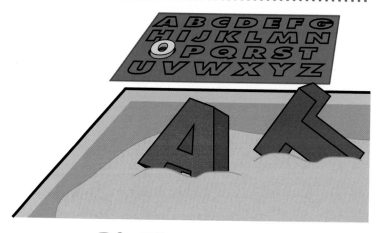

Dig Those Letters!

Here's a way to practice letter-identification skills that your youngsters will really dig! Program a sheet of tagboard with each letter of the alphabet. Bury a set of magnetic letters in your sand table; then place the prepared gameboard nearby.

To play, encourage each child in a small group to dig up a letter in the table. Have him identify the letter and then place it on the corresponding letter on the gameboard. When each letter has been discovered, have the children bury the letters in preparation for the next group. **Letter identification**

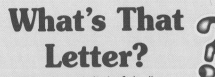

I Spy Collages

Creating these collages will help your students work out the riddle of learning letters. Prepare by stocking your art center with large paper plates, glue, scissors, and alphabet collage materials such as letter stickers, letters cut from newspapers, and Alpha-Bits cereal pieces. Also, include additional collage materials such as pom-poms, feathers, buttons, etc.

Invite each student to create his own letter collage by randomly gluing his choice of letters to a paper plate. Direct him to arrange additional collage materials around the letters and then glue them to his tray. When each child has completed a collage, have pairs exchange collages and try to spy specific letters. Then display the collages on a wall or bulletin board with the heading "I Spy Letters." **Letter identification**

What's That Letter?

Try this delightful ditty to help students practice letter identification. Randomly hold up an alphabet card; then quietly sing the first verse of the song shown, being sure to allow each child time to visually identify the letter on the card. Have each child silently indicate that she has identified the letter; then have students name the letter as you sing the second verse of the song together. Continue in the same manner until everyone is singing to the letter-recognition beat! **Letter identification**

(sung to the tune of "Bingo")

Oh, what's this letter?
Do you know?
Can you guess what it is now?

[B], [B], it's a [B].
[B], [B], it's a [B].
[B], [B], it's a [B].
This letter is a [B]!

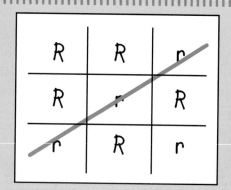

Alphabet Tic-Tac-Toe

This partner game gives youngsters loads of practice with writing uppercase and lowercase letters. To begin, give each twosome a copy of a blank tic-tac-toe grid. Announce a featured letter and have Player 1 write the uppercase version of the letter in a chosen box on the grid. Then have Player 2 write the lowercase version of the letter in a different box. Play continues in this manner until one player has written his version of the letter in three boxes in a row and is declared the winner. If all of the boxes are written in and neither player has three in a row, the game is a draw. To play again, have youngsters switch roles and repeat the game with a different letter of the alphabet. **Uppercase and lowercase letters**

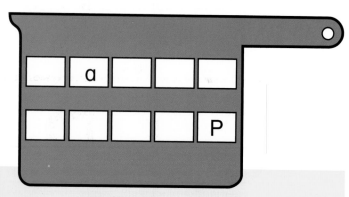

Soup's On!

Playing this partner game of Alphabet Soup Concentration helps youngsters match uppercase and lowercase letters. Copy and cut apart the uppercase and lowercase alphabet cards on pages 21 and 22. Then cut a large soup pot from tagboard and program it with ten spaces equal in size to an alphabet card. Place the resulting gameboard on the floor or a table. Choose five uppercase alphabet cards and their matching lowercase cards. (Set the other cards aside for later games.) Randomly place each of the ten cards facedown in a separate gameboard space.

To play, Player 1 turns over two cards. If the cards are a matching pair of an uppercase and a lowercase letter, she keeps them. If they are not, she returns them to their facedown position on the gameboard. Player 2 then takes a turn in a similar manner. The game continues until all the letters have been removed from the pot.
Uppercase and lowercase letters

Collecting Letters

Send your youngsters on a scavenger hunt to collect and then sort consonants and vowels. Set out two bins and label one "Consonants" and the other "Vowels." Then hide a set of alphabet cards around your classroom. (For a larger class, or a longer activity, hide more than one card for a letter or consonant, as desired.) Invite students to search the room to find the hidden letter cards. When a child finds a letter, he decides whether it is a consonant or vowel and places it in the corresponding bin. When all the cards have been found, enlist students' help in deciding whether each consonant and vowel has been correctly sorted.
Consonants and vowels

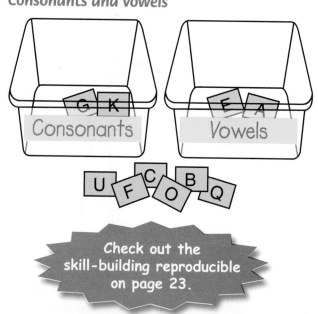

Check out the skill-building reproducible on page 23.

A	B	C	D
TEC61047	TEC61047	TEC61047	TEC61047
E	F	G	H
TEC61047	TEC61047	TEC61047	TEC61047
I	J	K	L
TEC61047	TEC61047	TEC61047	TEC61047
M	N	O	P
TEC61047	TEC61047	TEC61047	TEC61047
Q	R	S	T
TEC61047	TEC61047	TEC61047	TEC61047
U	V	W	X
TEC61047	TEC61047	TEC61047	TEC61047
	Y	Z	
	TEC61047	TEC61047	

Lowercase Alphabet Cards

Use with "Soup's On!" on page 20.

a	b	c	d
TEC61047	TEC61047	TEC61047	TEC61047
e	f	g	h
TEC61047	TEC61047	TEC61047	TEC61047
i	j	k	l
TEC61047	TEC61047	TEC61047	TEC61047
m	n	o	p
TEC61047	TEC61047	TEC61047	TEC61047
q	r	s	t
TEC61047	TEC61047	TEC61047	TEC61047
u	v	w	x
TEC61047	TEC61047	TEC61047	TEC61047
	y	z	
	TEC61047	TEC61047	

Blast Off!

 Draw a line in ABC order.

A B C D E F G H I J K L M N O P Q R S T U V W X Y Z

Phonological Awareness & Phonics

TRANSITION RHYME TIME

Move youngsters from one destination to another with this rhyme-time idea. In advance, color and cut out a copy of the rhyming pictures on page 38. Glue each cutout onto a separate card. To use, give each child a card. Ask him to say a word that rhymes with his card before he goes to his assigned destination (such as to a center, to the library, or to line up for dismissal). **Rhyming**

Rhyming With Shape Pads

Use this versatile seasonal center throughout the year. To prepare, photocopy the rhyming pictures on page 38. Glue each of the pictures onto a separate sheet from a seasonal-shaped notepad. Place the notepad sheets and spring-type clothespins in a center. To use this center, a child matches each picture to a corresponding rhyming picture and uses a clothespin to clip each pair together. **Rhyming**

A-Digging We Will Go

Your little ones will really dig rhymes when they use this fun center. In advance, collect a clean half-pint milk carton for each rhyming word family that you plan to study. Cut off the top of each carton; then glue a picture representing each different word family onto each carton. (You may find the pictures on pages 38 and 39 useful.) Place the cartons near your sand table. Bury in the sand a variety of small objects that rhyme with the pictures on the cartons. To use the center, a child digs an object out of the sand, then places it in the corresponding carton. **Rhyming**

Rhyming Show-and-Share Book

This book of rhymes is sure to become a class favorite. To begin, ask each child to bring in two rhyming items from home. During circle time, have each child, in turn, show and name her rhyming objects. Then photograph the child holding both objects or, if desired, have her draw both objects. Mount each photo or drawing onto a sheet of construction paper programmed with "[Child's name]'s rhyming objects." Write the label for the two objects under the picture; then bind the pages together to create a classroom rhyming book. **Rhyming**

Rhyming
Show-and-Share
Book

Ms. Kenneth's Class

Angela's rhyming objects

hat   cat

Magic Rhymes

A wave of this wand is sure to help youngsters create lots of rhymes! To make a wand, embellish a star cutout as desired and glue it to a large craft stick. During circle time, wave the wand while you chant the rhyme below. Then show students a simple sentence such as "There was a dog." Help youngsters name a few words that rhyme with *dog* and then have a volunteer use the rhyming word of his choice to make up a sentence that ends with it. Write his sentence beneath the first one. Before moving on to another pair of rhyming sentences, invite the volunteer to use the wand to point to each word as he and his classmates read the sentences to confirm that they end in a rhyme. **Rhyming**

Magic wand at circle time,
Help these students make a rhyme.

There was a dog.
He licked a frog.
He smelled like a hog.
He slept on a log.

A PAIR OF ILLUSTRATIONS

Students illustrate rhyming pairs with this cooperative activity. Write a different word on each of two cards to make a rhyming pair for every two students. Shuffle the cards, give one to each student, and help him read his word. Then invite a volunteer to stand and read his word aloud. Encourage the child who has the rhyming word on his card to stand, announce his word, and sit with his partner. Once each student is paired up, have each twosome glue its rhyming cards to a sheet of construction paper and illustrate its words. **Rhyming**

mouse   house

I Spy

Stretch your students' listening and observation skills with this rhyming version of I Spy. Have your students sit in a circle. Ask a student volunteer to be the caller. Have him whisper to you the name of an object in the room; then help him think of a rhyming word for the object. Have the caller then announce, "I spy something that rhymes with [the rhyming word]." Instruct the students to raise their hands when they think they have visually located the object. After a brief period of time, ask the caller to select a child to share his guess. If that child's guess is correct, he becomes the caller for the next round of play. **Rhyming**

Rhyming Lotto

This version of the ever-popular lotto game can be used as a center activity or as a take-home game. Duplicate the caller cards and make several copies of the gameboards (page 39) on construction paper; then cut them out. To use, place the gameboards and stacked caller cards in a center with a bowl of game markers such as pom-poms. Each player in a small group chooses a gameboard and eight markers. In turn, a caller draws the top caller card and announces the rhyming picture to be covered with a marker. When a player covers all of the rhyming pictures on his gameboard, he calls out, "Lotto!" Then that player becomes the caller for the next game.

If desired, put the game pieces in a large resealable plastic bag. Include a note explaining how to play the game and encouraging a child's family to play it together; then send the game home with a different child each day. **Rhyming**

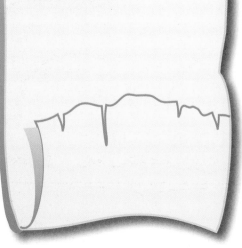

Connecting Word Parts

purple

Segmenting syllables is a snap with this whole-group activity! Give each child five Unifix cubes. Then say a word with two to five syllables and have her connect one cube for each syllable. Repeat the word slowly, as needed. After scanning for accuracy, have students disconnect their cubes. Then continue with more words for an assessment of each youngster's ability to represent syllables in words. **Syllables**

One-Syllable Words

book
chair
glue
chalk
flag
lights
door

fish!

Syllable Search

Foster student participation with this classroom exploration. Encourage each youngster to walk around the room in search of one-syllable word items. When an item is found, record his suggestion on a sheet of chart paper. After a desired amount of time, invite students to gather by the chart to confirm that each item named is a one-syllable word. To do this, have youngsters clap or tap the number of syllables in each word. For a new exploration, invite youngsters to search for two-syllable word items. **Syllables**

SWEET SCOOPS!

banana

Students count syllables to build these sundaes! Have each student color and cut out a copy of the dish and ice-cream scoop patterns on page 91. Next, say a chosen grade-appropriate word, emphasizing each syllable. As each student repeats the word, have him place one scoop per syllable in the dish. Then repeat the word and have students touch each scoop they placed to check their work. Confirm the number of syllables and then have students remove their ice-cream scoops to prepare for the next word. For an added challenge, provide extra scoops and have students segment sounds in a given word. **Syllables**

PUT IT ON A POSTER

Have your little ones chart their alphabet know-how with these letter posters. Use a wide marker to program tagboard sheets each with a different letter of the alphabet. Provide each youngster with a letter, a bottle of glue, and a container of glitter. Direct him to trace his letter shape with the glue and then sprinkle it with glitter. When dry, have him glue his letter to the top of a large sheet of construction paper to make a poster. As you are studying a particular letter of the alphabet, display the corresponding poster. Encourage students to decorate the poster with magazine pictures or drawings of things that begin with that letter. *Beginning sounds*

I'm going on a picnic,
So I'm in a happy mood.
I'll pack a nice large basket,
With lots of yummy food!
Here's what I'll take...

Picnic Plates

Food items are the center of attention with this beginning sound activity. Write each letter you would like to feature on an individual paper plate. Then invite youngsters to draw or cut out food pictures from magazines, labels, and boxes that begin with the corresponding letter sounds. Next, help youngsters sort the pictures by beginning sounds and glue them to the corresponding paper plates. Finally, encourage each youngster to use the plates to help her share what she might like to pack for a picnic. **Beginning sounds**

Splat!

Youngsters swat the letters representing beginning sounds of words with this small-group game! For each beginning sound you would like to review, cut out a copy of the corresponding letter cards on pages 33–37. Place the cards faceup on the floor. Then say a corresponding word and invite one youngster to use a clean flyswatter to swat the letter associated with its beginning sound. When he is correct, ask all team members to say, "Splat!" If he is incorrect, encourage youngsters to repeat the word until he identifies the beginning sound. Continue in this manner until each group member has had a turn. **Sound-letter association**

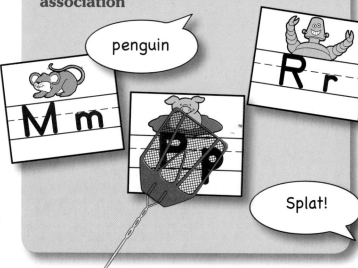

Pass and Play

Students identify beginning sounds with this circle game. Discuss with students the beginning sounds of two to five selected objects. Then gather youngsters in a circle, play some music, and have students pass the objects around the circle. After a desired amount of time, stop the music and say one of the five beginning sounds. Invite the youngster holding the item with the same beginning sound to stand, name the object, and say the beginning sound. If she is correct, have her give a little cheer and then sit down before resuming play with more rounds. If she is incorrect, guide youngsters to find the matching sound before moving on. **Beginning sounds**

Name Change

Silly names are the result of this beginning sound swap! Select a beginning sound you would like to review. Then replace the initial sound in your name with the selected sound. For instance, if the sound to review is /b/, Miss Wilson would change to Biss Bilson! Each morning, announce the featured letter sound for the day. Then encourage youngsters to use their new names to greet each other! **Phonemic manipulation**

LETTER LAUNDRY

String a clothesline in your classroom. Into a basket, place pictures and real items that begin with a desired letter. Add a couple of items that do not begin with the designated letter. Program a set of clothespins with the corresponding letter. Place the clothespins and the basket near the clothesline. Have each youngster search the basket for the items that begin with the selected letter, then clip them to the clothesline. When he has finished, have him tell you the names of the clipped items phand the name of the letter being studied. Vary the center by changing the letter or adding two or three different letter items to the basket. **Beginning sounds**

LET 'EM ROLL!

Label each side of a small empty tissue box with an ending sound you would like to review. Provide corresponding picture clues for students to use as a resource. To play, ask a volunteer to roll the box and announce the sound rolled. Then have each group member name a different word with that ending sound. For example, if /d/ is rolled, group members might say the words: *bed, mad, lid, lizard,* and *cloud.* After confirming the accuracy of each word, have the next group member roll to begin a new round! **Ending sounds**

Sounds in a Bottle

Shake up some final consonant practice with this partner-game idea. To prepare, partially fill a clear, dry plastic bottle with sand or salt. Write the letters *g, m, n, p,* and *t* on small pieces of foam, put them in the bottle, and secure the lid.

Supply each partner with a programmed sheet as shown. (Be sure to pick a word that will have several possibilities such as *ta___.*) To play, one partner shakes the bottle until he finds a letter. If the letter can be used to complete the word programmed on his page, he writes the word on his paper and passes the bottle to his partner. If it does not, his turn is over. The other child then shakes up the bottle and takes a turn in the same manner. Play alternates as time allows. **Ending sounds**

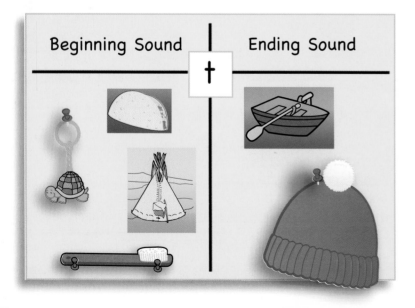

Super Sound Board!

Review beginning and ending sounds with this bulletin board display. Label two columns on the board as shown. Then post a letter whose sound you would like to review. Invite each youngster to find an object that either begins or ends with the desired sound. Then help her mount the object or a picture of that object on the board under the correct column. For a home connection, encourage youngsters to share family-related items. **Beginning and ending sounds**

Animal Word Families

Introduce word families with these cute critters! Program an enlarged copy of each animal pattern on page 40 as shown. Then program each of several copies of the pattern (page 40) with a corresponding word family word.

To begin, have youngsters sort the animals. Then use the large animal cutouts as headings for each word family. Tell students that the word on each matching cutout ends with the same sequence of letters. Invite a youngster to choose a large cutout, read the animal name, and spell the word ending. After helping youngsters read all of the words in the corresponding family, continue with another critter! **Word families**

CUTE CATERPILLARS!

Students assemble word family caterpillars at this center. To make one caterpillar, draw facial features on a construction paper circle (head). Glue a hat cutout programmed with a word family ending to the head. Then write corresponding word family words on colorful circle cutouts (body parts). Repeat this process to make a desired number of word family caterpillars. Store the pieces in a resealable plastic bag and place the bag at a center.

When a child visits the center, he identifies the word family on each hat. Then he places each circle cutout next to the correct word family as shown. After reading the words on each caterpillar, he returns the pieces to the bag for the next visitor. **Word families**

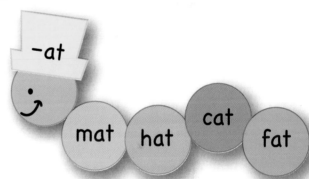

"Egg-citement" by the Dozen

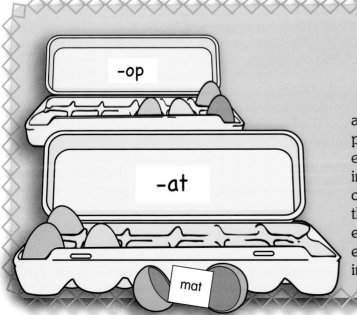

Here's a "Grade-A" way to sort the –at and –op word families! Cut out a construction paper copy of the word cards on page 41. Put each card in a plastic egg and place the eggs in a basket. Label one clean and sterilized egg carton "–at" and another carton "–op." Store the cartons and the basket in a center. To play, encourage each youngster to crack open an egg, identify the word family, and place the egg in the corresponding carton. **Word families**

Some Silly Spots!

To prepare for this center, cut out two extra large ladybugs from bulletin board paper. Draw a happy face on one cutout and a sad face on the other. Cut out a supply of black paper circles (spots). Use a white crayon to label some of the spots with *-ug* words and some with nonsense words. Place the ladybugs and spots at a center. When a youngster visits the area, she chooses a spot and reads the word. If it is a real word, she places the spot on the ladybug with the happy face. If it is a nonsense word, she places it on the ladybug with the sad face. She continues in this manner until she has sorted all of the spots. **Word families**

HEAR AND CHEER!

For this small-group activity, cut out a copy of a designated vowel card (pages 33-37) for each group member. After reviewing the sound of the featured vowel, call out a word that has a short-vowel sound. If the word contains the featured vowel, each youngster holds up his card and says, "Hip, hip, hooray!" If the word does not, students sit quietly. Continue in a like manner with a desired number of other words. **Short vowels**

Check out the skill-building reproducible on page 42.

Build-a-Word!

Youngsters make short-vowel *a* words at this center! In advance, gather foam letters (or construction paper letters) *b, c, f, m, r,* and *s* of the same color. Store the letters in a container. Also, program a large card as shown. Place the card, container, and a supply of paper at a center. When a child visits the center, he uses the letters to build short-vowel *a* words and writes each word on his paper. **Short *a***

Be sure to check out the letter cards on pages 33-37! They're perfect for a variety of skills.

Suggestions for using the Letter Cards

ABC order

Beginning sounds

Ending sounds

Letter identification

Letter matching

Handwriting

Word wall labels

Labels for class-made books

Labels for student-made books

Letter Cards

A a   TEC61047

B b   TEC61047

Letter Cards

C c

TEC61047

D d

TEC61047

E e

TEC61047

F f

TEC61047

G g

TEC61047

H h

TEC61047

I i

TEC61047

J j

TEC61047

K k

TEC61047

L l

TEC61047

M m

TEC61047

N n

TEC61047

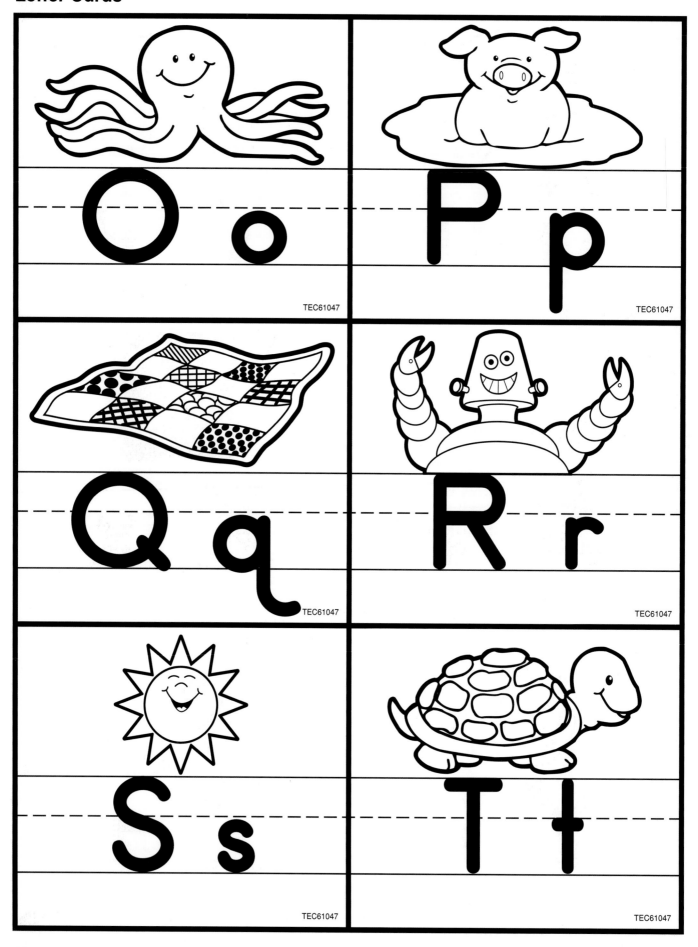

O o   TEC61047

P p   TEC61047

Q q   TEC61047

R r   TEC61047

S s   TEC61047

T t   TEC61047

U u

V v

W w

X x

Y y

Z z

TEC61047

Rhyming Pictures

Use with "Transition Rhyme Time" and "Rhyming With Shape Pads" on page 24.

TEC61047   TEC61047   TEC61047   TEC61047

TEC61047   TEC61047   TEC61047   TEC61047

TEC61047   TEC61047   TEC61047   TEC61047

TEC61047   TEC61047   TEC61047   TEC61047

Animal Patterns
Use with "Animal Word Families" on page 31.

bat TEC61047	cat TEC61047	chat TEC61047	fat TEC61047
flat TEC61047	hat TEC61047	mat TEC61047	pat TEC61047
rat TEC61047	sat TEC61047	splat TEC61047	that TEC61047
bop TEC61047	chop TEC61047	cop TEC61047	hop TEC61047
mop TEC61047	plop TEC61047	pop TEC61047	prop TEC61047
shop TEC61047	slop TEC61047	stop TEC61047	top TEC61047

Name _____

42

Owl's Books

 Cut.

Glue to match beginning sounds.

/p/ as in

/m/ as in

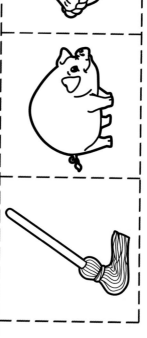

BIRD HOMES

I Can Read!

Animals at Night

All About Owls

Word Skills

Word Worms

Looking for a unique way for youngsters to practice sight words? Try worms and mud puddles! To make a mud puddle for each child, place brown paper shreds inside a personalized resealable plastic bag. Make worms by drawing simple faces on a supply of craft sticks. Store the worms in a container within student reach and place several fine-tip permanent markers nearby. When a youngster learns a new sight word, have him write it on a worm and then store the worm in his mud puddle. After a child accumulates several word worms, periodically have him take his mud puddle home overnight and read the words with his family. **Word recognition**

Hop and Read

To prepare for this two-player game, write six high-frequency words, each on a separate blank card. Laminate the cards, if desired, and tape them to the floor to resemble a trail. To begin, Player 1 rolls a die and moves that many spaces, hopping from card to card. He reads aloud the word on which he lands. (Have the other player offer assistance if necessary.) Then he leaves the path, and Player 2 takes a turn in the same manner. Players continue to take turns rolling the die, hopping, and reading as time allows. **Word recognition**

Freshly Popped Words

Here's an idea that gives students practice reading high-frequency words. Program each popcorn shape on a copy of page 48 with a different high-frequency word. Give each child a copy of the programmed sheet and tell students that since these words pop up frequently, you call them popcorn words. Then have each student write her name on her paper and practice reading the featured words. Periodically choose a student and assess her on the designated words. When a student has mastered a word, invite her to color the corresponding piece of popcorn.
Word recognition

Making Words

Give students hands-on practice with high-frequency words. To prepare, program each of several blank cards with a different word. Place the cards at a table along with play dough, rolling pins, and a set of alphabet cookie cutters. A child takes a card and reads the word. Then he flattens some play dough and cuts out the corresponding letters, arranging them to spell the word. After you check his work, ask the youngster to read the word. Then invite him to choose another card and make a new word.
Word recognition and spelling

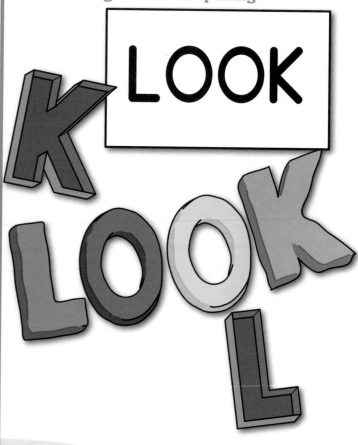

Ladling Letters

Warm up students' literacy skills with this center. To prepare, set a large plastic bowl (soup pot) containing letter manipulatives at a center along with a ladle and a supply of construction paper circles (soup bowls). A child takes a soup bowl and uses the ladle to scoop letters from the pot. Invite her to use the letters to spell as many words as she can on her soup bowl. When she is unable to make any more words, invite her to return her letters to the pot and scoop out a second helping. **Spelling**

Spelling Word Search

Keep students on the lookout for spelling words with this weekly display. Divide a length of bulletin board paper into the same number of sections as you have spelling words. Write one spelling word in each section. Then post the display on a classroom wall within students' reach. Challenge youngsters to find their spelling words on items—such as newspapers, cards, magazines, and cereal boxes—and cut them out. Have them attach each cutout to the corresponding section of the display. At the end of the week, evaluate the display to discover which words were found most and least often. Repeat the activity with each week's spelling words. **Spelling**

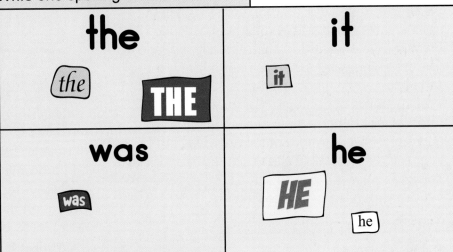

Sharing Letters

To prepare for this small-group game, write a different spelling word on a separate card for each group member. Collect letter manipulatives to spell each of the chosen words and scramble them in a container. Stack the cards facedown and place the container nearby. Have each student choose a card and place it in front of her. To begin, Player 1 takes a letter from the container. If her chosen letter matches a letter in her word, she places it above the card. If it doesn't, she finds the letter in another player's word and hands it to the appropriate player. Player 2 then takes a new letter from the container. Players take turns in this manner until each word is spelled. **Spelling**

Pitch a Word

This partner center is sure to be a hit with students! Cut out a baseball pattern (page 49) for each spelling word. Also cut out a brown construction paper copy of the bat pattern on page 50. Then laminate the patterns so they can be reused. Program each baseball with a different spelling word. Place the bat, the balls, wipe-off markers, and tissues at a center.

To play, one child is the pitcher and holds the programmed baseballs. The other student is the batter and holds the bat and a wipe-off marker. The pitcher "throws" a ball to the batter by reading a word on a baseball. The batter uses the wipe-off marker to write the word on a bat. Then the two players compare spellings. If the batter spelled the word correctly, he wipes off the bat and the pitcher throws him another ball. If he is incorrect, he corrects the word with the pitcher's assistance before being thrown another ball. Once the batter has correctly spelled each word, invite the players to switch roles and repeat the activity. **Spelling**

Word Rings

With students' help, this classroom study aid is simple to make! Program a class supply of blank cards, each with a different vocabulary word. Give one card to each student and help her read the word. Then ask her to draw on the back of the card a picture to illustrate the meaning of the word. (Offer assistance if necessary.) Punch a hole in each completed card and slide it onto a metal ring. Place the cards in an accessible classroom location. Invite a child to use the ring of cards for independent vocabulary practice. **Vocabulary**

Very Important Vocabulary

This ongoing display provides a way for students to build their vocabularies. Title a sheet of bulletin board paper "Vocabulary." Then display it in a prominent location. When an unknown word is discovered, tell youngsters its meaning and write it on the display. Periodically review any new words on the list. Then, several times during the year, send a copy of the list home for each student to review with her parents. **Vocabulary**

Vocabulary

roots

stem

leaves

Pass the Card

Keep vocabulary skills on the move with this small-group game. Program a set of index cards with different vocabulary words and place each card in an envelope. Gather a small group of students in a circle. Play soft music and begin passing one of the envelopes around the circle. When you stop the music, have the youngster holding the envelope read the vocabulary word aloud. (Provide assistance if necessary.) Then ask her to give the word's definition, or ask a volunteer from the group for help. For another round of vocabulary fun, restart the music and pass a different envelope around the circle. **Vocabulary**

Go Fish!

To prepare this small-group game, make a fishing rod by attaching a magnet to one end of a length of yarn and tying the other end to a dowel. Color and cut out a copy of the cards on page 51 and attach a paper clip to one card from each opposite pair. Cut a piece of blue bulletin board paper to resemble a pond and place it on the floor. Lay the paper-clipped cards facedown in the pond. Then stack the remaining cards and place them near the pond along with the fishing rod.

A child chooses a card from the stack and names the picture. Then she uses the rod to fish for a card. Once she "catches" a card, she determines whether it is the opposite of her chosen card. If it is, she keeps the cards. If it is not, she returns the paper-clipped card to the pond and places the other card at the bottom of the stack. Players continue in this manner until all of the opposite pairs have been caught.
Opposites

Concentrate on Opposites

Color and cut out a copy of the opposite cards on page 51. Then arrange the cards facedown in a pocket chart. To begin, ask a child to turn over two cards. Then have him use the picture clues to read the words. If his two chosen cards are opposites, have him leave the cards faceup. If they are not opposites, have him turn the cards over. Then ask another child to choose two cards to turn over. Continue the game in this manner until all of the opposite pairs have been revealed. **Opposites**

Animals in Action

Your students will quickly recognize opposites with some book-related dramatic play. Read aloud the wonderful descriptions of animal opposites in *Quick as a Cricket* by Audrey Wood. Read the text a second time, but pause after each introductory descriptive phrase. Ask your students to recall the phrase's opposite; then continue reading. Read the text a third time. Pause after each introductory descriptive phrase and ask students to act out the phrase. Then read the opposite phrase and have them act that out too. **Opposites**

Popcorn Words

Popcorn

Note to the teacher: Use with "Freshly Popped Words" on page 44.

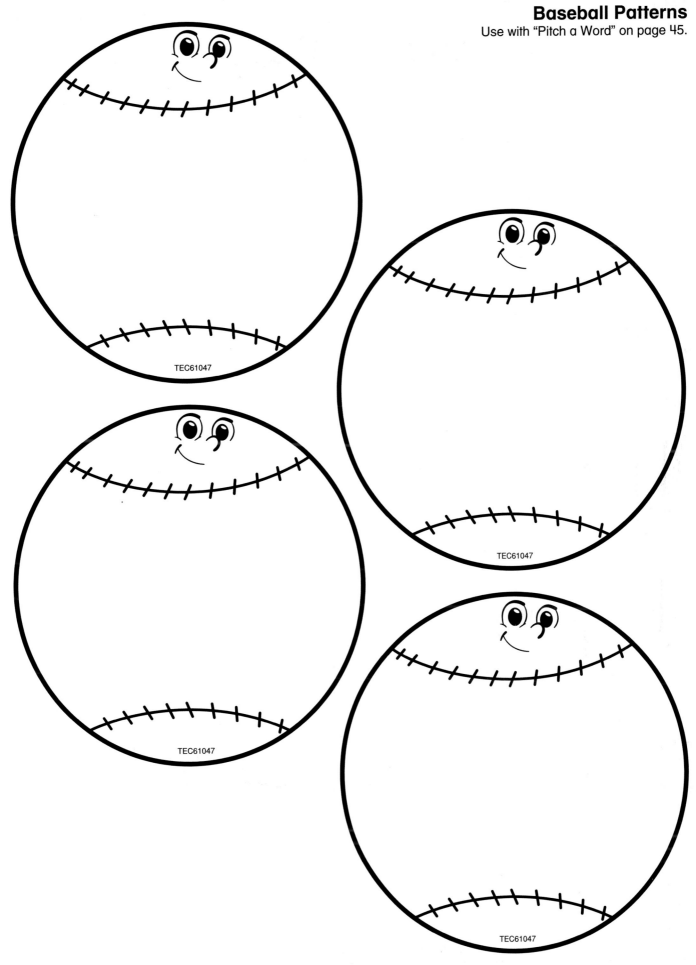

TEC61047

TEC61047

TEC61047

TEC61047

Baseball Bat Pattern

Use with "Pitch a Word" on page 45.

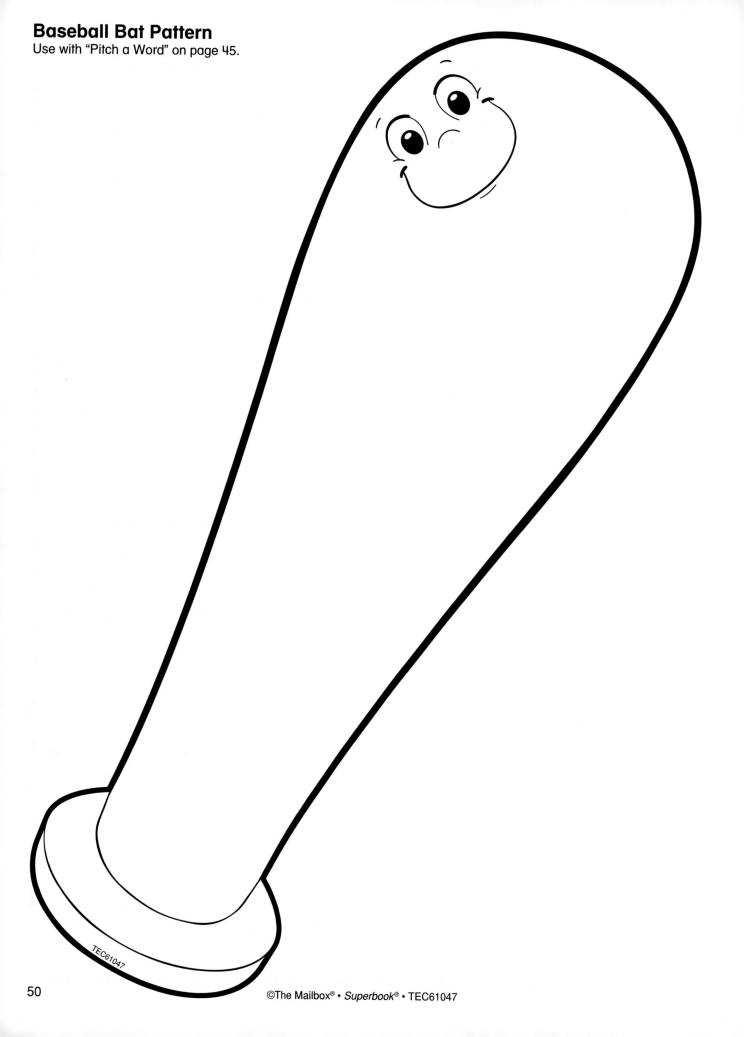

TEC61047

Opposite Cards

Use with "Go Fish!" and "Concentrate on Opposites" on page 47.

day

TEC61047

night

TEC61047

empty

TEC61047

full

TEC61047

happy

TEC61047

sad

TEC61047

big

TEC61047

little

TEC61047

up

TEC61047

down

TEC61047

front

TEC61047

back

TEC61047

READING COMPREHENSION

Silent Story Hints

Story props are just perfect to help little ones retell a story! In advance, gather props for a selected read-aloud and store them in a box. As you read the story aloud, pause when appropriate to remove corresponding props from the box and place them in full view in order of appearance. After reading the story, invite youngsters to retell the tale, using the sequenced props as their guide. **Retelling**

Tell It on Tape!

Try this retelling idea after a story read-aloud. Flip through the pages of a previously read book as you tape-record youngsters' retelling of the story. When finished, rewind the tape and let little ones listen to their recorded version. Continue to tape-record group retellings in this manner throughout the year. There's no doubt that the later versions will show improvement in youngsters' language development, vocabulary, and reading comprehension. **Retelling**

Does It Belong?

Students are sure to point out errors in this story-retelling activity! To prepare, make a set of cards showing several pictures related to a selected story. Then create a few more cards with unrelated pictures. Put the story cards in order, randomly place each unrelated card in the set, and stack them facedown. To begin, read the story aloud. Then tell students that you will retell the story using the cards. It won't take long before your students correct the new version whenever an unrelated card is introduced! **Retelling**

There wasn't a giraffe in the story!

Story Tower

Use building blocks to heighten student interest during story retelling! After a read-aloud, select a volunteer to begin a retelling of the story. Then have him place a block on the floor to begin building a tower. Invite different volunteers, in turn, to add a block to the tower when they share what happened next in the story. Finally, invite a student to place one block at the top of the tower and announce, "The end." **Retelling**

On the Cover

Compare students' story predictions with this graphing idea. Show the front cover of a storytime selection and read the title aloud. Then ask youngsters to share their predictions about the story. Write each prediction along the bottom of the board as shown. Then have each youngster write his name on a sticky note and place it in a column to vote for a story prediction. Finally, read the book aloud and encourage youngsters to evaluate each of the predictions on the graph. **Making predictions**

Open the Door

To prepare, fold a large piece of bulletin board paper in half to resemble a rectangular door. Draw a circle on the front to make a doorknob and label the resulting door with a selected story title. Then sit with youngsters to preview the book's illustrations and make predictions. Write their predictions on the closed door. After you read the story aloud, open the door and write students' comments about what really happened in the story. **Making predictions**

Periodic Predictions

Make several copies of the Story Stop marker on page 59 and color each stop sign red. Then preread a selected book and place a marker between ideal pages to stop and ask youngsters to make predictions. To begin, introduce the book and lead students in previewing the pictures. When you get to a marker, invite students to make predictions. Finally, read the story aloud and compare the author's written words to the student-made predictions. **Making predictions**

STOP

Make a prediction.

Which Fish?

Small groups are sure to enjoy matching details to main ideas with this idea. To prepare, program two copies of the fish pattern on page 59 with a different main-idea sentence. For each main idea, write a corresponding detail sentence on each of three circles (air bubbles). During your small-group time, help youngsters read the two main-idea sentences. Then help youngsters, in turn, read a detail sentence and match it to the correct fish.

Main idea and details

Sunny Details

To prepare for this small-group activity, write one main-idea sentence and several supporting-detail sentences on yellow paper strips. Place the strips and a yellow paper circle (sun) in your small-group area. To begin, help each youngster, in turn, read a sentence aloud. After each sentence has been read, challenge students to determine which strip is programmed with the main idea. Place the main-idea sentence on the sun. Then discuss how each detail supports the main idea as you place each one around the sun's center to resemble rays. **Main idea and details**

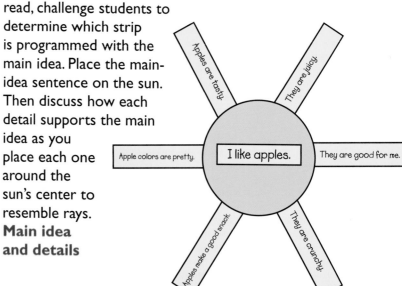

Story Order

To prepare, write on separate sentence strips a sentence that sums up each part of a selected story. Then invite youngsters to settle in for a read-aloud of the story. To follow up, write the words *beginning*, *middle*, and *end* on the board and then read one of the sentence strips aloud. Encourage students to determine which part of the story is described—the beginning, the middle, or the end. Have a youngster hold the sentence in front of him beside the corresponding story-part heading. Continue in this manner with the two remaining sentences. Then reread each strip, in sequence, to check the story order. **Beginning, middle, and end**

In Routine Order

These pictures provide real-world connections for students to sequence! Take four different pictures of youngsters at different times during a routine activity. For example, when preparing to go to lunch, take a picture of youngsters lining up. Take another picture of the children standing in line, ready to go. While walking by an obvious location on the way, take a third picture. Take a final picture of youngsters eating their lunches. Mount each photo on construction paper and number the backs in the correct sequence. Then encourage students to put the pictures in chronological order. Youngsters will be delighted by the opportunity to look at classmates while learning to sequence events! **Sequencing**

Favorite Scoops

Highlight favorite story parts with this display! Cut out a scoop of ice cream for each student. After reading a story aloud, have each youngster illustrate her favorite story part on the scoop. Then invite each student, in turn, to share her completed scoop and help her to determine when the event occurred: at the beginning, the middle, or the end of the story. Display each scoop in the corresponding section of a board similar to the one shown. **Beginning, middle, and end**

Character Cookies

In advance, write the name of each character in a selected story on a separate construction paper circle (cookie). Place the programmed cookies in a plastic cookie jar. After reading the featured story aloud, invite a volunteer to remove a cookie from the jar. Help him read the name on the cookie and encourage him to share details about that character as well as the character's role in the story. Continue in this manner until all of the cookies have been removed from the jar. **Story elements**

A Literary Treat!

This whole-group activity relates the many ingredients of a fruit salad to the many parts that make a good story. Have each youngster color and cut out a copy of the fruit patterns on page 60. Discuss with students the story element listed on each fruit cutout. Tell students that when a story element is heard during a read-aloud, they should hold up the corresponding fruit. Pause to allow time for students to identify the story part before continuing to read. At the story's end, review the characters, setting, problem, and solution as youngsters glue each corresponding fruit to a paper plate. Encourage little ones to take home their fruit plates and share the story with their families. **Story elements**

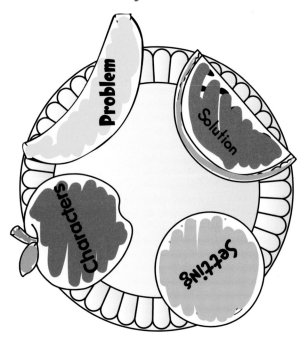

Adjusted Endings

Youngsters change a story element to explore new endings with this whole-group activity. After reading a selected story, identify a story element, such as the setting, that could be changed. Then ask individuals to share their thoughts as you record each change on the board. For example, a story that features a zoo could be changed to a circus setting. Then explore how the change might affect the story's ending and record the new endings next to the corresponding changes. **Story elements**

Change	New Ending
Duck goes to the circus.	Duck learns how to walk across the high wire.
Duck goes to the rain forest.	Duck finds many frog friends.

Text to Self

For this small-group activity, write the title of a selected story on a copy of page 61. Then copy the page for each group member. After reading the featured story aloud, discuss with youngsters whether any part of the book reminds them of personal experiences. Then have each group member complete the phrase on each side of her paper with corresponding words and illustrations.
Making connections

Can of Questions

Help youngsters make story connections with these thought-provoking questions. To prepare, decorate an empty container so that it looks similar to the one shown. Then cut out the question cards on a copy of page 62 and place them in the container. After a read-aloud, select a volunteer to remove a card from the container and help him read the question. Then invite youngsters to share and compare their responses.
Making connections

Then What?

Magazine pictures can help students illustrate cause-and-effect relationships. Give each student a picture from a magazine. Have him use his imagination to draw what might have happened right after the pictured event. When students are finished with their work, invite them to share their magazine pictures and illustrations with the class. For a variation, show youngsters the same image and see how different their effects are from one another. **Cause and effect**

Animal Character Comparisons

Use this idea to help youngsters distinguish between the characteristics of a real animal and a fictional animal character. After reading a story aloud that features an animal with human characteristics, label a chart similar to the one shown. Invite youngsters to share real and make-believe traits that correspond with the animal in the story. Then review the completed lists to compare interesting character traits. **Reality and fantasy**

Real dog	Clifford
is brown, black, white, or tan	is red
is small or large	is a giant
barks	talks like a person

Picture Posters

The difference between real and pretend pictures is on display with these visual aids. To prepare, label a sheet of bulletin board paper "Reality." Cut a second sheet of bulletin board paper to resemble a cloud shape and label it "Fantasy." Then ask students to look through magazines to find sample pictures for each title. Have youngsters cut out the pictures and place each one on the corresponding poster. After a generous supply of pictures has been collected, lead youngsters to agree on the best examples for each title and glue them to the poster. Finally, refer to the posters when little ones try to determine whether a story is real or make-believe. **Reality and fantasy**

Is It Real?

Incorporate real and make-believe pictures into your morning routine! Place two empty tissue boxes, labeled as shown, and a class supply of cubes or counters in an easily accessible classroom location. Each day, display a different picture that is either real or make-believe. When each student enters the classroom, she looks at the picture, decides whether it is real or pretend, and places a cube in the corresponding box. Later in the day, check student votes by having a volunteer shake each of the boxes. Students are sure to recognize unanimous decisions when one of the boxes sounds empty! **Reality and fantasy**

Fish Pattern
Use with "Which Fish?" on page 54.

Fruit Patterns

Use with "A Literary Treat!" on page 56.

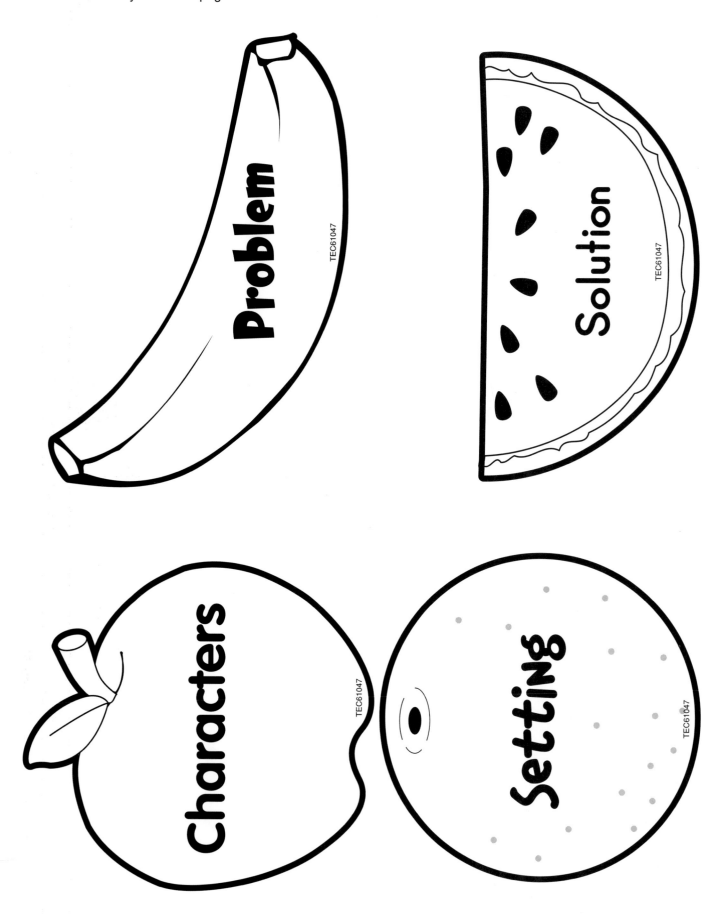

Name _____

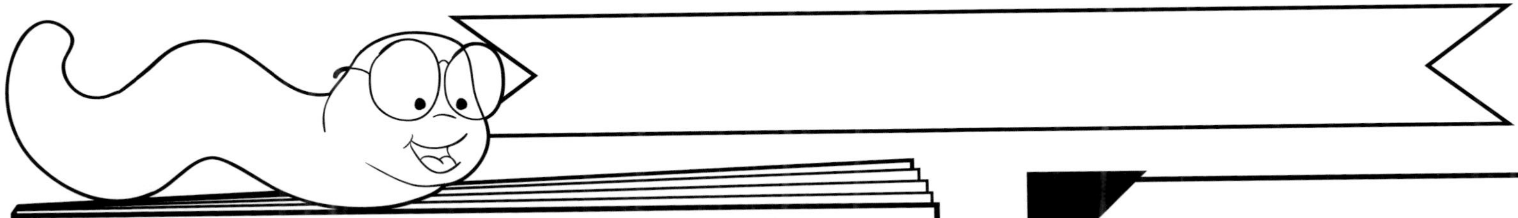

That reminds me of

In the book,

©The Mailbox® • Superbook® • TEC61047

Note to the teacher: Use with "Text to Self" on page 57.

Question Cards

Use with "Can of Questions" on page 57.

Did this story make you laugh? Explain. TEC61047	Has something like this ever happened to you? TEC61047	What does this remind you of in the real world? TEC61047
Have you ever been to a place like the one in the story? TEC61047	What does this remind you of in your life? TEC61047	Have you read about something like this before? TEC61047
Does this story remind you of another story? TEC61047	How did this story make you feel? TEC61047	Does this story remind you of a time when you were with your family? TEC61047

Literature Links

Motivate your kindergartners to read and encourage a love of literature with the following ideas that can be used with any book.

A New Ending

Here's a fun way to extend a literature lesson into a language experience activity. When you reach the end of a story, have students brainstorm other possible endings for it. Instruct each student to write and illustrate another ending for the story. Then invite each student to share his ending with his classmates. You're sure to see bunches of creativity with this activity!

Josh

The litl pigs mad frens with the wulf.

ROAR!

SOUND EFFECTS

Encourage good listening skills by inviting children to make sound effects as you read aloud a poem or story. Before reading, identify several sounds that students can make. For example, a lion might say, "ROAR!"; the wind could blow, "WHOOSH"; or a giant might stomp, "THUMP, THUMP, THUMP." As you read the poem or story, pause each time you read one of the sound effects previously identified so that students may contribute that sound. For variety, assign each sound to a small group.

Pop-Up Puppets

Spice up your literature retellings with a puppet that identifies both character and setting! After reading a book to your youngsters, have students decorate a large paper cup to resemble a key location in your literature selection. Then have them make a stick-puppet character and insert it into a slit in the bottom of the cup. Invite little ones to move their puppets appropriately during a second reading of the book.

Reading at Home

Celebrate youngsters and parents reading together with this home-school connection! When a parent reads a book aloud to her child, invite the youngster to share a quick synopsis of the book at school the next day. When the child is finished discussing the book, have him write his name and the book's title and author on a colorful construction paper book cutout (patterns on page 65). Then attach it to a bulletin board decorated with a house cutout and the title "We Read at Home!"

Joshua

Red Leaf
Yellow Leaf

by
Lois Ehlert

Dear Bear,

We like your story Mooncake. You are very silly. Why did you think the moon would taste good?"

Let's Write a Letter!

No doubt youngsters will have plenty of things to say to the characters in a book! After sharing a read-aloud, encourage students to suggest things they would like to ask or tell a character as you write their ideas on a sheet of chart paper. Next, use the ideas on the paper to compose a letter as a class on a second sheet of paper (or help students compose individual letters). What a fun way to reflect on a storytime selection!

The Cookie Jar

Motivate students to read independently or at home with their families by challenging them to achieve a group reading goal. To create this display, cut a large cookie jar from bulletin board paper and mount it on a classroom wall. Copy the patterns on page 66 onto tan construction paper, cut them out, and place them near the display. (If desired, have youngsters use crayons to decorate the edges of the cookies.) Tell the class that for every book a student reads either on his own or with a family member, a cookie will be added to the jar. The student must write (or dictate for you to write) his name, the author's name, and the title of the book on a cookie cutout; then he has you initial it to indicate that he told you about the book. Youngsters will be amazed at how fast the cookie jar fills up!

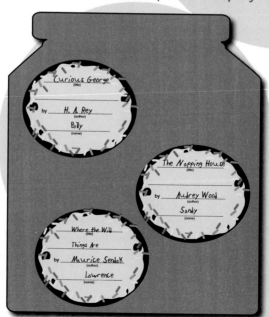

Cookie Patterns
Use with "The Cookie Jar" on page 64.

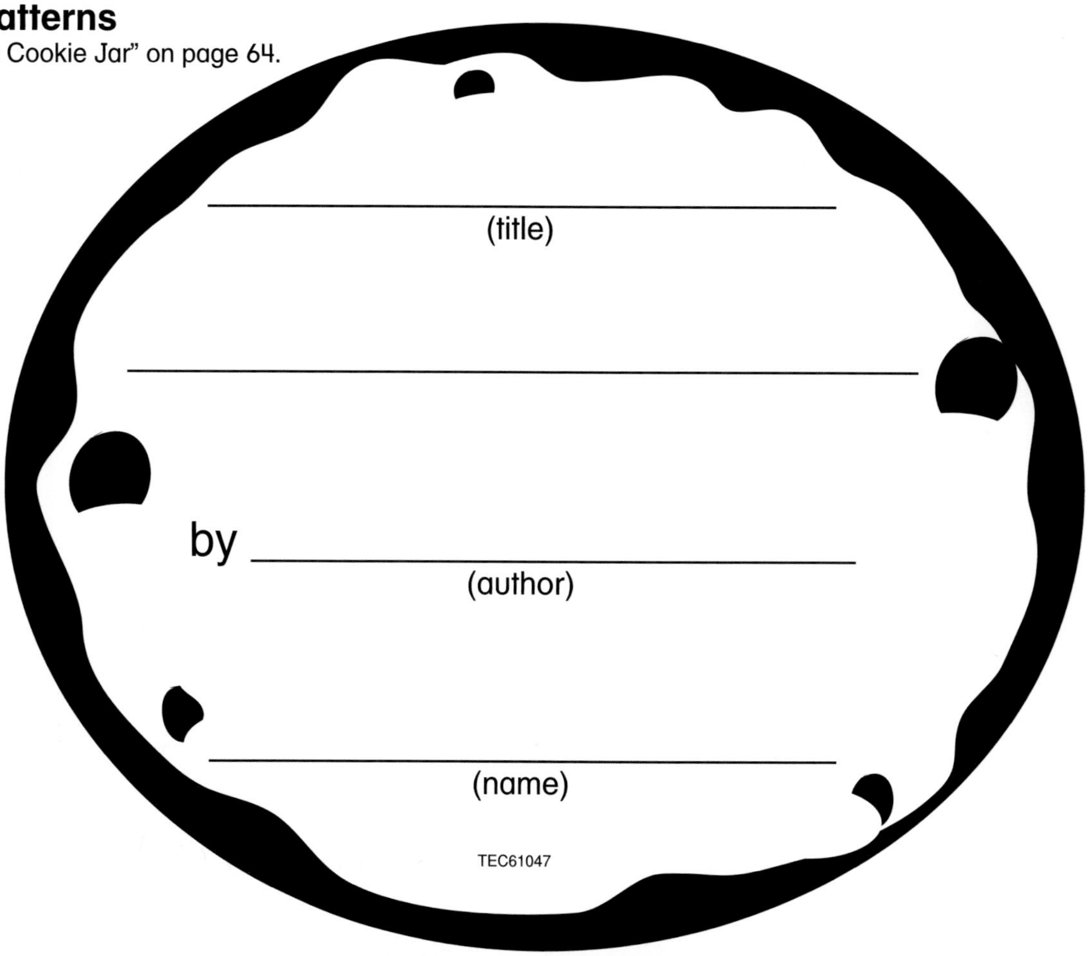

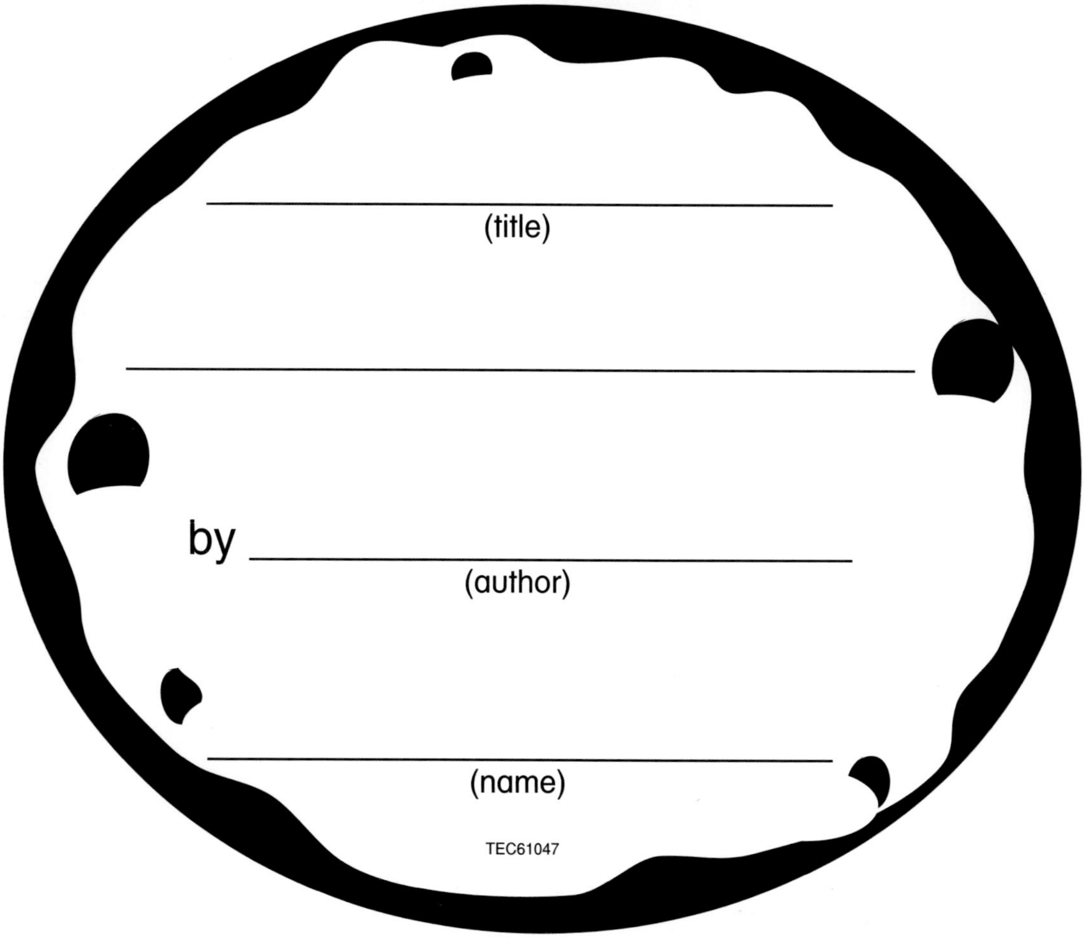

_____
(title)

_____

by _____
(author)

_____
(name)

TEC61047

_____
(title)

_____

by _____
(author)

_____
(name)

TEC61047

Wipe-Off Writing

Provide plenty of handwriting practice with wipe-off writing paper! Mount several sheets of writing paper on separate sheets of construction paper. Then laminate each sheet. Place the laminated sheets, wipe-off markers, tissues, and a set of letter cards at a center. When a child visits the center, he copies selected letters onto a wipe-off sheet. When his sheet is full, he uses a tissue to wipe it clean and continues with more letters. For more advanced students, provide word cards. **Handwriting**

Frog Spacers

Help little ones remember to leave space between words with these frog spacers! Have each child paint both sides of a jumbo craft stick green. After the paint is dry, help her use a permanent marker to draw a small frog on one end of the stick. (Or give each child a small frog sticker to attach to the stick.) Tell students that, when writing sentences, their frogs need to jump between each word. The result will be appropriate spacing between words. *Handwriting*

I li,Ke to meet

Handwriting Hall of Fame

Recognize outstanding handwriting with this display idea! To create a hall of fame display, mount a plastic page protector (trim off the holes) in the center of a 12" x 18" sheet of construction paper. Decorate the resulting border to resemble a frame and attach a paper plaque titled "Honorable Handwriting." Display the frame in a prominent classroom location. Each week, recognize one student for his outstanding handwriting and slide his work sample into the page protector. Students are sure to try their best to be inducted into the handwriting hall of fame! Handwriting

My name is Ethan.
My cat is black.

Honorable Handwriting

Roll and Write

Keep sentence writing rolling along! In advance, cover two small empty square tissue boxes (or similar-size boxes) with paper. Choose six picture cards from page 74 and glue each one to a different side of one box. Write a different action word on each side of the other box. Invite two students to each roll one box and identify the word or picture rolled. Then invite a volunteer to dictate a sentence using both words as you write his response on the board. If desired, ask more students to compose different sentences with the two words before having youngsters roll again. **Dictating sentences**

The bird jumps out of its nest to catch a worm.

One day a prince went to the park. He lost his crown when he was hanging on the monkey bars. He was sad. Then a little frog found the crown and gave it to the prince.

a prince — the park

Silly Story

For this shared writing activity, prepare a supply of tagboard strips in two different colors. Label one set of strips with different story characters. Label the other set with different settings. Place each set of strips in a separate container. Invite a student to remove a strip from each container. After you read aloud each strip, invite students to dictate a story that involves the chosen character and setting. Write the dictations on a sheet of chart paper. When the story is complete, have each child draw a picture about the class story; then display the pictures along with the story. **Shared writing**

Special Storybook Visitors

Stimulate young writers by incorporating storybook characters into their writing. Share several classics with your students, such as *Cinderella*, *Snow White and the Seven Dwarfs*, and *Little Red Riding Hood*. After completing each story, ask students to imagine how the characters from these stories would act if they visited the classroom. Then have students choose one of the characters. Enlist youngsters' help in writing a class story about the character's visit to the classroom. When the story is complete, invite little ones to read it aloud and act out the events. **Interactive writing**

Journal Joggers

Looking for some fun and fresh journal prompts you can use anytime of the year? Try these! **Journal prompts**

- If I had three wishes…

- If I could fly like a bird…

- If I were a(n) [animal]…

- If I were the teacher…

- If I were as small as a ladybug…

- If I were invisible…

- The Yummiest Dinner

- The Yuckiest Dinner

- The Best Treasure

- The Best Day Ever

- A good friend is…

- At the end of the rainbow…

Write Through the Seasons

Prepare a journal for each child by stapling several sheets of story paper into a 9" x 12" construction paper folder. Have each child personalize and color a copy of the appropriate seasonal journal cover (pages 75–77). Instruct him to glue the cover onto the front of his journal. Several times during each season, have each student use the word bank on his journal cover to write and illustrate a seasonal journal entry. **Journal prompts**

Look What I Did!

Use center time to build background experiences for writing! During journal-writing time, encourage each student to write about her experience at a learning center that day or on a previous day. Invite her to illustrate her page and share the entry with a partner. **Journal writing**

Take a Topic

Use this idea to help students think of a writing topic. Cut out several copies of the cards on page 74. Store the cards in a container; then place the container in an easily accessible location. When a child needs a writing topic, invite her to choose a picture from the container and glue it to a sheet of paper. Then direct her to incorporate the picture into a scene and write about the illustration. Refresh the box with more pictures as needed. **Writing prompts**

He Said, She Said

What do your little ones remember most about different staff members at your school? Find out with this caption-writing idea! In advance, take pictures of several different staff members. Enlarge the photos, mount them on separate sheets of construction paper, and display them on a bulletin board. For each child, trim a sheet of white paper into a speech-bubble shape. Then have her choose a pictured person and help her write something that person might say. Mount the completed speech bubbles near the corresponding photos. Lead youngsters in reading each pictured person's captions. **Writing captions**

Kindergarteners in Action

In advance, take photos of youngsters participating in different activities, such as recess, writing on the board, working at centers, or eating lunch. Each morning, post a few photos in an easily accessible location for students to view during their free time. Later in the day, attach each photo to a sheet of construction paper. Ask students to think of a caption for each photo that includes who is in the photo, where the activity is taking place, and what the students are doing. Write the student-generated captions below the photos. Then repeat the same process each day for any remaining photos. Display the sheets around the room for students to view. **Writing captions**

Lots of Lists

A student-generated list becomes a word bank for independent writing with this idea! Label a sheet of chart paper with a chosen list topic (see the suggestions). Invite each student to contribute to the list and write her response on the chart. Once the class is satisfied with the list, have each student choose one specific list entry to write about or illustrate independently. Display students' completed work around the list for all to see! **Writing lists**

Suggestions
Animals on a farm
Types of cookies
Ice-cream flavors
Games with balls
Pizza toppings
Sticky things

Games With Balls
basketball
soccer
football
tennis
racquetball
catch
dodgeball
volleyball
four square

I play basketball wif mi dad.

All in Order

Here's a hands-on way for little ones to practice sentence order. Write a simple sentence on a sentence strip. Cut the strip apart between each word, leaving the punctuation attached to the last word. Place the resulting word cards in random order along the top row of a pocket chart. Also, write the sentence several times on a sheet of paper to make a class supply; then cut apart the strips and set them aside.

To begin, read aloud each word on the pocket chart. Ask youngsters to identify the capital letter and the punctuation mark to determine the beginning and end of the sentence. Then have student volunteers rearrange the words to form a sentence. After the class reads the sentence aloud, give each child a prepared strip to cut apart between each word. Direct each child to scramble the words, glue them in order on a sheet of paper, and add an illustration. **Complete sentences**

The | mice | ran | into | the | hole.

The prite btrfli flis to the sun.

by Juliet

Squiggles of the Week

Encourage creative thinking and writing with this idea! Each week, draw a simple squiggle on the top of a sheet of story paper. Copy the paper to make a class supply. Have each student incorporate the squiggle in an illustration. Then have her write or dictate a sentence about her picture. Display students' completed papers with the title "Squiggles of the Week." Replace the work samples each week for a fresh display. **Creative writing**

The brwn bar is in the cav.
He wnts to eet the red barees.
—by Devon

A Perfect Setting

Discuss with youngsters different story settings and write a student-generated list of settings on the board. Then give each child a clip art animal to color. Have him glue his animal to a half sheet of construction paper and incorporate it into a setting. Then, on a sheet of writing paper, have him dictate or write a description of the animal in its setting. Invite students to share their work with the class; then post each child's paper and illustration on a display titled "Sensational Settings." Descriptive writing

CARDS BY DESIGN

Birthday greetings will abound in this writing center. Brainstorm with your students a list of birthday-related words. Write each word on a separate birthday-cake cutout. Display the cutouts in a center along with birthday gift wrap, construction paper, stickers, construction paper shapes, old birthday cards, curling ribbon, and envelopes. Encourage a student in this center to create a birthday card using his choice of materials. Have him place his completed card in an envelope and deliver it to the birthday child on the child's birthday. **Writing a card**

Create an Alien

Here's a small-group writing activity that is out of this world! Prepare a supply of colorful construction paper shapes in a variety of sizes. Work with a small group of students to use the shapes to create a unique alien. Have youngsters glue the shapes to a large sheet of construction paper and draw details to resemble an alien. Then, as group members compose sentences to describe their alien, help them write their descriptions on a sheet of chart paper. After you have met with all students, invite each group to share its work. *Descriptive writing*

The alien is funny. It has a triangle head with three eyes. It is orange, red, blue, yellow, and purple. It has three fingers. The alien lives in outer space.

Fantastic Fish

Youngsters create and describe prize-winning fish with this writing idea! Draw a large fish on a sheet of paper; then copy it to make a class supply. On each paper, write a prize-worthy description, such as the funniest fish, the most colorful fish, the scariest fish, or the slimiest fish. Give each child a prepared sheet and read the text aloud. Have her decorate her fish to fit the description. Then have her dictate or write a sentence telling why her fish fits the description. Post each child's fish and writing on a display titled "Prize-Winning Fish." **Descriptive writing**

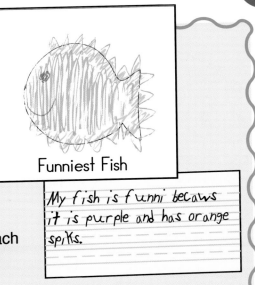

Funniest Fish

My fish is funni becaus it is purple and has orange spiks.

Writing Wrap

Let each student know his writing is important with this decorative carrier. Have each student decorate a cardboard tube using an assortment of art supplies. Label each child's tube with his name. When a youngster completes a piece of writing of which he is especially proud, help him roll up the paper and insert it into his tube. Provide a basket in which youngsters may place their special writing. During center time, encourage students to visit the basket and read their classmates' best work! Publishing

Reusable Class Book

Here's a quick way to publish students' writing. Stock a view binder with a class supply of clear page protectors. When you are ready to publish a class book, slip each child's writing and illustration into a page protector. Then slide a cover into the clear front pocket of the binder. Display the book in your classroom library for all to enjoy. In addition to being durable, this book can be used again and again by replacing the student work and the cover! Publishing

Picture Cards

Use with "Roll and Write" on page 68 and "Take a Topic" on page 70.

My Fall Journal

leaves

acorns

tree

rake

squirrel

apple

turkey

pumpkin

Name _____

Note to the teacher: Use with "Write Through the Seasons" on page 69.

My Winter Journal

snowflake

shovel

mittens

skates

hat

cocoa

coat

snowman

Name _____

Note to the teacher: Use with "Write Through the Seasons" on page 69.

My Spring Journal

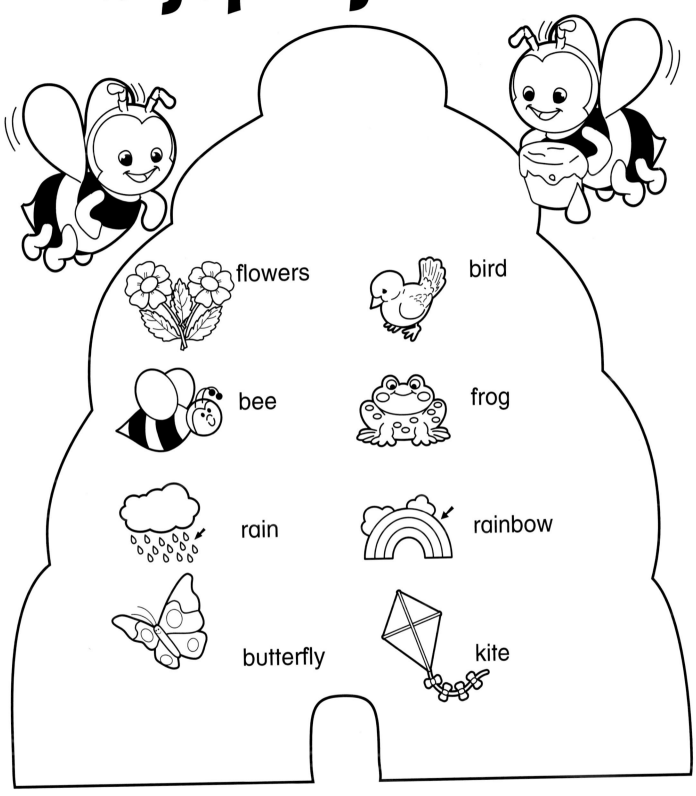

flowers

bird

bee

frog

rain

rainbow

butterfly

kite

Name _____

Note to the teacher: Use with "Write Through the Seasons" on page 69.

NUMBER & OPERATIONS

Plenty of Parking

Students are in the driver's seat for this center activity. Use a white crayon to draw ten parking spaces on a sheet of 12" x 18" black construction paper and laminate the paper if desired. Then tape the paper to a hard surface and place ten toy cars nearby. A child determines whether there is a parking space for each car by "driving" each car into a separate space. When she is finished, she "drives" each car out of each space to ready the center for the next visitor. **One-to-one correspondence**

Busy Bees

This small-group activity keeps your youngsters bustling around the beehive! To prepare, gather a resealable plastic bag for each child in a small group. In a few bags place exactly ten yellow pom-poms (pollen), and in the other bags vary the number of pom-poms by one or two. Give each child in the group a bag of pom-poms and a yellow construction paper copy of the honeycomb card on page 89. Ask him to place one pom-pom in each honeycomb cell. Then lead him to determine whether he has more pom-poms, more cells, or the same number of pom-poms and cells. Ask him to place his pom-poms back in his bag, trade bags with another child, and repeat the activity. **One-to-one correspondence**

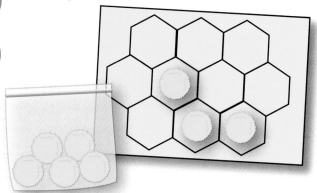

Number Chant

Improve little ones' number recognition skills with this rhythmic chant. Make a set of large number cards. Hold up one card and ask your youngsters to identify the number. Then invite them to clap and chant the verse below. Repeat the verse with the remaining numeral cards as time allows. **Reading numbers**

I went to school,
And what did I see?
The number [four]
In front of me.
[One, two, three, four]!

(Clap on the offbeats: "went," "school," "what," "see," "num-," "four," "front," "me.")

(Clap and count to each number.)

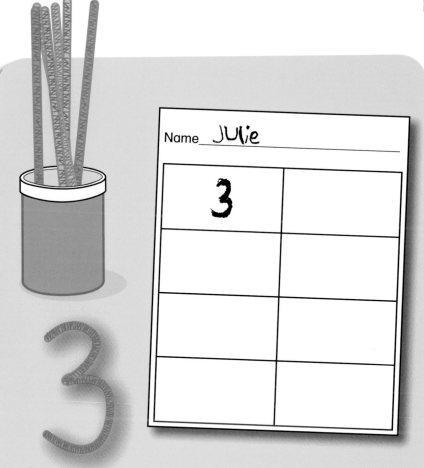

Numbers With a Twist

Place a container of pipe cleaners and a class supply of a recording sheet, similar to the one shown, at a center. A child visits the center and twists a pipe cleaner into the shape of a number of her choosing. When she is pleased with her number, she writes it on her recording sheet. She repeats the process for each box on the sheet, forming and writing a different number each time. **Writing numbers**

High-Five Switch

This version of the traditional game of Hot Potato will have your youngsters jumping up as they recognize numbers. For every two students, label a blank card with a different number. Then make an identical set of number cards. (Plan to play if you have an odd number of students.) Tape a card to each child's shirt and then direct the group to sit in a circle. Play music and have students pass a ball around the circle. After a short time, stop the music. Instruct the youngster holding the ball to jump up and announce his number. Then ask the child wearing the matching number to jump up, meet his partner in the middle of the circle for a high five, and switch places with him. Continue playing in this manner until each pair has had a chance to jump up and switch places. **Reading numbers**

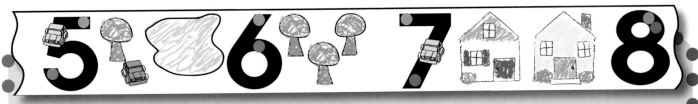

Numberville

Invite youngsters to practice number formation in the block center by driving through Numberville. To create Numberville, paint the numerals 0–9 on a length of bulletin board paper. Use green and red sticky dots to show where each numeral starts and stops. If desired, provide markers and crayons and invite children to draw more scenery. Lay the paper town in the block center and encourage children to say each number as they "drive" a toy vehicle over it. **Reading and writing numbers**

Count on Exercise

Try this number warm-up for some counting practice. Have a student volunteer stand in front of the group. Whisper a number in her ear and have her perform an exercise, such as jumping jacks, a corresponding number of times. Challenge her classmates to count in unison as she performs. After the volunteer confirms the number, repeat the activity with a different volunteer and number. **Counting**

Ten Little Froggies

Your little ones will hop with delight when you teach them this counting rhyme. As they say each verse, encourage them to use their fingers to count the number of times they hop. On the last verse, have students gently fall to the floor on "Drop!" **Counting**

One little froggie goes hop.
Along comes another and they just can't stop, so…

(Hop once and hold up one finger.)

Two little froggies go hop, hop.
Along comes another and they just can't stop, so…

(Hop twice and count on fingers.)

Three little froggies go hop, hop, hop.
Along comes another and they just can't stop, so…

(Hop three times and count on fingers.)

Continue in this manner and end as follows:

Ten little froggies go hop, hop, hop, hop, hop….
Drop! Time to stop!

(Hop ten times and count on fingers.)
(Fall gently to floor.)

Fill the Tray

To begin this partner game, give each child a plastic ice cube tray and a supply of pom-poms. To play, Player 1 rolls a jumbo die and places the corresponding number of pom-poms in his tray, one per section. Then Player 2 rolls the die and places the corresponding number of pom-poms in his tray. Alternate play continues in this manner until one child has filled his entire tray with pom-poms. **Counting**

Counting Classroom Objects

This activity works well as an individual assessment or a whole-group activity. To prepare, number a set of ten large cards. For an individual activity, have a child spread the cards out in number order in a designated location. Then encourage him to collect small objects from the room to match the number shown on each card. For example, he might put three blocks on the 3 card and ten crayons on the 10 card. After checking his work, ask the youngster to put the objects back in their original locations and place the cards in a stack for the next youngster. **Counting**

More Peas, Please!

Looking for a unique item to place in your math center? Try pea pods! Make several pea pod cutouts and label each with a different number. Place the pea pods at a center along with a supply of green play dough. A youngster chooses a pea pod and uses the play dough to roll the corresponding number of "peas." Then she counts orally as she places the peas on the pea pod. She continues in this manner until she has matched the corresponding number of peas to each pod. **Counting**

Counting in Season

This partner activity provides youngsters with some simple counting practice. Provide each twosome with a supply of seasonally themed cutouts and a set of number cards. Partner 1 chooses a card and reads the number aloud. Then Partner 2 counts out the corresponding number of cutouts. If Partner 2 is correct, the partners switch roles and repeat the activity. If Partner 2 is incorrect, Partner 1 helps her correct her work before they switch roles. **Counting**

How Many Animals?

To prepare this center activity, number ten inverted containers to represent cages and place them at a center along with a separate container of plastic animals. A child visits the center and places the corresponding number of animals under each cage. To check her work, invite each youngster to remove each cage, one at a time, and count each group of animals again as she places them back into the original container. **Counting**

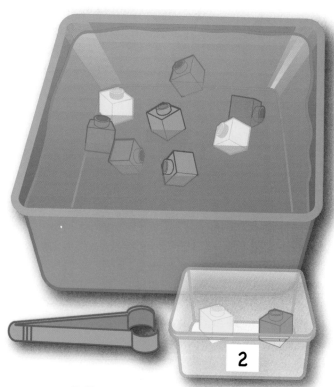

Floating Cubes

Count on this idea to float your students' boats! To prepare, number a set of plastic containers from 1 to 10 and place them near a large tub of water. Float a supply of cubes in the water. Then encourage a youngster to use tongs to remove the cubes from the water and then place the appropriate number of cubes into each container. After checking her work, ask her to put the cubes back into the water tub to prepare for the next child. **Counting**

Counting Cash

Use youngsters' curiosity about money to cash in on counting practice. To prepare for this activity, draw a simple wallet on each of ten envelopes similar to the one shown. Seal the envelopes and laminate them if desired. Then slit the top of each envelope front. Use a permanent marker to program the front of each envelope with a different number from 1 to 10. Provide a supply of play money, or make your own from green construction paper. To complete the center activity, have a student place the appropriate number of bills in each wallet. **Counting**

Backward Countdown

This whole-group activity has students counting from ten to one. To prepare, number ten large blank cards and give each card to a different child. To begin counting backward, the child holding the card labeled "10" goes to the front of the classroom. The child who has the card labeled "9" should follow and stand beside the first student. The remaining students join the lineup, one at a time, in backward number order. When all of the students are in place, lead the class in the chant shown and invite each child to hold up his number card at the appropriate time. Then collect the cards and give each card to a new student to begin the countdown again. **Counting backward**

We can count backward from ten to one.
10, 9, 8, 7, 6, 5, 4, 3, 2, 1.
Yay! Counting backward is fun!

Count on Cookies

Here's a display project that provides some tasty skip-counting practice. Give each youngster a cookie cutout and a piece of brown construction paper. Have her cut or tear the paper to resemble ten chocolate chips and then glue them to her cookie.

To promote counting by tens to various numbers, arrange students' completed projects in different-size groups on the wall. Then help students post number cards to label the projects in each group by tens. **Counting by tens**

Make a Match

In advance, gather a class supply of index cards and, beginning at 1, number half of the cards. Punch holes in each of the remaining cards to correspond with each numbered card. (Make a card for yourself if you have an odd number of students.) Give each child a card and have him read the number or count the number of holes on his card. Then invite him to find the student holding the corresponding card. Once the child has found his partner, invite the pair to sit down. After each child has found his match, collect the cards and redistribute them to play again. **Matching sets to numbers**

Who Has More?

Students compare sets in this fast-paced partner game. Have each child color and cut out a copy of the cards on page 90. Assign each child a partner and have members of each twosome mix their cards together and stack them facedown between them.

To play, each player takes a card, turns it over, and counts the shapes on each of the cards. The player who has the larger set on his card takes both cards and sets them aside. If the players have the same size sets, they each take one of the cards. The players continue in this manner with the remaining cards. **Comparing sets**

Colorful Apples

To prepare, make a desired number of two-sided apple cutouts from red and green construction paper. Draw a tree on a large paper bag and place the apples inside the bag. Invite a youngster to shake the bag as you lead the class in the rhyme shown. At the end of the rhyme, have the youngster open the bag and dump out the apples. Invite another student to sort the apples by their faceup color into two piles. Next, lead the class in counting the apples in each pile. Then ask a volunteer to identify which color pile has more apples and which has less, or whether the two piles are the same. Place the apples back into the bag and repeat the activity with different student volunteers as time allows. **Comparing sets**

Apples, apples from the tree. How many red ones will I see?

There are more green apples than red apples.

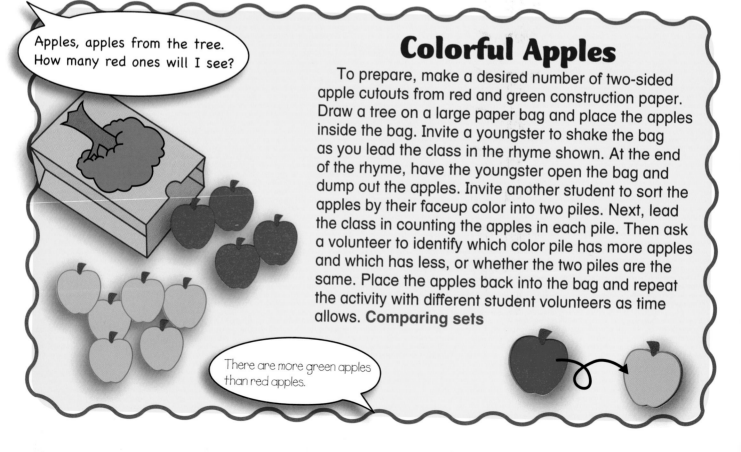

Sequenced Scoops

Serve up number-sense practice with this small-group activity. Cut out several copies of the ice-cream dish on page 91. Then cut out three colorful copies of the scoops on page 91 for each dish. Program each set of scoops with three consecutive numbers. Give each child a dish and a set of three scoops. Have her order her scoops from smallest to largest on her dish. After checking each student's work, encourage each youngster to trade scoops with another student and repeat the activity. **Ordering numbers**

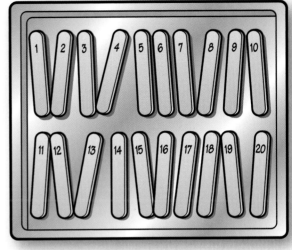

A Number Lineup

Sequencing numbers is a snap with these magnetic sticks. Program several craft sticks with a desired range of numbers, writing one number per stick. Attach a piece of magnetic tape to the back of each stick and place the sticks at a center along with a metal cookie sheet. A child visits the center and places the sticks on the cookie sheet in numerical order. **Ordering numbers**

Dig In!

Invite your little ones on a treasure hunt to find numbers. In advance, bury two sets of number manipulatives from 0 to 9 in a large tub of sand and place two plastic shovels and buckets nearby. Invite two students to the area and encourage each child to find one of each number buried in the sand. Once a child has found the numbers, have him lay them beside the tub in number order. After checking his work, have him hide the numbers in the sand for the next visitor. **Ordering numbers**

Which Animal?

Line up ordinal number practice, critter by critter. Position a desired number of different stuffed animals or plastic animal counters in a line. Ask a question that includes an ordinal number, such as "Which animal is third in line?" When a student supplies the correct answer, have her point out the correct animal. Continue in this manner with the remaining animals until each animal has been named. Then mix up the animals and repeat the activity as desired. **Ordinal numbers**

Nifty Number Line

Make great strides toward teaching youngsters about addition when you create a giant number line! Number a set of cards from 0 to 9 and laminate them for durability. Tape a length of string to the floor in an open area and attach the cards to the string at evenly spaced intervals. Gather youngsters around the number line and call out an addition problem such as "Four plus two." Have a student volunteer stand on the number 4 and then take two steps forward as his classmates count from 4. Then ask a different volunteer to solve a new problem in the same manner. For an added challenge, have students try some simple subtraction problems too. **Number line**

Gumballs Galore

To prepare this center, number ten gumball machine cutouts and program each one with a different addition problem. Place the cutouts and a container of colorful pom-poms (gumballs) at a center. A child uses the gumballs to help him solve each problem. For an added challenge, set a supply of paper and pencils at the center for the child to record each problem as he solves it. **Addition with manipulatives**

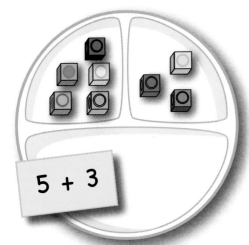

Serving-Size Addition

For this center activity, obtain a few disposable plates that are divided into three compartments. Program several blank cards with addition problems and place them in a resealable plastic bag. Place the bag, the plates, and a supply of manipulatives at a center stocked with paper and pencils. A child takes a plate and chooses a card. He sets the corresponding number of manipulatives in the two smaller sections of his plate to represent the problem. Then he writes the addition problem on his paper. He moves both sets of manipulatives into the larger compartment and counts them to determine the sum. After he writes his answer on his paper, he clears his plate and repeats the process with a new card. **Addition with manipulatives**

Beautiful Butterflies

Use this colorful idea to help youngsters practice addition facts. Make several large butterfly cutouts and program each with a different addition problem as shown. For self-checking, write the answer to each problem on the back of each butterfly. Then set the butterflies at a center with a supply of colorful pom-poms. A child chooses a butterfly and places the corresponding number of pom-poms on each wing. She counts the total number of pom-poms to solve the problem and then flips over the butterfly to check her work. She continues in this manner with each of the remaining butterflies. **Addition with manipulatives**

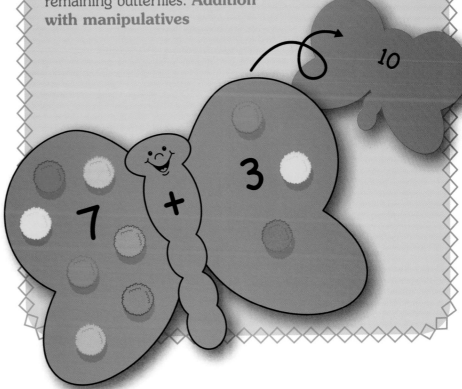

Linking Learning

Illustrate the connection between addition and subtraction with this small-group idea. Connect a number of linking cubes and have the group count them. Then place the cubes behind your back and break the rod into two pieces. Show students one piece of the rod and ask them to figure out how many cubes are still behind your back. Guide students in solving the problem. Once they have reached the correct conclusion, show them the remainder of the cubes to check their work. **Addition and subtraction**

Stegosaurus Subtraction

Set the stage for subtraction with these prehistoric pals. To prepare for this partner activity, make one copy of the stegosaurus and plate patterns on page 92 for every two students. (If desired, enlarge the patterns for easier handling.) Give each twosome a copy of the patterns along with a pair of jumbo dice and a recording sheet similar to the one shown. Then ask the twosome to color and cut out the patterns.

Partner 1 rolls the dice. He writes the number rolled in the corresponding blank on his recording sheet and places the corresponding number of plates on the dinosaur. Then Partner 2 rolls one die, writes the number in the corresponding blank, and removes that many plates from the dinosaur. After they solve the resulting number sentence, one partner writes the answer in the appropriate blank on the sheet. Then the partners switch roles and repeat the steps as time allows. **Subtraction with manipulatives**

How Many Blocks?

Pattern blocks add a unique element to estimation practice. Fill a see-through container with a variety of pattern blocks as desired. Give each student a copy of a recording sheet similar to the one shown. Then invite students to estimate the number of each shaped block in the container. Next, lead youngsters in counting the actual number of each shaped block in the container. Invite each youngster to share her estimate and comment on how accurate, high, or low her estimate was. **Estimation**

A Handful of Cereal

Here's an estimating activity that packs a handful of learning opportunities. Have each child fold a large sheet of construction paper in half. Then help her open the paper and trace one hand on each half of the paper. Show students a container of cereal pieces. Challenge each youngster to guess the number of cereal pieces she thinks she can pick up in one hand. Help her label the top left side of her paper "I guessed…"; then have her write her guess on the hand outline. Have her grab a handful of cereal and count the number of pieces. Next, ask her to write, "I counted…" on the top right side of her paper, and the actual number of cereal pieces that she picked up below that hand outline. Then have her glue the cereal pieces to the second hand outline. **Estimation**

Check out the skill-building reproducibles on pages 93–94.

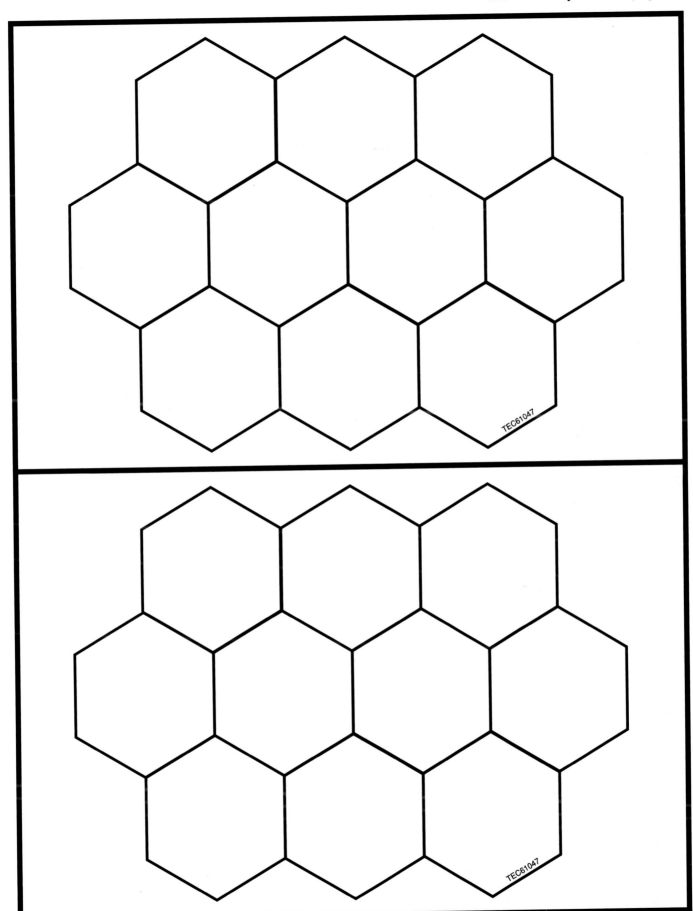

TEC61047

TEC61047

Game Cards

Use with "Who Has More?" on page 84.

TEC61047

TEC61047

TEC61047

TEC61047

TEC61047

TEC61047

TEC61047

TEC61047

TEC61047

TEC61047

TEC61047

TEC61047

TEC61047

Stegosaurus and Plate Patterns

Use with "Stegosaurus Subtraction" on page 88.

Plenty of Peanuts

 Count. ✏️ Write.

✏️ Draw a line to match sets.

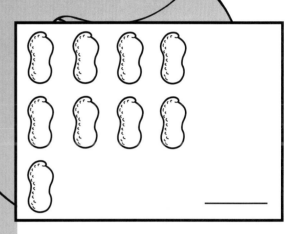

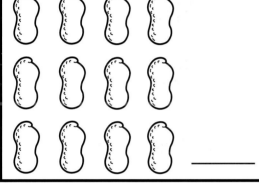 _____
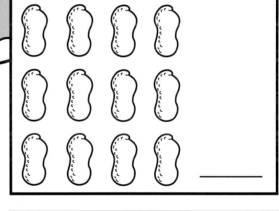 _____

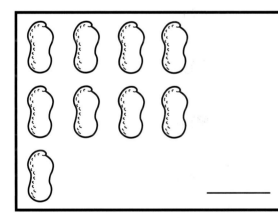 _____
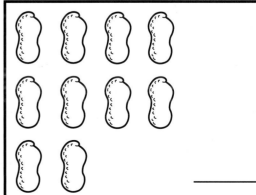 _____

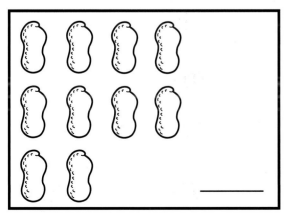 _____

Chow Time

✂ Cut.

Add. Use the bones to help you.

Max

4 + 4 = ___   5 + 2 = ___

3 + 2 = ___   3 + 3 = ___

6 + 1 = ___   7 + 1 = ___

2 + 4 = ___   1 + 3 = ___

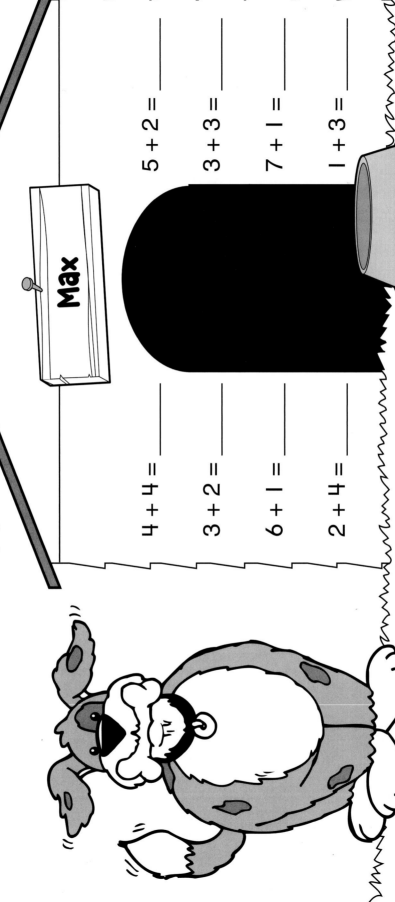

Fractions

Sweet Shares

Youngsters learn about equal shares with this sweet idea! Gather a variety of candy-bar wrappers. Cut some of the wrappers in half; then cut each remaining wrapper into two unequal pieces. Mount the pieces on separate blank cards. To begin, choose two youngsters and explain that you're going to let the two of them share one of your candy bars. Choose two coordinating cards and give one card to each child. Have students discuss whether the candy bar has been divided fairly, prompting them to describe the candy bar as being *divided in half* or *not divided in half.* Then repeat the process with other student pairs and different coordinating cards. **Halves**

Missing Pieces

For this small-group activity, gather six sheets of construction paper of the same color. Use a black marker to divide two sheets into halves, two sheets in thirds, and two sheets into fourths. Cut one sheet from each matching pair into separate pieces; then place the pieces into a bag. Gather a small group of youngsters around the three intact sheets. Instruct a child to choose a piece from the bag and then match it to a section on one of the sheets. When she makes a correct match, point out to the youngster that the piece is one of two (or three, or four) equal pieces that make up a whole sheet of paper. Continue in the same way with each remaining piece in the bag until all sections of the sheets have been covered. **Parts of a whole**

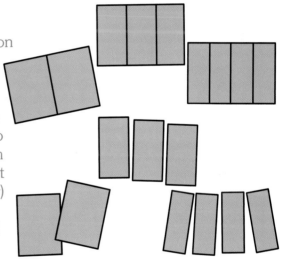

Train Time

Provide access to a supply of Unifix cubes and have each child make a length of four attached cubes. Ask youngsters to pretend they have each made a train with four cars. Next, write the fraction ¾ on the board and explain that three out of the four cars need to disconnect for repairs. Encourage youngsters to snap a group of three cars off of their trains and hold the sections up in the air. After scanning for accuracy, explain that the repairs are finished and the cars can be reconnected. Repeat the process with different fractions and trains with larger numbers of cars. **Parts of a whole**

Is It Equal?

Gather a small group of youngsters and give each child a paper plate visually divided into fourths. Have students pretend that their plates are pizzas. Ask students if there is a way they can prove that all of the slices of pizza are the same size. After listening to several suggestions, have students cut out the slices and stack them so they can see that they are all equal. Next, give each child eight red circle cutouts to resemble pepperoni. Have her place the pepperoni slices on her pieces of pizza so that each piece has the same number. **Equal parts**

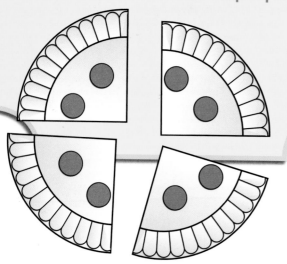

Snacks Are Served!

Youngsters serve up equal-size portions of pretend snacks at this center! In advance, make simple food cutouts such as those shown. Draw lines to equally divide some of the foods. On the remaining foods, draw lines to show unequal portions. Place the snacks at a center with a paper plate. Encourage a center visitor to choose a snack and decide whether it's divided into equal parts. If it is, he places it on the plate. If it is not, he sets it aside. He continues in this manner for each remaining snack. **Equal parts**

Bears in the Bed

Introduce little ones to writing fractions with this adorable class book! For each child, make a copy of page 97 and fold a 12" x 18" sheet of construction paper to resemble a bed and blanket as shown. To begin, have each child cut out the text box and a desired number of bear patterns; then encourage her to color some of the bears red and some blue. Have her glue the bears to the bed so they are peeking out from under the blanket and then glue the blanket in place. Next, have her fill in the blank on the text box with the appropriate number. After she glues the box to the project, help her write the corresponding fraction under the box. Bind the completed pages together with a cover titled "Bears in the Bed." Read aloud this adorable book to your youngsters. **Writing fractions**

4 little teddy bears are lying in bed.

How many bears are the color red?

$$\frac{2}{4}$$

Check out the skill-building reproducible on page 98.

_____ little teddy bears are lying in bed.

How many bears are the color red?

A Fair Share

🖍 Color each cracker that shows $\frac{1}{2}$ orange.

🖍 Color the other crackers yellow.

Patterns & Sorting

Follow Me!

Patterns and movement go hand in hand in this activity. Gather your little ones around you; then pat your legs as you say the rhyme below. At the end of the rhyme, create a simple pattern using claps, snaps, and pats. Invite each child to join in as he discovers the pattern. Then repeat the rhyme with a new pattern. Clap, clap, snap, snap! **Copying a pattern**

Patterns, patterns all around.
See them, feel them, hear their sound.
Watch to see just what I do,
Then everybody do it, too!

People Patterns

Arrange a small group of student volunteers into a pattern such as *stand/sit/stand/sit* or *front/front/back/ back*. Encourage the other students to examine the arrangement and reveal the pattern. Then ask a few students to place themselves in the line and extend the pattern. Continue until each child has had a chance to participate in the pattern. **Extending a pattern**

What Comes Next?

To begin this pattern-building activity, create a simple pattern using a set of blocks. Ask your youngsters to study the pattern and secretly guess which block will continue the pattern. Then sing the song below and, at the end, ask a child to choose the block he thinks would come next. If he is correct, invite him to add the correct block to the end of the pattern. If he is incorrect, help him find the appropriate block and add it to the pattern. Repeat this activity by creating a new block pattern, or use other materials such as Unifix cubes. **Extending a pattern**

(sung to the tune of "Are You Sleeping?")

Pattern pieces, pattern pieces,
In a row, in a row.
Show me what comes next.
Show me what comes next.
Do you know? Do you know?

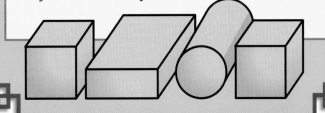

Colorful Copying

Make a supply of pattern strips by hot-gluing crayons in a pattern onto tagboard strips. Place the strips at a table along with a supply of loose crayons. A youngster chooses a strip and then uses the crayons to reproduce and extend the pattern. He continues in this manner with each remaining strip. **Copying and extending a pattern**

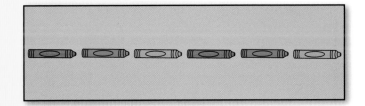

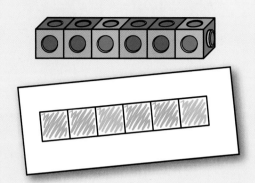

Linking Patterns

Help your youngsters see the patterns in these colorful designs! Give each child a supply of linking cubes in two colors and a paper strip. Then ask her to find crayons that match the colors of her linking cubes. Instruct her to connect her cubes to make a two-colored pattern. Then have her reproduce her pattern by tracing each cube onto her paper using the corresponding colored crayon and coloring in the resulting square. **Creating a pattern**

Pretty Petals

Patterns will be in full bloom when youngsters complete this activity. Set a supply of paper and crayons at a center along with glue and a supply of different-colored plastic spoons. When a child visits the center, she draws a picture of a flower stem on a piece of paper. Then encourage her to arrange the spoons in a circular pattern on the mat as shown to create a unique flower. Finally, she glues the spoons in place to complete her beautiful blossom. **Creating a pattern**

Monkeying Around

Youngsters will go ape over this small-group patterning activity. Make several copies of the monkey patterns on page 103 onto red, yellow, green, and blue construction paper. Cut out the monkeys and store them in a basket. Teach a small group of little ones the first verse of the rhyme at the right, inserting a student's name as indicated. Once the child creates a monkey pattern, chant the second verse of the rhyme together, and select a volunteer to extend the pattern. Continue with the remaining groups until all of your students have had a chance to monkey around. **Creating and extending a pattern**

Verse One:
Down, down in Jungle Town,
There's monkey madness all around.
Silly monkeys can be seen
In blue and red, yellow and green.
No other monkeys are quite like these.
[Student's name], make a pattern, please.

Verse Two:
Down, down in Jungle Town,
A monkey pattern can be found.
They're in a row, looking fine.
Each with a special place in line.
Let's add more. Here we go!
Who can make this pattern grow?

Cereal Sorting

This center is a sorting activity and a snack rolled into one! For each color in a box of Froot Loops, cut a circle from a matching color of tagboard. Laminate the cutouts and place them at a center with a supply of plastic cups and a supply of Froot Loops. A child visits the center and spreads the circles out. She fills a cup with cereal pieces and then sorts each onto the corresponding circle. After she has sorted all of her cereal pieces, she nibbles on her tasty treat! **Sorting by color**

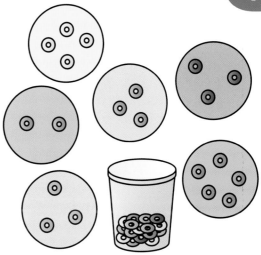

All Aboard!

Invite your little ones to take a ride on the sorting express! In advance, color and cut out a copy of the train engine on page 104. Add a different-colored piece of construction paper to make each train car; then add wheels and other details as desired. Cut several pictures from magazines that match the color of each train car. Then enlist students' help in sorting the pictures and attaching them to the corresponding car. Display the train under a desired title. **Sorting by color**

The Sorting Express

Tidy Picnic

Students use their sorting skills to organize picnic supplies at this center. Fill a picnic basket with a jumbled supply of paper plates, napkins, and a variety of plastic silverware. Set the basket at a center, along with a tablecloth. A child visits the center and lays out the tablecloth. He takes each item out of the basket and sorts it into a corresponding pile. Once a youngster has all the picnic supplies correctly sorted, he mixes up the items and returns them to the basket for the next visitor. **Sorting by shape**

Stuck on Sorting

Looking for an inexpensive sorting manipulative? Try stickers! To make sorting mats, adhere one each of several sets of stickers to a separate sheet of construction paper. Then cut the remaining stickers apart and store them in an envelope along with the sorting mats. Invite a youngster to spread out the mats and sort each sticker onto the corresponding mat. **Sorting by one attribute**

Perfectly Placed Pom-Poms

Encourage your youngsters to sort by color, size, or both with this idea. Place pom-poms of various sizes and colors in a basket. Invite a student to first sort the pom-poms by color. When she is satisfied with her sorting, tell her to sort the pom-poms again, this time using a different attribute such as size. Then invite her to sort the pom-poms another time using both attributes. **Sorting by more than one attribute**

Animal Attributes

Animals are the perfect tool to help youngsters practice sorting one set in a variety of ways. Have each student color and cut apart a copy of the animal cards on page 105 and then sort them by an attribute such as size. Once each student has her cards sorted, ask for volunteers to suggest alternate ways to sort the cards. After hearing several suggestions, invite each youngster to sort her animal cards again, this time using a different attribute. After she's completed the task, invite each student in turn to share how she sorted her cards. **Sorting a set in different ways**

I sorted by the number of legs each animal has.

Check out the skill-building reproducible on page 106.

TEC61047
TEC61047
TEC61047
TEC61047
TEC61047
TEC61047

Train Engine
Use with "All Aboard!" on page 101.

The Sorting Express

TEC61047

TEC61047

TEC61047

TEC61047

TEC61047

TEC61047

TEC61047

TEC61047

TEC61047

TEC61047

Shapely Patterns

 Cut.

Glue to finish the pattern.

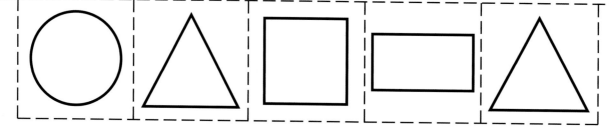

Shape Hunt

Youngsters sort shapes with this whole-group activity. In advance, label each of four sheets of newsprint with a different shape. Then display the papers in your classroom. Make several shape cutouts to match the ones shown on the papers. Hide the shapes throughout the classroom and then have students go on a shape hunt. When each child finds a shape, have him write his name on it and then use a glue stick to attach it to the appropriate paper. **Plane shapes**

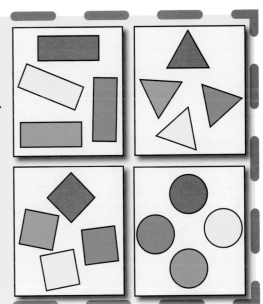

Pleasing Pipe Cleaners!

Your kindergartners can form a variety of shapes with a simple supply of pipe cleaners! Give each child several long and short pipe cleaners. Name a shape and then encourage students to arrange their pipe cleaners to form the shape. When you've had a chance to check everyone's work, name a new shape and have students continue as before. **Plane shapes**

Colorful Shapes

Provide students with a supply of crayons in varying lengths. Name a shape; then have students arrange the crayons into the appropriate shape. For a variation, have youngsters form letters or numerals. Plane shapes

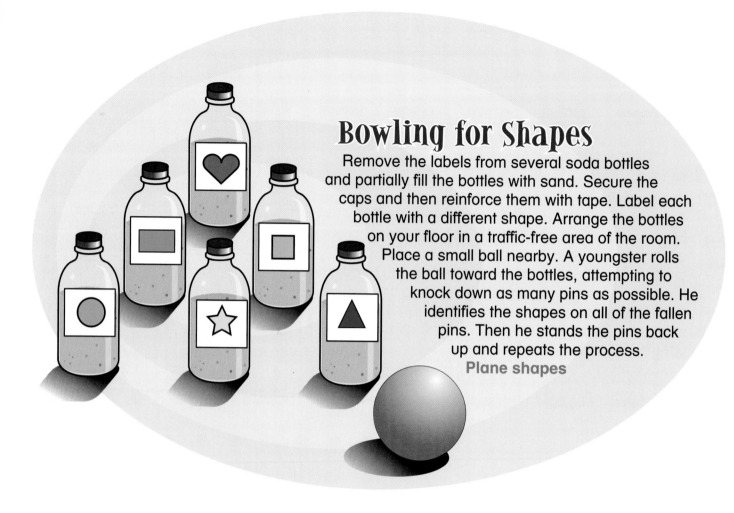

Bowling for Shapes

Remove the labels from several soda bottles and partially fill the bottles with sand. Secure the caps and then reinforce them with tape. Label each bottle with a different shape. Arrange the bottles on your floor in a traffic-free area of the room. Place a small ball nearby. A youngster rolls the ball toward the bottles, attempting to knock down as many pins as possible. He identifies the shapes on all of the fallen pins. Then he stands the pins back up and repeats the process.
Plane shapes

Shape Buddies

Draw sets of small, medium, and large shapes on separate pieces of construction paper to make a class supply. Give each child a paper and encourage him to cut out his shape. Next, instruct him to find his shape buddies (the classmates who have the same shape) and sit with them in your large-group area. When everyone has found his buddies, have each group, in turn, stand up and arrange itself in a row from the smallest shape to the largest shape. **Plane shapes**

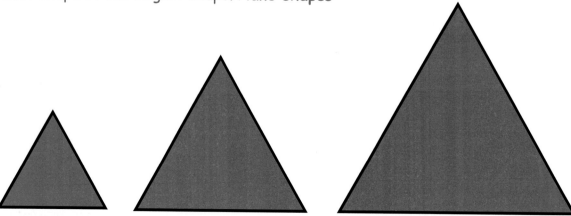

Collage Game

The result of this game is a colorful shape collage! To begin, gather six different shape stampers (or trim sponges into six different shapes). Place the stampers at a table along with colorful, shallow containers of paint and a large sheet of paper. Make a die similar to the one shown by attaching a matching set of shape cutouts to a small tissue box. To begin, invite a child to roll the die and name the shape. Then encourage him to go to the table and use the corresponding stamper to make a print on the paper. Continue in the same way until each youngster has had a chance to add a print to the collage. When the paint is dry, display this shapely artwork in your classroom. Plane shapes

Let's Draw!

Gather a few nine-pocket sports-card holders. Use a permanent marker to draw a different shape in the first pocket in each row as shown. In the second pocket, repeat the shape drawing with dashed lines. Leave the final pocket in each row blank. Place the cardholders at a center along with dry-erase markers and a cloth for erasing. A youngster visits the center and chooses a cardholder; then she uses the marker to trace the shape in the first two pockets and then to draw the shape on her own in the final pocket. She repeats the procedure for each row and then she erases her work for the next visitor. **Plane shapes**

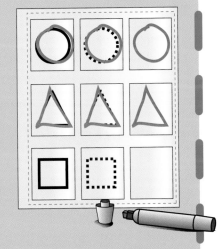

A Splendid Skyscraper

Reinforce rectangles with this picture-perfect project! Give each child a copy of page 112 and two yellow strips of construction paper. Provide access to crayons, including unwrapped black crayons. The youngster colors the scene as desired. Next, she colors the entire page with the side of a black crayon so it resembles a night scene. Then she snips the strips into rectangles and glues them to the building to resemble lighted windows. The youngster then identifies the shape of the building and the windows, noting that all rectangles have two long sides, two short sides, and four corners. **Plane shapes**

A Photo Book

In advance, take photographs of objects in your school that represent solid figures. Glue each photo on a 6" x 9" sheet of construction paper. Then, on the back of the paper, write the name (or draw a picture) of the solid figure it represents. Compile the pages into a class book titled "Name the Shape." Place the book at a center. A youngster studies each photo, determines the solid shape it represents, and turns the page to check her answer. **Solid figures**

Roll, Slide, and Spin

Youngsters identify the properties of solid shapes with this fun learning opportunity! In advance, make a simple chart labeled as shown. Then display the chart and show youngsters a square box (cube), a ball (sphere), and an oatmeal canister (cylinder). Next, invite a child to roll the ball. Since the ball will roll, have the youngster place a check in the appropriate location on the chart. Continue in the same way, checking to see if the ball will spin and slide. Repeat the process with each of the figures, having youngsters note that the cylinder can move differently depending on how it is placed on a flat surface. Solid figures

	roll	slide	spin
sphere	✓		✓
cube		✓	✓
cylinder	✓ on side	✓ on end	✓ on side and end

Shopping for Shapes

To set up this center, display a variety of common objects that represent solid figures. Consider items like cube-shaped tissue boxes, candy kisses, and balls. Label each item with a price tag. Then place a container of cardboard penny manipulatives at the table. Invite a group of youngsters to the table to go shopping for shapes. Encourage each student to choose something he wants to buy and identify the solid figure it represents. Then instruct him to count out the appropriate number of pennies to purchase the item. Solid figures

In or Out

Target the position words *in* and *out* with this nifty song. To begin, take youngsters to your school gymnasium or outside. Then place a plastic hoop in front of each child. Lead students in singing the song provided as they move in and out of the hoop as indicated. **Position words**

(sung to the tune of "Three Blind Mice")

Hoop-de-doo! Hoop-de-doo!
Where are you? Where are you?
Hop *in* the hoop and turn round and round.
Hop *out*; then reach out and touch the ground.
Hop *in*; now let's all jump up and down.
Hoop-de-doo! Hoop-de-doo!

Table Chant

This quick chant can be used prior to snacktime or anytime students are seated at a table or their desks! When youngsters are seated, guide them in performing the chant shown, emphasizing the position words shown and checking students for position-word understanding. **Position words**

One hand *on* the left,
One hand *on* the right.
Both hands *over* the table
And shake with all your might.
Both hands *under* the table
And then *on* the table flat.
Fold them together
And that is that!

Place left hand on table.
Place right hand on table.
Place both hands over the table.
Shake hands.
Place both hands under the table.
Place hands on tabletop.
Clasp hands.
Brush hands together.

Position-Word Practice

Cut out a copy of the cards on page 113 and stack them facedown on a tabletop. After a child chooses a card, quietly read the instruction to him and then have him follow the direction given. Next, have the child call on a classmate; then encourage the classmate to describe what the child has done using an appropriate position word. He put the book beside the chair! Position words

Place a book **beside** a chair.

Check out the skill-building reproducibles on pages 114–115.

Note to the teacher: Use with "A Splendid Skyscraper" on page 109.

Place a book **beside** a chair.

TEC61047

Place a crayon **under** a table.

TEC61047

Hold a pencil **over** a piece of paper.

TEC61047

Place a paper **on** a chair.

TEC61047

Place a small block **in** your pocket.

TEC61047

Place a chair **next to** your teacher.

TEC61047

Shapely Sweets

Color by the code.

Color Code

○ — red   △ — brown

▭ — orange   ▢ — green

Name_____

Turtle Trouble

Trace the shapes. Name each shape.

Measurement, Time, & Money

Furry Friends

Give youngsters an opportunity to compare different heights with the help of some furry friends! In advance, invite each child to bring a stuffed animal to school. (Have several extra stuffed animals available for those youngsters who might need them.) Gather a group of four or five youngsters and have each child get his animal. Prompt youngsters to compare the heights of their animals, using words such as *taller* and *shorter*. Then help students place their animals in a row from shortest to tallest.
Measurement

Rotating Tubs

Provide small groups of students with a tub of same-shaped pattern blocks and a tub of small classroom items such as a ruler, a pencil, and a crayon. Encourage youngsters to measure the items using the pattern blocks. When each group has measured the items in its tub, rotate the tubs.
Measurement

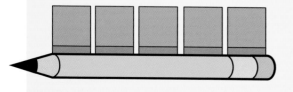

An Interesting "Pasta-bility"

Students are sure to enjoy practicing seriation skills with a supply of spaghetti! Give each youngster a piece of uncooked spaghetti; then encourage him to break the spaghetti into four or five different segments. Have each child arrange the segments in a row from shortest to tallest on a brightly colored piece of paper. After you've had an opportunity to check the arrangement, invite him to glue his spaghetti in place.
Measurement

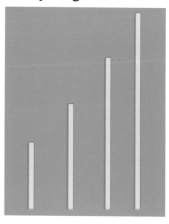

Measuring Up

With this activity students can measure, then compare, the length of their feet. To begin, place each student with a partner. Then have both partners trace a foot on the same sheet of paper. Instruct the partners to help each other cut a piece of yarn the length of each foot. Then have each child use a sticky dot to attach her piece of yarn to the bottom edge of the pair's paper (near her own illustration). Encourage the partners to compare the lengths of each piece of yarn. Which child has the longer foot? **Measurement**

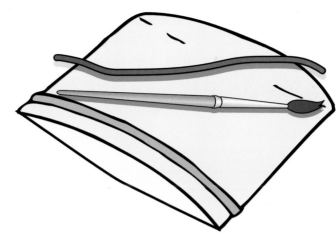

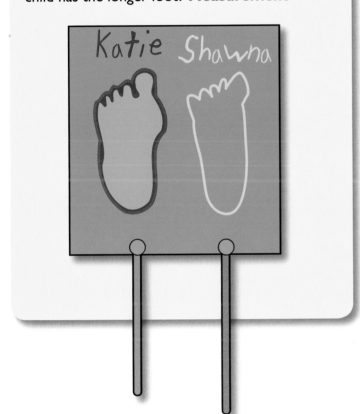

Make a Match!

To prepare, collect a number of items that vary in length and will fit easily into a large zippered plastic bag. You might select common items such as a pencil, a craft stick, a book, and a paintbrush, or toys such as a small car and a block. Measure and cut a length of yarn to match the length of each item; then place the items and pieces of yarn into a large zippered plastic bag. To use, invite a youngster to remove each object from the bag and find the piece of yarn that matches its length. **Measurement**

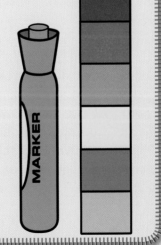

Measurement Freeze

Get little ones moving with this measurement game! Have each child snap together ten Unifix cubes. Then encourage youngsters to walk around the room, comparing the length of their cube constructions to items in the classroom. When a youngster finds something that is shorter than his length of cubes, prompt him to freeze next to the object and hold up his cubes. When everyone has frozen, have each child name the object he has found. Repeat the process, encouraging students to find objects that are longer than their cube constructions. **Measurement**

One Tall Teacher

Students use craft sticks to measure your height with this fun learning opportunity! Have a classroom helper (or a child) trace your body on a sheet of bulletin board paper to make an outline. Draw lines to mark the bottom and the top of your outline as shown. Then place the outline in a center along with a supply of craft sticks. A child places sticks from the bottom mark to the top and then counts the number of sticks used. **Measurement**

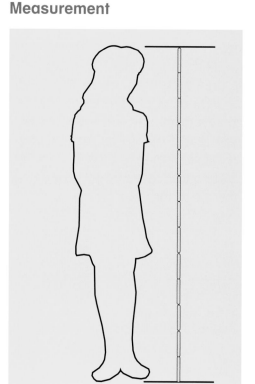

Hands-on Capacity

This engaging activity gives youngsters plenty of hands-on experience with capacity! Explain to students that *capacity* is how much an object can hold. Then show youngsters a container of foam peanuts (or other small objects). Have students estimate how many peanuts they think you can scoop out of the container with one hand. Encourage each child to write his estimate on a hand cutout and attach it to the board. Then scoop a handful of peanuts from the container and have students help count the total amount. Finally, prompt youngsters to compare the number with their estimates. Repeat this activity, having a youngster or special classroom visitor scoop out the peanuts. **Measurement**

Weighty Decision

Fill several 20-ounce soda bottles with varying amounts of sand. To seal, line the caps with hot glue and screw them in place. Then invite students to order the bottles from the lightest to the heaviest. Make this activity self-checking by numbering the bottoms of the bottles. **Measurement**

Supersize It!

Youngsters are sure to have an enormous amount of fun with this extralarge clock! In advance, use spray paint to make a large clockface on a bedsheet. Make an hour and a minute hand from poster board. To begin, place the sheet on the floor and encourage youngsters to sit near the bottom of the clock. Invite a child to write a time on the board. Then give a second youngster the hour and minute hands and encourage him to place the hands on the clock to show the time. Continue in the same way with several different youngsters. **Time**

Time Tags

Incorporate telling time into your daily activities! Cut out a class supply of colorful clocks (pattern on page 123). Then laminate and hole-punch the clocks. Divide the clocks into several small sets; then use a dry-erase marker to label each set with a different time. At the beginning of the school day, help each child pin a clock to his shirt. Then incorporate the times into your daily activities. For example, request that all youngsters wearing the time 6:00 line up for lunch or that all students wearing matching times form small groups. Repeat the process the next school day, switching the tags so that each child is wearing a new time. **Time**

It's a Match!

For every two students, program a clock cutout (pattern on page 123) with a different time; then label an index card with the matching time. To begin, gather youngsters in your large-group area and give each child either a clock or an index card. Encourage each student to read the time on his card and then find the student who has the matching time. Have each youngster sit down when he finds his partner. After all the matches have been made, collect the cards and then play another round! **Time**

AM and PM

Help youngsters understand AM and PM with this simple activity. For each youngster, fold a sheet of drawing paper in half; then unfold it and label each side as shown. Explain that AM refers to a time in the morning. Have students draw a picture of something they do during the AM hours on the appropriate side of the paper. Repeat the process with the remaining side of the paper, explaining that PM refers to the afternoon and evening hours. If desired, encourage students to share their drawings with their classmates. Time.

Personal Preferences

Label a simple graph with the headings shown. Also make a supply of sun and moon cutouts. To begin, explain to youngsters that a *morning person* is someone who enjoys morning more than other times of the day. Further explain that a *night owl* is someone who likes the nighttime the best. Invite each child to share whether he's more of a morning person or a night owl. Then have each youngster place a corresponding cutout on the graph. Finally, discuss the results of the completed graph. Time

Morning, Noon, and Night

In advance, make a chart with three columns and then label each column with the heading shown. Color and cut out a copy of the cards on page 124. To begin, show the students a card and have youngsters identify what is happening in the picture. Next, instruct a child to name when the event would most likely occur: morning, noon, or night. Have the youngster attach the card to the appropriate column. Repeat the process for each remaining card. Time

Marvelous Motions!

Help little ones understand the concepts of *yesterday, today, and tomorrow* with some simple hand motions! To begin, show youngsters the hand motions below, explaining that yesterday is already behind them, today is right now, and tomorrow is coming up next. Then, during your calendar routine, have students use the three signs as they identify the names of the days for yesterday, today, and tomorrow. **Calendar**

What's the News?

Label three cards with the words shown and post them near your class calendar. During calendar time, ask a volunteer to share some news with the class as you write her name and her words on a sheet of paper. Post the paper below the today card. Also select a student to share the next day; then write her name on a paper and post it below the tomorrow card. During the next school day, shift each paper to the left. Review yesterday's news. Then continue in the same way, having the designated youngster share her news for today and choosing a future newscaster to place below the tomorrow card. **Calendar**

yesterday	today	tomorrow
Jana I have a new puppy.	Eric My big brother has a soccer game after school and I'm going to go.	D'Shaun

Day by Day

With this idea, you can reinforce the days of the week *and* transition students one at a time to their next activity. To begin, have youngsters sit in a circle. Then choose a child and encourage him to say, "Sunday." Prompt the classmate next to him to say, "Monday." Then continue in the same way for each remaining day of the week. The child who says, "Saturday" is the one designated to leave the group. Repeat the process several times until all youngsters have transitioned to the next activity. **Calendar**

Fill the Bank

At this math center, youngsters sort coins onto adorable piggy banks. To begin, enlarge the piggy bank on page 125; then make three pink construction paper copies. Cut out the banks and label them with the amounts shown. Then place the banks at a center along with a supply of penny, nickel, and dime cards (patterns on page 125). A child chooses a coin, identifies how much it is worth, and then places it on the corresponding bank. He continues until all of the coins have been sorted onto the banks. **Money**

The Banker Says...

Reinforce coin recognition and listening skills with this variation of Simon Says. Gather a small group of students and give each child a penny, nickel, dime, and quarter cutout (patterns on page 125). To play, take the role of the banker and tell the group to pick up a specific coin. The group members should respond only if your request is prefaced by "The banker says." Verify the coins that were selected. If a child chooses an incorrect coin, guide him to select the correct one. If a child responds without the banker's okay, he sits out for one round of play. Continue in this manner as time allows. **Money**

Seasonal Sales

Invite students to go on a seasonal shopping spree! Clip pictures of items in newspaper flyers during seasonal sales, such as Christmas items in December or beach-related items in June. Glue each picture to a small tagboard card and print an imaginary price (from 1¢ to 25¢) on the back of each card. Give each child in a small group a supply of penny cards (patterns on page 125) and let the buying begin! Have each child choose a specified number of items and count out her pennies to "pay" for them. Gotta stay within your budget! **Money**

Check out the skill-building reproducible on page 126.

Time of Day Cards
Use with "Morning, Noon, and Night" on page 120.

©The Mailbox® • *Superbook*® • TEC61047

TEC61047

Coin Cards
Use with "Fill the Bank," "The Banker Says…," and "Seasonal Sales" on page 122.

Measure. ## LEAP, FROG!

 Write the answer in each box.

 Circle the frog that leaped the highest.

Graphing

What Color Is Your Door?

When you do this data-collection activity, you'll be making your home-school connection right at your students' front doors. In advance, duplicate the parent note on page 130 to send home with each child. When your students return their completed notes, label a large graph so that each child's door color is represented. Then have each child cut out his door pattern. During group time, sing the song below. As each child's door color is mentioned in the song, invite her to tape her door cutout in the appropriate column on the graph. Repeat the song as much as necessary, filling in a different color name each time, until every child has attached her cutout to the graph. Then discuss the results. **Data collection**

What Color Is Your Door?
(sung to the tune of "The Farmer in the Dell")

What color is your door?
What color is your door?
Heigh-ho, at home, you know.
What color is your door?

Is your front door [color name]?
Is your front door [color name]?
Heigh-ho, at home, you know.
Is your front door [color name]?

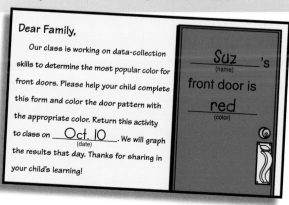

Dear Family,

Our class is working on data-collection skills to determine the most popular color for front doors. Please help your child complete this form and color the door pattern with the appropriate color. Return this activity to class on ___Oct. 10___ *(date)*. We will graph the results that day. Thanks for sharing in your child's learning!

___Suz___'s *(name)* front door is ___red___ *(color)*

A Sweet Graph!

To prepare for this activity, obtain a bag of miniature candy bars. (Be sure to use a bag that contains several different varieties.) Label each row on a blank graphing grid to correspond to a different candy bar. Then post the grid in your large-group area. To begin, give a candy bar to each child and invite him to eat his treat and save the wrapper. Instruct each youngster to tape his wrapper to the appropriate row on the grid. When the graph is complete, have students identify which variety of candy bar has the most wrappers on the graph and which has the fewest. **Object graph**

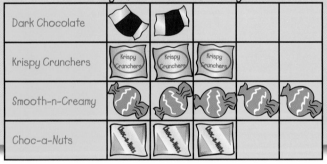

How Many of Each Kind of Candy Bar?

So Many Colors

Have students sort a supply of new crayons into color families, such as reds, greens, and yellows. When the crayons have been sorted, help youngsters count the crayons in each family and lay them end to end to create a graph. Which color family has the most? Which has the least? Are any equal? **Object graph**

Pleasing Pasta

Supply each child in your class with a handful of different pasta pieces. Encourage her to sort the pieces. Then have her identify her most common pasta shape and glue it onto a class graph. Discuss which shape is most common and which is least common. Are any shapes equal? **Object graph**

Our Favorite Holidays

Happy Holidays

Which holidays are favorites of your youngsters? Find out with this nifty graph! Choose four different pieces of clip art, each representing a different holiday. Make several copies of each picture. Color one of each type of picture and attach it to a graph as shown. Place the other copies of the clip art pictures in stacks near the graph. To begin, prompt students to discuss holidays they enjoy. Then present the four different choices on the graph. Instruct each child to choose a picture that represents his favorite holiday of the four shown. After each student colors his picture, encourage him to place it on the graph in the appropriate row. Then lead youngsters in a discussion about the results of the graph. **Picture graph**

A Birthday Graph

The result of this graph is a display of student birthdays that you can leave up all year. Create a chart listing the months of the year on a large paper cupcake. Next, have each child draw a self-portrait on a small paper card and sign her name. Then help her write the date of her birthday in the top right corner. Once each child has finished, have each child, in turn, tape her card to the correct row. Then pose questions about the completed graph for youngsters to answer. **Picture graph**

Happy Birthday!

January	
February	
March	
April	
May	
June	
July	
August	
September	
October	
November	
December	

Yes or No

Students will learn plenty about each other with this daily (or weekly) graphing activity. In advance, label two sheets of tagboard as shown and place them in an easily accessible location for your students. Set a basket containing a class supply of Unifix cubes nearby. Each morning, post a different question and read it aloud. As students have time throughout the day, invite each youngster to place a cube on one of the tagboard sheets to answer the question, attaching his cube to any others placed there by classmates. Then, at the end of the day, lead students in counting the cubes in each tower and interpreting the data. **Symbolic graph**

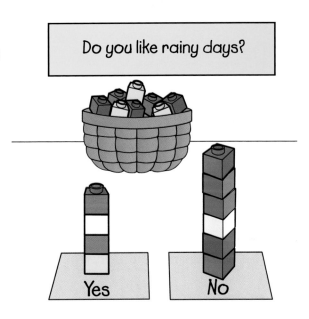

Do you like rainy days?

Yes   No

Just Rollin' Along

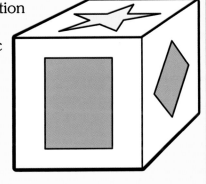

Youngsters will roll right into this data-collection activity while learning some basic shapes along the way. In advance, convert a cube-shaped, empty tissue box into a large die by covering it with a piece of bulletin board paper. Glue a different shape cutout onto each side of the die. (See the shapes on page 131.) Make a copy of page 131 for every two students in your class. Then divide your class into pairs, appointing a roller and a recorder for each pair. Give each pair a copy of the recording form. In turn, have each roller roll the die. His recorder will then color a graph square corresponding to the shape rolled. After several rounds, ask the partners to count the number of colored squares in each column. Which shape was rolled most often by each pair? Then give each pair a new recording form, have the partners switch duties, and roll forward with another round of this activity. **Bar graph**

3-D Graph

Try this twist on the traditional graph. Create a three-dimensional graph by inserting pipe cleaners into balls of clay. Press the balls onto a shoebox lid as shown; then label each pipe cleaner with a graphing category. Provide each child with one Mathlink cube (or Unifix cube). To record his vote, a child slides his cube onto the appropriate pipe cleaner. **Symbolic graph**

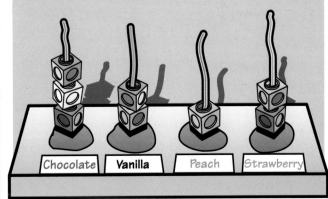

Chocolate   Vanilla   Peach   Strawberry

Check out the skill-building reproducible on page 132.

Dear Family,

Our class is working on data-collection skills to determine the most popular color for front doors. Please help your child complete this form and color the door pattern with the appropriate color. Return this activity to class on _____. We will graph
(date)
the results that day. Thanks for sharing in your child's learning!

©The Mailbox® • *Superbook®* • TEC61047

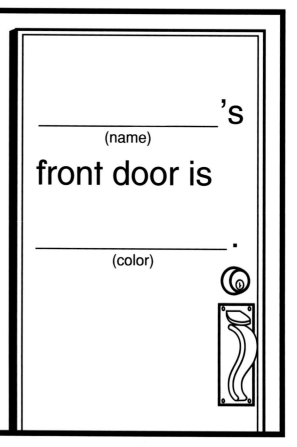

_____'s
(name)

front door is

_____.
(color)

Dear Family,

Our class is working on data-collection skills to determine the most popular color for front doors. Please help your child complete this form and color the door pattern with the appropriate color. Return this activity to class on _____. We will graph
(date)
the results that day. Thanks for sharing in your child's learning!

©The Mailbox® • *Superbook®* • TEC61047

_____'s
(name)

front door is

_____.
(color)

Name _____

Note to the teacher: Use with "Just Rollin' Along" on page 129.

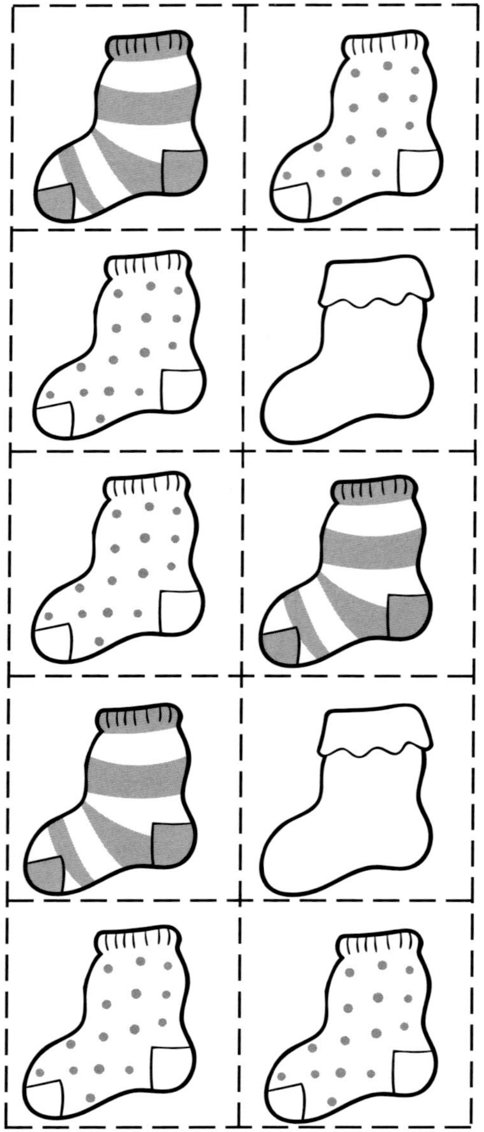

Name _____

Lunching on Laundry

✂ Cut. Graph.

Glue in place.

Goat's Socks

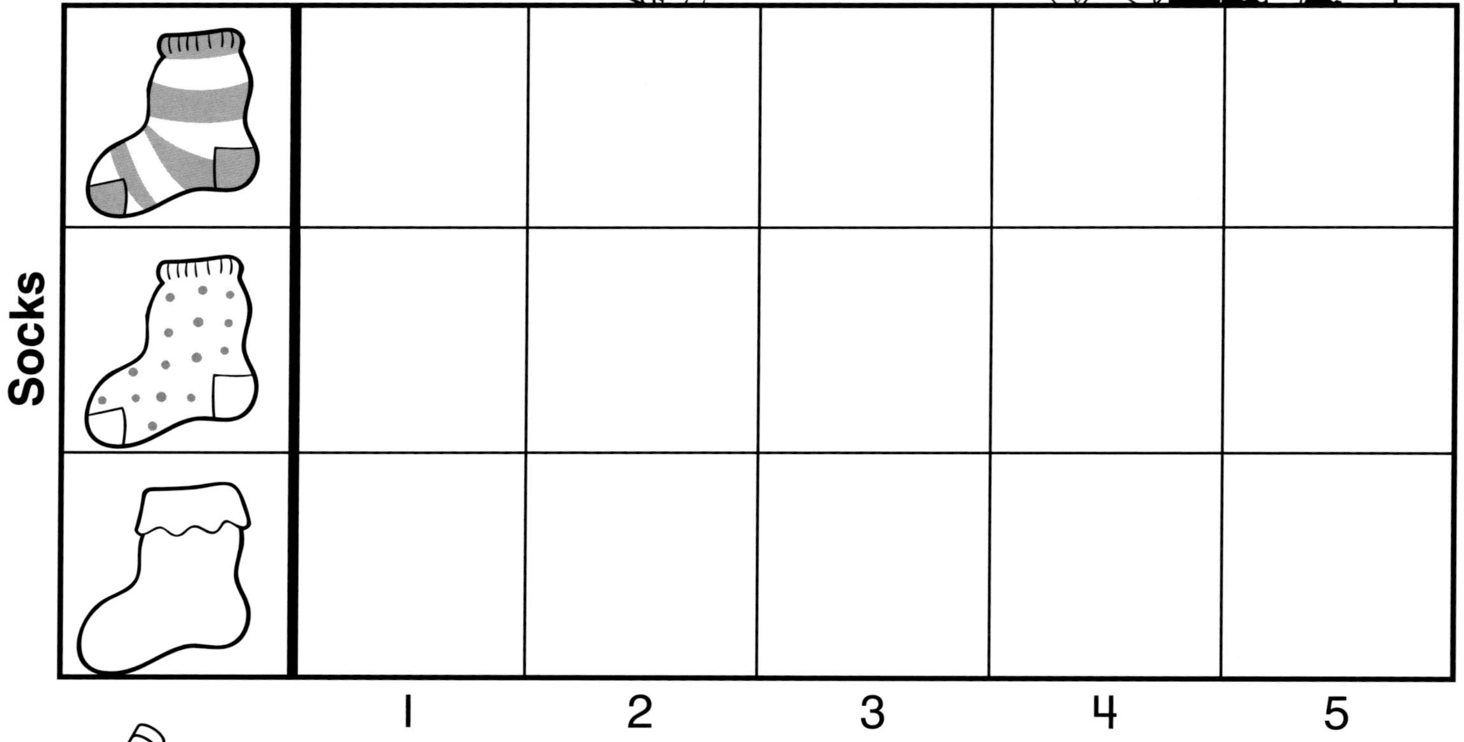

Socks

	1	2	3	4	5

Number of Socks

✏ Circle.

1. Which has more?    or

2. Which has less?    or

Plants

From Seed to Flower

Lead youngsters in performing this fun action chant to help them better understand the parts of a plant.

Plant a seed in a little cup.
The roots grow down
And the sprouts grow up.
It grows quite tall
And soon you'll see
A flower as pretty as can be!

Pretend to drop a seed in a cup.
Point down.
Point up.
Stand on tiptoes.
Place hand above eyes and look up.
Make a circle with arms to resemble a flower.

Alike	Different
Both have stems. Both can have petals. Both have leaves. Both are alive. Both need water.	Trees have fruit, and flowers don't. Trees are big, and flowers are small. Trees are made of wood.

Terrific Trees, Fabulous Flowers

Youngsters compare trees and flowers with this easy activity! To prepare, make a chart similar to the one shown and post it in your large-group area. Present a potted flower to your youngsters and have them describe what they see. Next, have youngsters visit a tree near your school (or look at photographs of trees) and repeat the process. Invite students to describe how trees and flowers are alike and different as you write their words on the chart in the appropriate columns. Conclude by asking youngsters to describe what they like about trees and flowers.

A Super Salad

People eat many different plant parts, and all of them can go into this super salad! Send a note home requesting parents to provide the different plant parts needed for the salad. Some options include lettuce (leaves), carrots (roots), celery (stems), broccoli (flowers), tomatoes (fruit), and sunflower seed kernels (seeds). Explain the plant part represented by each ingredient. Wash the ingredients; then have youngsters use butter knives to chop any large ingredients into smaller pieces. Assemble the salad in a large bowl and then serve it to your youngsters with kid-friendly dressing. Yum!

Build a Plant

To prepare for this partner game, color and cut out two copies of the plant parts on page 135 and one copy of the spinner on page 136. Place each set of plant parts in a resealable plastic bag. Then place the bags at a center along with the spinner, a pencil, and a jumbo paper clip. Two youngsters visit the center and each child takes a bag. One child uses the pencil to hold the paper clip on the spinner; then she spins the spinner by flicking the paper clip. She removes the corresponding part from her bag and places it in front of her. Her partner repeats the process. Each young-ster continues in the same way to build a plant, missing a turn if the spinner lands on a plant part that she has already removed from the bag. The first person to completely build a flower names all the parts and is declared the winner!

Water, Soil, and Sun

Spotlight the basic needs of plants with this simple tune!

(sung to the tune of "The Farmer in the Dell")

Water, soil, and sun.
Water, soil, and sun.
Three things a plant must have
Are water, soil, and sun.

A Texturized Tree

To make this classroom tree display, give each youngster a sheet of copy paper and an unwrapped brown crayon. Take students outside and have them use their supplies to make a rubbing of tree bark. (If a tree isn't available, have youngsters make a rubbing of corrugated cardboard to resemble bark.) Collect students' papers and display them on a wall as shown to make a tree trunk. Have students cut strips of brown construction paper; then help them attach the strips above and below the trunk to make branches and roots. Encourage students to add leaf cutouts to the branches. Finally, enlist students' help in labeling index cards with the different parts of a tree and attaching them to the display.

leaves

branches

trunk

roots

TEC61047

Spinner Pattern

Use with "Build a Plant" on page 134.

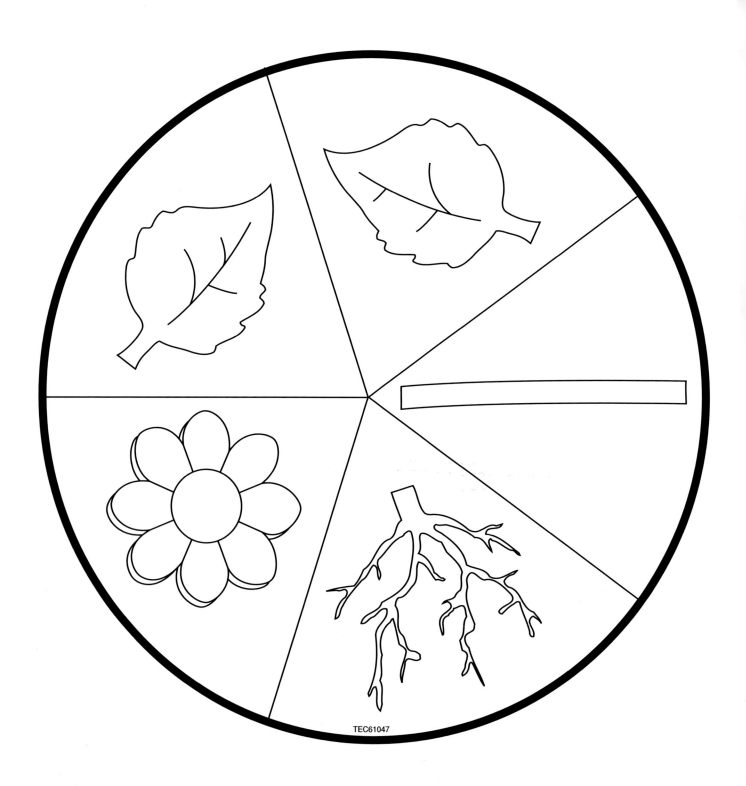

TEC61047

ANIMALS

Leo Lion's Needs

Review the needs of animals with this fun game. Have students practice roaring like a lion. To play, say a phrase such as "Leo Lion needs water." If the named item is something a lion needs, youngsters respond by roaring. If it is not, the children remain quiet. Continue to substitute different items in this manner, saying realistic needs of a lion as well as giggle-worthy statements such as "Leo Lion needs tennis shoes." If desired, play another round by substituting a new animal name and sound.

Animals All Around

Animals love the great outdoors as much as children do—maybe more! After all, for most of them, it's their home! Discuss with youngsters the many types of animal homes they might see outdoors, such as a spiderweb, an anthill, a nest, and a tree stump. Then give each child a copy of page 139 and a crayon. Take the children on a walk to hunt for animal homes. Invite each child to draw an animal home that she spots and to write or dictate the name of the animal that she thinks lives there. When you return to the classroom, have youngsters share their findings with the class.

Name _Jamie_

Home Hunting

Who lives here?
a spider

ALL GROWN-UP

To prepare for this small-group game, color and cut out a copy of the picture cards on page 140, omitting the fish, snake, and lizard cards. Post the cards where students can see them and then secretly choose an animal from one of the cards. Lead youngsters in reciting the first three lines of the poem, inserting the name of the baby animal that corresponds with the chosen animal. Ask a student volunteer to choose the corresponding adult animal card. If she is correct, lead students in reciting the last line of the poem, inserting the appropriate adult animal name. If she is incorrect, help her find the correct card before completing the poem.

Adult Animals	Baby Animals
duck	duckling
bear	cub
dog	puppy
kangaroo	joey
chicken	chick
goose	gosling

I'm a baby [duckling];
I will change and grow.
When I grow up,
I'll be a [duck], you know!

Lovely Life Cycles

Youngsters illustrate the life cycle of a butterfly by making these delightful projects. To begin, give each child a strip of construction paper divided and labeled as shown. Then lead each student in following the steps below to create his own project. After the paint dries, help youngsters use a fine-tip marker to add desired details to each box.

Steps:
1. In the first box, draw a leaf. Then dip a finger in white paint and press it onto the leaf to create an egg.
2. Dip a finger in green paint and press it onto the second box several times in a row so that the paint resembles a caterpillar.
3. Draw a tree branch in the third box. Then dip your thumb in white paint and press it against the tree branch to make a chrysalis.
4. Dip a finger in colorful paint and press it onto the paper four times to create butterfly wings.

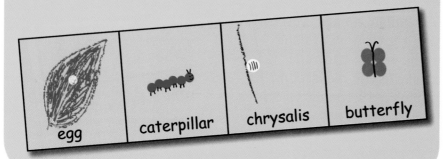

egg   caterpillar   chrysalis   butterfly

Savvy Sorting

This interactive activity helps youngsters identify animals' body coverings. Write the following words on separate index cards: *fur, scales,* and *feathers.* Post each card in a different location in the room. Color and cut apart several copies of the animal cards on page 140 and give one animal card to each child. Ask her to determine the pictured animal's body covering and stand near the appropriate posted card. Quickly scan for accuracy. To play again, collect the cards, shuffle them, and give each youngster a new card. If desired, play a similar game, posting index cards identifying habitats or different kinds of movement.

Home Hunting

Who lives here?

_____

Note to the teacher: Use with "Animals All Around" on page 137.

Animal Cards

Use with "All Grown-Up" and "Savvy Sorting" on page 138.

The Five Senses

Get the Picture?

Open students' eyes to the importance of the sense of sight with this activity. Have each child draw a simple picture, such as a house, on a sheet of paper. Then ask him to close his eyes and draw the same picture on another sheet of paper. Once his drawings are complete, invite him to open his eyes and compare his two drawings. Engage youngsters in a discussion about the importance of the sense of sight and how it affects their daily activities.

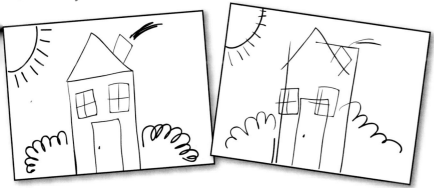

Follow Your Nose

Since many products have distinctive aromas, challenge your students to a scent-matching activity. Collect 12 empty, plastic film canisters; then prepare a smelling center. To do this place a cotton ball inside each film canister. Choose one of the spices or extracts listed below and sprinkle a bit of it into a pair of canisters. Program the bottoms of the paired canisters with matching-colored dots for self-checking. Repeat for each of six spices or extracts.

- allspice
- almond extract
- banana extract
- cinnamon
- chocolate syrup or extract
- coconut extract
- cloves
- vanilla extract
- lemon extract or peel
- orange extract or peel
- nutmeg

SNAP, CLAP, STOMP!

The actions at this center become music to your little ones' ears! Cut apart three copies of the sound cards on page 143 and stack them at a center. A youngster chooses several cards and arranges them in a row. Then he performs the corresponding actions to hear the sounds produced by each. He returns the cards to the bottom of the stack and chooses new cards to repeat the activity.

   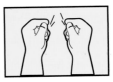

Sweet or Not Sweet?

Tempt your youngsters' sense of taste with a delicious selection of fruits. In advance, prepare a large graph as shown. Set up a taste test with sliced oranges, pink grapefruits, apples, and bananas. Place corresponding colored stickers in front of each fruit. Instruct each student to taste each fruit, then decide whether it tastes sweet or not. Then have him take a corresponding sticker and place it on the graph in the appropriate column. Which fruits did your class think were sweet?

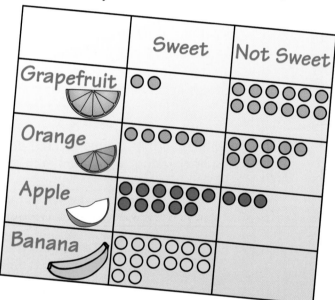

THERE'S THE RUB!

Bark provides a perfect introduction to the sense of touch. In advance, make a class set of page 144. Find a location with several kinds of trees. Provide crayons in various shades of gray and brown. Give each child a copy of page 144; then head outside to touch trees. As each student feels a tree, ask her to make a bark rubbing on her handout. Then have her write or dictate the color of the bark and decide whether the bark is smooth, rough, or shaggy. After returning to the classroom, have students fill in the final blank on their papers by writing or dictating a description of what the bark felt like. Bind all your students' rubbings between two sheets of construction paper to make a class book.

Feely Sacks

Prepare this center for tactile matching fun. Gather two of each of the following items.

cotton balls   silk flowers
lemons   cinnamon sticks
blocks   crayons
pinecones   sandpaper pieces

Then make eight simple feely sacks. To make one, fold a paper lunch bag lengthwise. Draw a half circle the size of a child's fist on the fold. Divide the half circle into four equal slices. Beginning at the fold, cut each slice to the edge of the circle. Then open the bag, place one item from a pair inside, fold the top down, and staple the bag closed. Place all the bags and the matching items in a center. Can your students find the match for each item by touch alone?

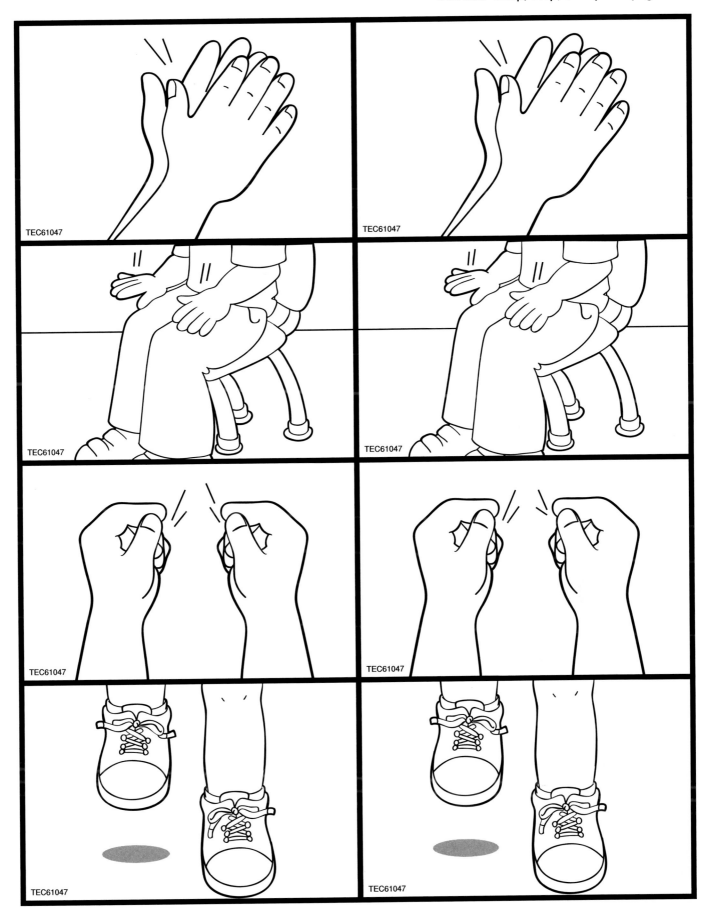

Here is my rubbing of a tree's bark.

The bark is _____ and _____.
                                  (color)   (smooth, rough, or shaggy)

It feels like _____.

©The Mailbox® • Superbook® • TEC61047

144   **Note to the teacher:** Use with "There's the Rub!" on page 142.

WEATHER & SEASONS

What's the Weather?

Add this song to your daily weather routine to remind youngsters of possible weather conditions. Each day lead students in singing the song; then ask a volunteer to describe the current weather.

(sung to the tune of "Found a Peanut")

Is it rainy? Is it sunny?
Is it cloudy? Is there snow?
What's the weather? What's the weather?
Come and tell us so we'll know.

Weather Watchers

Youngsters take these supersimple projects home and make daily weather observations. To begin, give each student a paper plate that has been divided into four sections. Help him label each section as shown and draw a picture to match the corresponding weather. Then glue a strip of magnetic tape to the back of each plate. Clip a clothespin to each completed project and have each student take his project home and attach it to his refrigerator. Encourage each child to have his family help him check the weather each day and move the clothespin to the appropriate section of the plate.

A Week of Weather

To prepare, cut out five copies of the journal page on page 147 for each student. Stack each child's pages between construction paper covers and staple each journal along the left edge. On Monday, invite students to look out a window or step outside to observe the weather. Lead a discussion of how the weather affects our feelings and choice of surroundings. Then help each child complete the sentence on the first page of her weather journal and illustrate her statement. (If the weather stays the same for more than one day, encourage youngsters to draw a unique illustration on each page.) Repeat this activity with a new journal page each day. At the end of the week, invite youngsters to take their weather journals home to share with their families.

Sensational Seasons

Play this action-packed game to review the four seasons. Divide students into four groups and assign each group a different season. Demonstrate the movements shown below and have each group practice the movement that corresponds with its assigned season. To play, have the groups listen as you name seasonal items one at a time. When a youngster hears an item that corresponds with his group's assigned season, he performs his designated movement. Continue to play in this manner as time allows.

Fall—Flutter to the ground like a leaf.
Winter—Shiver and clutch shoulders as if it's cold.
Spring—Jump up like a growing flower.
Summer—Fan face with hands as if it's hot.

What to Wear

These creative booklets are a fun way for youngsters to review appropriate seasonal clothing. To begin, lead students in a discussion of the typical weather conditions in each season. Continue the discussion by asking volunteers to share examples of appropriate clothing to wear in each season. Then give each child a copy of page 148. Have her draw a picture of herself on each page, dressed in appropriate clothing for the corresponding season. Next, have her cut out the pages and stack them between two construction paper covers. Help each child staple her booklet and add a title and illustration to her cover.

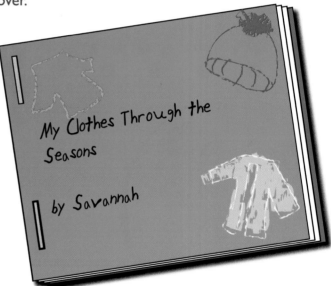

My Clothes Through the Seasons

by Savannah

Seasonal Reminders

Make this thought-provoking class book to review an individual season. To prepare, program a sheet of paper similar to the one shown, and copy a class supply. Then create a student-generated list of things that remind youngsters of the designated season. Have each student choose an item, write it on his page, and add an illustration. Stack the completed pages between two construction paper covers and add an appropriate title. If desired, repeat the activity during the remaining seasons.

Fall reminds me of _pumpkins_.

because it is a _____

_____ day!

_____ is where I'd like to stay

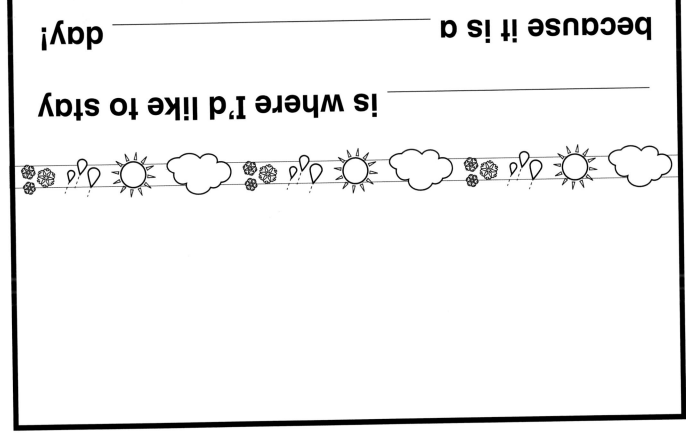

because it is a _____

_____ day!

_____ is where I'd like to stay

Journal Pages
Use with "A Week of Weather" on page 145.

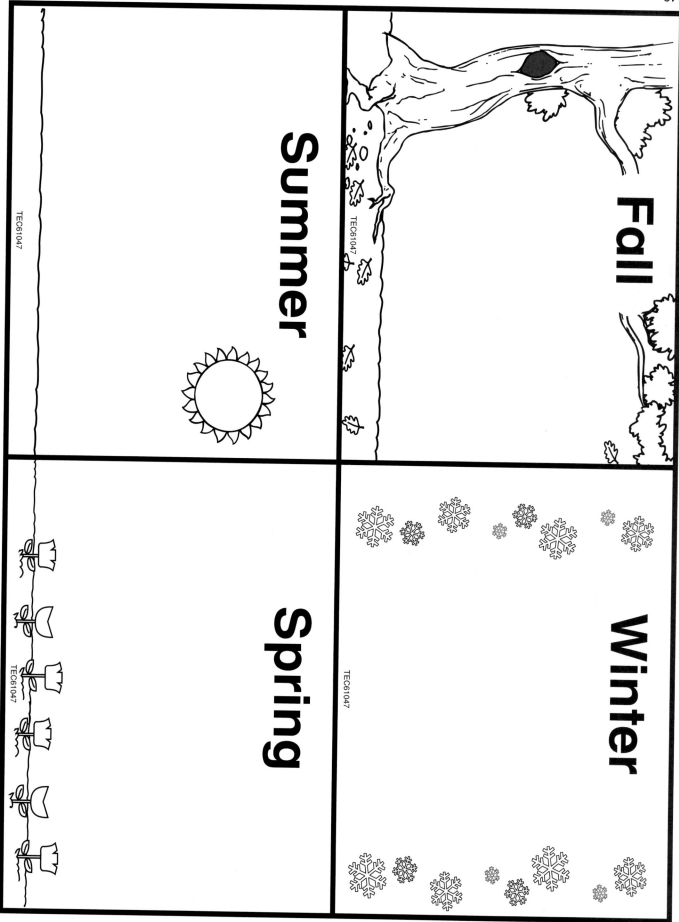

Fall

TEC61047

Summer

TEC61047

Winter

TEC61047

Spring

TEC61047

Booklet Pages
Use with "What to Wear" on page 146.

Tooth Fairy Facts

Display dental information about your class with this tooth fairy glyph! Post an enlarged copy of the legend and make a white construction paper copy of the tooth fairy pattern on page 151 for each student. Read aloud the legend, pausing after each listing so students may color their pages. Display the completed fairies; then pose glyph-related questions for students to answer, such as "How many girls eat apples?" or "How many boys brush their teeth more than once a day?"

Legend

Clothes
purple = girl
red = boy

Star
orange = lost a tooth
yellow = never lost a tooth

Fairy Dust
green = visit the dentist
yellow = never been to the dentist

Hair Color
yellow = like to eat apples
brown = do not like to eat apples

Wings
blue = brush teeth once a day
green = brush teeth more than once a day

Brush the outside of your top teeth.

Brush the inside of your top teeth.

Brush the outside of your bottom teeth.

Brush the inside of your bottom teeth.

Brush the places your teeth touch.

Brush your tongue.

Big Brushes!

Youngsters are sure to show off good brushing habits with these toothbrushes! Give each child a copy of the toothbrush bristles on page 152. As you read aloud the text on each bristle, invite a volunteer to use a clean, dry toothbrush to demonstrate the corresponding brushing technique on a hand puppet or stuffed animal. Then have each youngster cut apart his bristles and glue each one to one end of a long construction paper rectangle (toothbrush). Encourage youngsters to take their supersize brushes home to share with their families.

Fun to Be Fit!

Emphasize the importance of physical activity every day with this little ditty. After several rounds of the song, ask youngsters to share physical activities they participate in.

(sung to the tune of "I'm a Little Teapot")

I'm a little active every day.
I like to run and jump when I play!
When I'm with my friends,
We all will say,
"Hooray for fitness every day!"

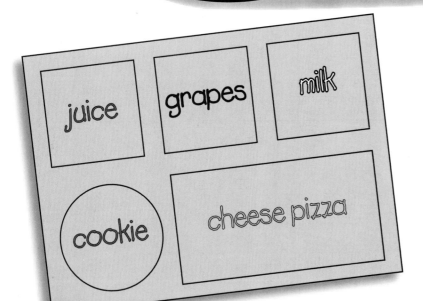

juice
grapes
milk
cookie
cheese pizza

Hot Lunch Lessons!

Where can you find an example of a meal with all of the food groups? Why, the school cafeteria of course! Draw a school lunch tray on a large sheet of tagboard and laminate. Each morning, use a wipe-off marker to write the day's menu on the tray. Then ask individual volunteers to identify the food group(s) for each item. For an added challenge, encourage youngsters to compare the number of servings for each food group.

Food for Thought

Youngsters' food descriptions are perfect for this whole-group activity. Whisper the name of a food in a student's ear. Then encourage him to describe the food and identify its food group. Invite group members to use the clues and guess the name of the food. When a student names the food described, continue in the same manner having him give clues for a new mystery food.

It is orange.
It is crunchy.
It is in the vegetable group.

Brush the outside of your top teeth.

TEC61047

Brush the inside of your top teeth.

TEC61047

Brush the outside of your bottom teeth.

TEC61047

Brush the inside of your bottom teeth.

TEC61047

Brush the places your teeth touch.

TEC61047

Brush your tongue.

TEC61047

Toothbrush Bristles
Use with "Big Brushes!" on page 149.

All About My Family and Me

You Know What You Like

A week filled with favorite things will help students enjoy their differences and similarities. Explain to the class that since each of us is different; we like different things, such as different games, toys, and foods. Ask students to discuss some of their favorite things. Then plan a Favorites Week.

Send a note home to parents asking that each child bring in his favorite toy on Monday, his favorite game on Tuesday, a picture of his favorite people on Wednesday, a favorite book on Thursday, and a favorite food on Friday. Each day set aside some time for students to play with or discuss their favorite objects. On Friday, celebrate with a feast of favorite foods.

You and I

Support a celebration of individual differences with this poetic display. Encourage each youngster to draw on a sheet of paper a full-length picture of himself. Arrange the completed self-portraits around a copy of the poem shown. After reading the poem several times, encourage your little ones to use the portraits to identify individual differences. For a more realistic version of the display, replace the self-portraits with student photos.

Different

You and I have different eyes,
And we each have a different nose.
Let's face it—we're different
Down to our toes.

You and I have different ears,
And we each have different feet.
Let's face it—we're different.
Isn't that neat?

You and I have different hair,
And we each have different hands.
Let's face it—being different
Is just grand!

A Family "Photo-Graph"

Youngsters compare the sizes of their families with this graphing activity. In advance, number each row of your pocket chart as shown. Ask each student to bring in a photograph of her family. (Or, if desired, have each student draw her family on a blank card.) When all of the photos are in, have each child count the number of people in her family. Then direct her to place the photo in the corresponding row in the pocket chart. After posing questions about the completed graph, lead students to conclude that, no matter what size the family is, each one is special!

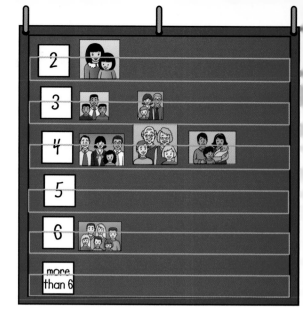

Wyatt's 's family likes to go sailing.

Family Time Together

Little ones showcase their favorite family activities in this student-made scrapbook. Have each child write his name on a copy of page 156. Then have him write or dictate a favorite family activity to complete the sentence. Encourage him to include all of his family members as he illustrates the page in the space provided. Finally, bind the pages into a book with a title such as "A Scrapbook of Family Fun!"

Hoppin' Families!

Students identify their very special family members with this lily pad project. Make a construction paper copy of the frog and flower patterns on page 155 for each child. Be sure to make extra copies of the frog for students who have more than four family members. To begin, help each child write his family's last name on the flower pattern and the name of each family member on an individual frog. Then have him cut out the patterns and glue them to a lily pad shape. Arrange the completed projects on a blue-covered bulletin board titled "Our Hoppin' Families." Finally, invite each youngster to introduce his family and share one special quality about each family member.

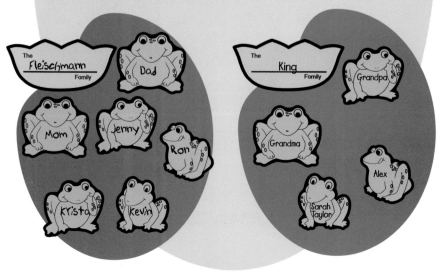

The

Family

TEC61047

TEC61047

TEC61047

TEC61047

TEC61047

155

_____'s family likes to _____

Note to the teacher: Use with "Family Time Together" on page 154.

Favorite Places

Have students describe places in their community such as parks, restaurants, and stores. List the place names on a sheet of chart paper. Next, give each youngster a sheet of construction paper programmed as shown. Have him draw a picture of one of his favorite locations in the community. Then help him fill in the spaces to complete the sentence. Assemble the drawings into a class book titled "Community Favorites."

Ian's favorite place in the community is <u>Johnson's Ice Cream</u>.

A Career Chorus

A community is home to people who have a variety of different jobs. Highlight a few of these jobs with this snappy song. Then have youngsters share other common careers.

(sung to the tune of "She'll Be Comin' Round the Mountain")

There are many jobs in our community.
There are many jobs in our community.
You could teach or be a writer,
Or a big brave firefighter.
There are many jobs in our community.

There are many jobs in our community.
There are many jobs in our community.
You could be a veterinarian,
Or a nurse or a librarian.
There are many jobs in our community.

Tools of the Trade

To prepare, gather several tools that might be used in a variety of jobs, such as a rolling pin, a hand-held gardening spade, a hammer, a piece of chalk, and a tongue depressor. Place the items in a large grocery bag and then show the bag to your youngsters. Invite a student to remove an item from the bag and identify it. Then help youngsters name careers that might use the item. Continue in the same way with each remaining item in the bag.

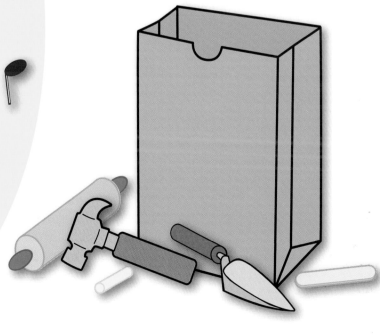

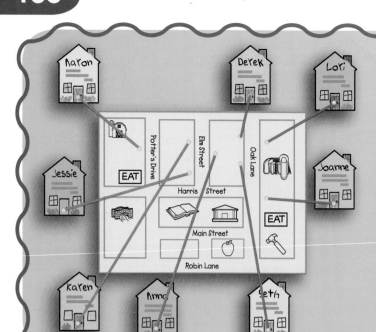

Home, Sweet Home

Youngsters see which classmates live near each other with this fun learning opportunity! To begin, help each child write his name and address on a house cutout (pattern on page 159). Invite each student to decorate his house. Then display the houses around a map that shows the city or town the youngsters live in. Tack a length of yarn from the child's house to his home's location on the map. Finally, discuss the map with your students, drawing attention to youngsters who live near each other and near specific landmarks.

Neighborhood Noises

Have youngsters suggest sounds they might hear in their neighborhoods as you write their ideas on chart paper. After you've listed several sounds, choose two volunteers. Whisper to the volunteers the name of one of the sounds and then encourage them to imitate the sound. After the students' performance, have the remaining youngsters guess which sound they were imitating. Repeat the process with several student pairs.

car horn beeping
cat meowing
pigeon cooing
tires screeching
doors shutting
people walking
dog barking
siren wailing

Where do you like to play in your community?

What is your favorite restaurant in your community?

What kinds of jobs do people have in your community?

Community Questions

Here's a circle-time game that's sure to get little ones talking about their community! Cut out a copy of the cards on page 160 and place them in a decorative gift bag. Gather students around the bag and invite a child to draw a card. After you read the question, invite several youngsters to provide an answer. Then continue in the same way with the remaining cards until all students have had a chance to share.

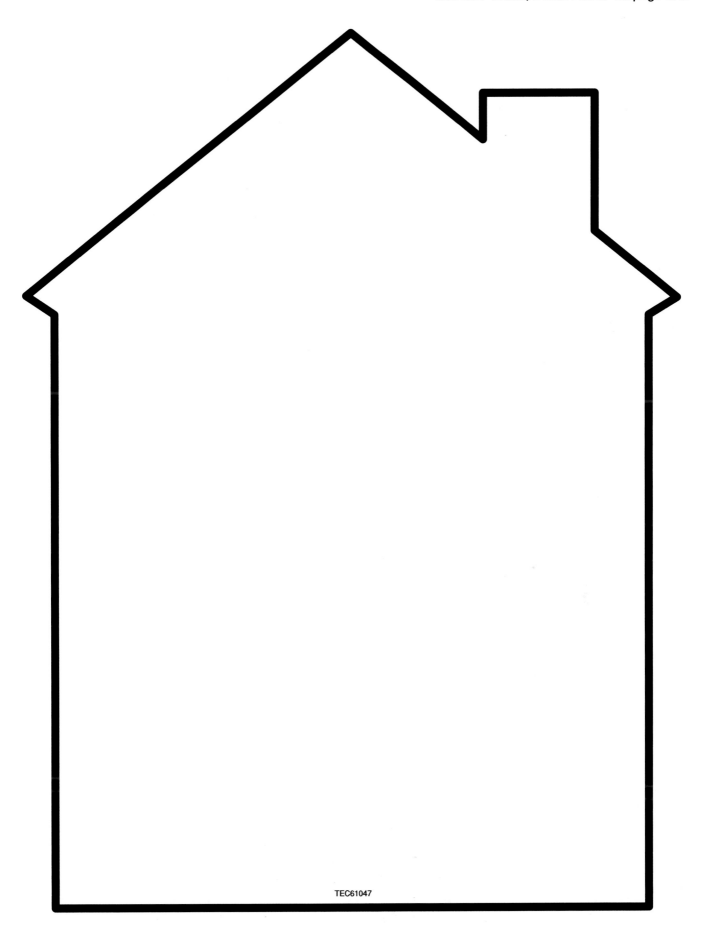

TEC61047

What is your favorite restaurant in your community?

TEC61047

Where do you like to play in your community?

TEC61047

What kinds of jobs do people have in your community?

TEC61047

Have you ever visited a bigger or smaller community than yours? What was it like?

TEC61047

Do you have special events in your community, such as parades and celebrations? What are they?

TEC61047

Name a person you know who lives in your community.

TEC61047

Citizenship

Constitution Day, celebrated annually on September 17, marks the anniversary of the day in 1787 when delegates completed and signed the United States Constitution.

Star Students

Encourage youngsters to shine as good citizens with this classroom display. Post a large paper flag (without stars) on a classroom wall and place a supply of white star cutouts nearby. Discuss with students ways they can be good citizens in the classroom, such as treating classmates with respect or keeping the classroom clean. When a child exhibits a good citizenship trait, invite her to add her name to a star and attach it to the flag. When 50 stars (or another predetermined number) have been posted on the flag, reward students with a special treat or privilege.

Better Citizens

This idea reminds youngsters that they can practice good citizenship in more than one location. Invite student volunteers to share ways they can be better citizens at school, at home, or in their neighborhoods as you list their ideas on chart paper. Then give each child a sheet of paper programmed like the one shown. Have each child draw a picture of himself being a good citizen in a chosen location and help him fill in the blank on his paper. If desired, invite each youngster to share his project with the group.

I am a good citizen _in my neighborhood_.

Valued Voting

The Constitution helps to ensure that United States citizens are guaranteed many rights, such as the right to vote. Discuss with youngsters the importance of voting. Then invite students to participate in one or more classroom elections throughout the day. For example, invite students to vote on things such as a storytime book for the day or a game to play at recess. Have each youngster complete a ballot similar to the one shown and deposit it in a designated container. After all the votes are cast, enlist students' help in tallying the results on the board and then announce the winning outcomes.

Check out the skill-building reproducible on page 162.

Sensational Symbols

Listen and do.

©The Mailbox® • Superbook® • TEC61047

flag	Statue of Liberty	Liberty Bell
bald eagle	Capitol building	Uncle Sam

Note to the teacher: Name each patriotic symbol and read each word aloud. Have each child cut out the words and glue them beside their corresponding symbols.

Social Skills

In Full Bloom

Plant the seeds of good behavior and encourage youngsters to follow the rules with these beautiful blossoms. In advance, place a large ball of play dough into the bottom of a flowerpot. Using the patterns on page 169, prepare a colorful flower cutout for each of your classroom rules and write one rule on each. Tape a jumbo craft stick to the back of each flower and insert the sticks into the play dough. When it's time to introduce or review a rule, simply pull that flower out of the pot and discuss it.

Listen Carefully

A code word and a special signal help youngsters become good listeners. At the beginning of group time, announce a special code word such as a color, a book character's name, or a nonsense word. Next, show students a silent signal such as waving the arms above the head. Explain that each time students hear the featured word, they are to perform the silent signal to let you know they are listening. Then proceed with your planned activities, inserting the code word randomly throughout group time.

Tell Me About It

This partner activity is the perfect way to help students practice taking turns speaking and listening. Begin by giving each youngster three circle cutouts. Announce a topic for each twosome to discuss, such as what they did over the weekend or a current topic of study. To begin his turn, a youngster sets one of his circles aside and then briefly talks about the subject while his partner listens. Next, his partner sets a circle aside and takes her turn speaking in a similar manner. Students continue using this approach to take turns speaking and listening until each student has used all of his circles.

We Can Share

Incorporate sharing with letter recognition to double the learning fun! Write each child's first name on a chart, and add the words *can share* after each name. Help each child think of an item she could share that starts with the same letter as her name. Extend this activity by having your students think of things to share that begin with each letter of the alphabet; list them on a chart called "Things We Can Share From *A* to *Z*."

Things We Can Share

Angie can share apples.

Lori can share Lincoln logs.

Nick can share neon crayons.

Mary can share markers.

Beth can share books.

Paul can share puzzle pieces.

Sarah can share scissors.

Eddie can share erasers.

Sharing Buddies

Pick a time once a week for Sharing Buddies. Have each child choose a game or book to share. Put everyone's name in a bag; then draw two names at a time. Encourage each pair of children to share their chosen items with each other during this special time. For a slightly different twist, play Sharing Buddies Switch-e-roo. Put all the names back in the bag every ten minutes or so, and draw new buddies.

The Art of Sharing

Teach youngsters the art of sharing with some fun art materials. In advance, cut out a paper heart for each of your kindergartners. Fill a plastic bag for each child in a small group with a different type of collage item, such as glitter, sequins, yarn, or colorful paper scraps. Invite each student in the group to take one plastic bag. Then provide glue and invite students to decorate their paper hearts collage-style. By sharing his art materials with his group members, each child will have a variety of materials with which to decorate his heart.

The Sharing Chair

Your children will become more aware of all the ways they share with others when you transform your rocking chair or another comfy chair into a Sharing Chair once a week. Model the procedure first by sitting in the chair and telling about how you have shared your possessions, time, or talents with others that week. Then invite each child, in turn, to sit in the chair and tell about how he has shared with others that week. For a variation, have each child tell how someone else has shared with him.

Share a Story

Invite your youngsters to share a story with friends and families by compiling this class book. Collect a story written and illustrated by each of your kindergarten authors to include in the book. Add your own story, as well as a few blank pages. Then fasten the pages between construction paper covers. Let each student have a turn taking the book home to share with his family. If desired, invite parents to share stories by writing on the blank pages provided.

If your students like this book, continue the fun with additional books such as *Share a Picture* and *Share a Happy Thought*. Your students may come up with ideas for more shared books.

Share a Story

The Together Tower

Show your budding architects how they can create something together by sharing ideas. Invite each student to select a block from the block center. Have the children sit in a circle and explain that they will be working together to build a tower one block at a time. Choose a student to begin the tower as you recite the following poem; then repeat the poem each time you choose another builder.

Look at the idea [child's name] has got!
If we all build together, we all gain a lot.

Have the first child place his block somewhere in the open area inside the circle. Invite the second student to place his block on or near the first block. Remind your construction crew that each person's building idea is special and that no one knows what the tower will look like until every block has been placed. Label your finished product "The Together Tower," and leave it standing for a while for all to appreciate.

Give Yourselves a Hand

Show everyone how much your little ones share with a "We Share, We Care" bulletin board. Each time someone shares, write down what was shared on a colorful hand cutout and staple it to the board. Remind youngsters that sharing includes not only sharing toys and games with their classmates, but also sharing possessions, time, or talents with others in school, the community—even the world! If your class collects canned goods for charity, participates in a recycling project, or performs a skit for the class next door, be sure to record it!

Arrange the hand shapes randomly, or section off the board with areas for sharing with friends, family, school, the community, and the world. If there's room, add a section for how others have shared with your students.

Need a Hug?

Encourage children to attend to others' feelings when they share a hug with a friend in need. Make a colorful supply of the hug cards on page 170 and place them in a designated spot in your classroom. To begin, lead a discussion about how hugs make people feel and when they are given and received. Then share one of the hug cards and tell youngsters to be on the lookout for a classmate who needs a hug. When a student sees someone in need, she gets a card from the stack and gives it to that person to cheer him up.

Self-Service With a Smile

Dish out some practice in self-help skills with this small-group idea. Fill each of several plastic serving dishes with one of the following: rice, play-dough balls, shaving cream, or packing peanuts. Set an appropriate serving utensil—such as a fork, a spoon, or tongs—inside each dish; then give each child a foam plate. Have youngsters pass each serving dish and its utensil so each child can carefully serve herself a portion of each item. Encourage students to try not to spill anything over the dish edges or off the serving utensils. Continue in this manner until each youngster has had a chance to serve herself from each of the serving dishes.

Pastry Party

Invite students to show off their table skills during this special play-dough pastry party. Give each child in a small group a set of plastic tableware and a portion of play dough. Ask her to form her play dough into some type of pastry, such as a pie, cake, or bread loaf. Then have her place her pastry on a foam plate. Encourage her to use her plastic knife to cut her play-dough pastry into serving portions. Then have her use her fork to pierce each pastry portion and serve one to each of her groupmates.

Designer's Delight

This partner center provides youngsters with plenty of buttoning practice. Collect a quantity of front-buttoning shirts and place them at a center. To begin, invite each child at the center to select a shirt from the collection. Then ask one youngster to create a pattern with the button closures on her shirt. For instance, she might button every other button on a shirt, leaving the remaining buttons unfastened. Have each child at the center duplicate the buttoning pattern on his shirt. Then have a new youngster create a pattern. Continue in this manner until each child at the center has had a turn creating a pattern.

Bow-Tying Practice

Try this idea to help youngsters learn to tie laces into bows. Create a tying board by punching two holes two inches apart in the center of a 4" x 5" piece of sturdy cardboard. Attach hole reinforcers to each hole on both the front and back of the board. Lace one end of a length of yarn through one hole in the back of the board and the other end up through the other hole. Then secure the yarn to the back with a piece of masking tape. To use, have a child tie traditional or bunny-ear bows with the resulting laces.

I Can Do It!

Wearing one of these teacher-made bracelets helps build a child's self-esteem. Cut a supply of 1½" x 7" construction paper strips and keep the strips and some stickers handy. When you observe a child doing something special, label a strip "I can!" and describe the accomplishment. Invite the child to choose a sticker to decorate his bracelet. Then wrap the strip around his wrist to resemble a bracelet and tape the ends together.

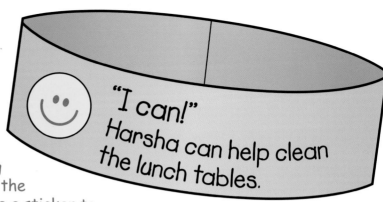

"I can!" Harsha can help clean the lunch tables.

Special Songs

Celebrate the special traits of each student by leading youngsters in singing these self-esteem-boosting songs.

You Are Special
(sung to the tune of "The Wheels on the Bus")

The [Lucy] in our class is [very kind, very kind, very kind].
The [Lucy] in our class is [very kind] all through the day.

I Am Special
(sung to the tune of "London Bridge")

I am special.
Yes, I am. Yes, I am. Yes, I am.
I am special.
Yes, I am.
I am very special.
No one has [a nose] like mine,
[A nose] like mine, [a nose] like mine.
No one has [a nose] like mine; I am very special!

Yes, It's Me!
(sung to the tune of "Frère Jacques")

I am special. I am special.
Turn around; you will see
Someone very special, someone very special.
Yes, it's me! Yes, it's me!

TEC61047

TEC61047

Here's a hug...

just for you!

TEC61047

Here's a hug...

just for you!

TEC61047

Here's a hug...

just for you!

TEC61047

Here's a hug...

just for you!

TEC61047

Box It!

Organize your individual centers with this tip! Store the pieces of an individual center in a shirt-size gift box. Label one side of the lid with the title and label the contents on top of the lid. Stack the boxes on a shelf with the titles facing outward to provide youngsters with easy access to the centers. **Center management**

gameboards
letter cards
game markers

Letter Lotto

Dino Counting

Color Sorting

Center Choices

Here's an easy way to manage your center time! Along the left side of a sheet of poster board, write the title of each center and add a simple illustration to each. For each student allowed in the center at one time, attach the hook side of a Velcro fastener next to the title. Program a card with each student's name and attach the loop side of a Velcro fastener to the back. At center time, invite each child to attach her name card to the desired center. When no more spaces are available for a center, then that center is full. **Center management**

Clip and Go!

Youngsters can independently choose and change learning centers with this colorful tip! To prepare, cut a different-colored tagboard square for each of your centers. Label each sign with the center name and add an illustration, if desired. Color the same number of clothespins to match a sign indicating how many children you will allow in each center at one time. Clip the clothespins to the appropriate signs; then place the signs at their corresponding centers. When a child visits a center, he removes a clothespin from the sign and clips it to his clothing. When no more clothespins are available, that center is full. When leaving a center, a child replaces the clothespin on the sign. **Center management**

It's Center Time!

Keep track of students' center use with a handy checklist! Program a copy of page 185 with each student's name and each center. After daily center time, ask each child which center(s) she visited; then mark it on the chart. **Center management**

Abuzz With Letters

Youngsters are sure to make a beeline to this partner center for some letter-matching practice! Copy and cut out a supply of the bee cards on page 186. Program half of the cards with uppercase letters and the other half with the matching lowercase letters. Place the cards at a center. When a twosome visits the center, it spreads out the cards facedown. A player flips over two cards. If they match, he says, "Buzz" and removes the cards from the playing area. If the cards do not match, he flips them back over. Players take turns in this manner until all of the cards are matched. **Uppercase and lowercase letter matching**

Sound Off!

The result of this center is a letter-perfect classroom display! At a center, tape a large sheet of bulletin board paper to a tabletop. Draw lines to divide the paper into several sections; then label each section with a different consonant. Place a supply of crayons or markers nearby. When a child visits the center, he announces a posted letter and its sound. Then he draws a small picture whose name begins with the sound in the corresponding section. He repeats this process for the other letters as time allows. When the paper is full, display it in the classroom, and then program another sheet of paper with different consonants.
Initial consonants

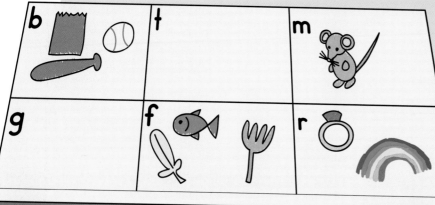

Spelling Squares

Nurture beginning spelling skills with letter tiles. Bring in squares from a Scrabble game, or visit a home improvement store to find small tiles and make your own low-cost letter tiles. Use a permanent marker to label one tile for each letter of the alphabet. Make multiples of often-used letters. Place the letter tiles in your writing center along with a list of seasonal or sight words. Then invite your youngsters to let their fingers do the writing as they use the tiles to copy the words on the list. **Word recognition**

Buddy Bookmarks

Turn reading buddies into writing buddies by inviting youngsters to create buddy bookmarks. Place a supply of tagboard strips at a center. A center visitor uses his best handwriting to write his name on a strip. Then he flips the strip over and illustrates it. Encourage students to trade strips with a buddy. What a great way to always have a buddy with you when reading! **Making a bookmark**

Reading Is Everywhere!

Expose your bookworms to the power of print by including lots of reading materials. Use the following list to get you started. Incorporating these materials into your reading center will show youngsters that reading has many purposes and is essential to living in our world. Reading material

- posters
- fiction and nonfiction books
- pictures
- magazines
- newspapers
- brochures and pamphlets
- menus
- store circulars and advertisements
- receipts
- coupons
- telephone books
- food-box front panels
- maps
- junk mail
- catalogs
- wordless books
- recipes
- greeting cards
- old grocery lists
- calendars
- class photo album/scrapbook
- picture dictionaries

High-Interest Reading Center

Change your reading center periodically to keep it fresh and exciting in order to entice new readers and welcome back frequent visitors. Consider organizing it by theme to correlate with your current unit of study, or seasonally to associate it with upcoming holidays and celebrations. Fill the center with stories related to your topic. Then, for added interest, include a space (table, shelf, or corner of the floor) for manipulatives and props related to the theme. For example, if your current unit is "The Farm," you might want to include plastic farm animals, miniature garden tools, a barn replica, and a toy tractor. Invite students to contribute to the collection and to take turns choosing a book from the center for storytime. Reading materials

Classroom Clip Art

The result of this writing and art activity is a collection of student-created clip art that's just perfect for jazzing up your notes to parents. Stock your writing center with 3" x 5" blank cards and black fine-tip markers. A child draws a picture on a card that illustrates an upcoming theme or season and adds a caption. Place several completed cards on a copy machine and reduce them to approximately 1" x 2". Cut out the pictures and messages as needed to enhance newsletters or parent communications. Youngsters will be eager to pass along your notes to parents when they see their own clip art decorating the page. **Writing a caption**

Personalized Stationery

Introduce letter writing with a personal touch by encouraging youngsters to design their own stationery. On sheets of white paper, mark off a one-inch border. Instruct each child to use crayons or rubber stamps to create a design within the border. Make a small supply of each student's design so she can have a personal pack of her own paper. Store each pack in a personalized folder. Place the folders at a center along with pencils, envelopes, and markers. A student writes or dictates a friendly letter to a family member or classmate on a sheet of her stationery. Then she colors the border, decorates an envelope, and tucks her letter inside. Your students will be bursting with pride when they deliver their personalized letters. **Letter writing**

Pretty Printing

Motivate your youngsters to write with some interesting implements. Join together two to four different colors of crayons, pens, pencils, or fine-line markers with a rubber band. Place these multicolored writing utensils where little ones can use them to add a fanciful touch to their writing. **Writing**

Card Stock

Coax creative writing from your youngsters with festive writing prompts. Gather a supply of used greeting cards and cut off the fronts of them. Place the card fronts in a basket at the writing center. Encourage each student to select a card. On a sheet of paper, have him write imaginative words or sentences inspired by the card. Continue collecting cards throughout the year to keep your writing center stocked and students' interest piqued. **Writing**

Hooked on Numerals

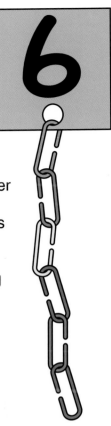

Label each of ten blank cards with a different number from 1 to 10. Punch a hole in the bottom of each card. For each numeral card, connect an equal number of learning links together to form a chain. Place the chains and cards at a center. A child attaches the corresponding chain to each card. **Matching numerals to sets**

Leafy Ladybug Math

Your little ones will go buggy over matching numerals to sets with these fun props! In advance, copy and cut out a leaf pattern for each numeral you want youngsters to practice. Program each leaf with a different numeral. Place the leaves and a jar of red pom-poms (ladybugs) at a center. Have students place the matching number of ladybugs on the leaves. If desired, expand youngsters' counting skills by teaching the song shown below. **Matching numerals to sets**

Ten Little Ladybugs
(sung to the tune of "Ten Little Indians")

One little, two little, three little ladybugs,
Four little, five little, six little ladybugs,
Seven little, eight little, nine little ladybugs,
Ten ladybugs on a leaf.

Matching Presents

To prepare for this concentration-style game, collect an even number of small gift boxes. For half of the boxes, write a different number inside each one. Program the remaining boxes to match. Attach a bow to the top of each box; then mix up the boxes and arrange them in rows at a center.

To play, a child opens two boxes and names the numbers shown. If the numbers match, she removes the boxes from the playing area. If the numbers do not match, she replaces the lid on each box. Play then passes to the next child. Players continue in the same manner until all the matches have been found. *Identifying numbers*

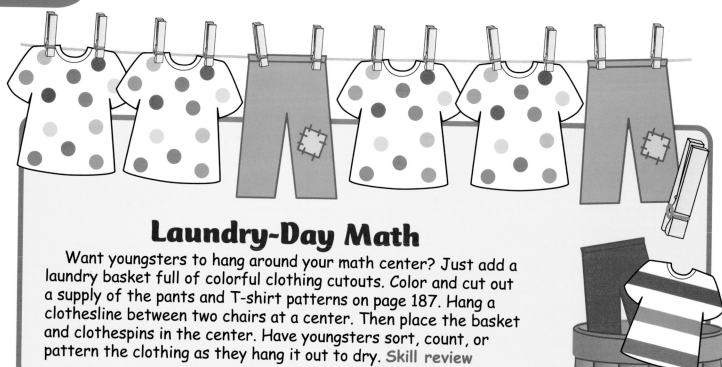

Laundry-Day Math

Want youngsters to hang around your math center? Just add a laundry basket full of colorful clothing cutouts. Color and cut out a supply of the pants and T-shirt patterns on page 187. Hang a clothesline between two chairs at a center. Then place the basket and clothespins in the center. Have youngsters sort, count, or pattern the clothing as they hang it out to dry. Skill review

Estimation Station

Gather several clear plastic containers and fill each one with a different item, such as pom-poms or Unifix cubes. A child at this center selects a container and estimates the number of objects inside. He records his estimation on a slip of paper. Then he counts the objects and records the correct number. After he compares his estimation to the actual count, he selects another container and repeats the process. For added fun, teach your students the song shown to sing as they work. Estimating

(sung to the tune of "Jingle Bells")

Estimate, estimate, estimate today.
Guess how many in the jar,
Then count them right away. Hey!

Walking the Dog

To prepare for this math center, gather a pile of multi-colored learning links. Draw various chain-link patterns of varying difficulty on sentence strips, making sure that they match the colors of your learning links. Place them in a tub with three or four small stuffed dogs. Encourage youngsters to pretend the stuffed animals are their pets. Invite each child to select a pattern strip and use the learning links to create a matching pattern collar and leash for her dog. After the proud owner takes her furry friend for a walk around the room, invite her to choose another pattern strip and begin again. **Patterns**

Seeing Spots!

Just how many spots are on the dogs at this center? Invite your youngsters to find out! Cut out two copies of the dog cards on page 188. Label each of 11 blank cards with a different numeral from 2 to 12; then draw a corresponding dot set on the back of each card. Store each set of cards in a separate bag and place the bags at a center. A child randomly chooses two dog cards and counts the total number of spots. Then she removes the corresponding number card from the bag and flips it over to check her answer. She returns each card to its bag and plays again. **Adding sets**

A Full Hive

To prepare for this partner center, cut out two construction paper copies of the beehive pattern on page 186. Place the hives, two large dice, and a supply of honey-flavored cereal pieces at a center. When a twosome visits the center, each child rolls a die. Youngsters compare the number of dots on the dice and the child with the larger amount places a cereal piece on his hive. Play continues in the same manner until a child collects ten cereal pieces. If desired, invite youngsters to snack on some cereal after completing the center. **Comparing sets**

Clothing That Measures Up

Challenge students to measure various classroom objects using T-shirts and pants. Copy and cut out the patterns on page 187. Before children begin, review measurement tips, such as measuring in a straight line and evenly spacing the cutouts. Have each student measure an object using the T-shirt cutouts and then using the pants cutouts. Afterward, have students discuss which items are the longest, the same size, and the shortest. If students get different measurement results for the same object, have them discuss possible reasons why. Provide additional practice with other nonstandard units of measurement, such as blocks, tennis shoes, or seasonal cutout shapes. **Nonstandard measurement**

"A-maze-ing" Water

This water experiment will make a big splash with students. Draw a simple maze on a piece of tagboard. Laminate the tagboard or cover it with clear Con-Tact covering. Place the maze, a container of blue-tinted water, paper towels, eyedroppers, and toothpicks at a center. Challenge students to place one drop of water at the start of the maze and move it with a toothpick to the end of the maze. Invite youngsters to experiment with different-size drops or more than one drop at a time on the maze. As they work, encourage them to discuss their observations about the drops of water.
Water

Window on the World

Create a simple weather station by placing your science center in front of a window. Cut streamers from a plastic garbage bag to make a wind gauge, and use duct tape to hang it outside the window. Mount a thermometer with suction cups on the outside of the window. Make weather watching a regular activity by asking one student or a small group of students to report on the weather each day. They may describe the strength of the wind and keep track of the temperature on a monthly graph, or they may try to draw the cloud formations they see each day on a blank calendar. Encourage students to discuss the patterns they see by asking questions such as "What do the clouds look like before it rains?" and "What time of year is the weather the warmest or the wettest?"
Weather

The Magic Paper Clip

Young minds will find themselves attracted to this fun puzzle. Fill a plastic jar with water. Drop a large paper clip into the jar, and screw the lid on tight. Place the jar and a strong magnet at a center. Challenge students to make the paper clip move without touching the jar with their hands. Let the children discover they can move the paper clip with the magnet. Magnetism

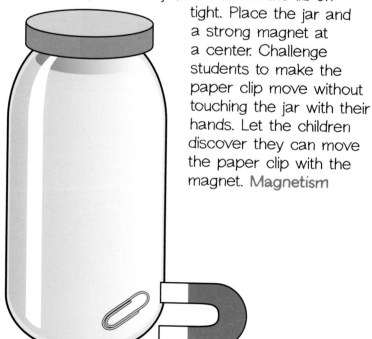

Mix It!

Little ones mix up secondary colors at this science center! Place red, yellow, and blue play dough at a center stocked with copies of the recording sheet on page 189. A child writes her name on a recording sheet and colors the play dough in the first column as indicated on the sheet. Then she takes equal amounts of red and blue play dough and makes a prediction about what color they will form when mixed together. After she colors the play dough in the second column to represent her guess, she mixes the dough together until blended. Next, she records the actual color formed on her sheet. She continues in the same manner for each remaining row. **Color mixing**

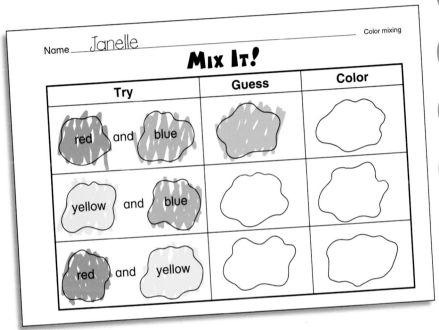

Name Janelle   Color mixing

Mix It!

Try			Guess	Color
red	and	blue		
yellow	and	blue		
red	and	yellow		

Sink the Bottle!

How many pebbles will it take to sink a bottle at the water table? Challenge little ones to find out! Gather a supply of pebbles that are small enough to fit into a small water bottle; then store them in a plastic pail. Place the pail and several empty plastic bottles of various sizes by your water table. When a child visits the center, he chooses a bottle and predicts how many pebbles it will take to sink the bottle. Then he counts as he places one pebble at a time in the bottle. After the bottle sinks, he compares his prediction to the actual count. He continues in the same way for each remaining bottle. Floating and sinking

Touchy, Touchy

Give students a feel for their sense of touch with a touching box. Cut a circle in the side of a box. Glue the top edge of a square of material over the circle so students cannot see inside. Place common items inside the box, such as a paper clip, a glue bottle, an unsharpened pencil, and a block. Tape the top of the box shut. Invite youngsters to visit the center in pairs and take turns reaching inside. Ask them to identify the items they feel inside the box. Once all students have made their guesses, reveal what is inside the box. Sense of touch

Spring Cleaning

Add a touch of springtime freshness to your housekeeping center! Stock the area with some spring-cleaning essentials, such as small buckets; a feather duster; a child-size broom, dustpan, and mop; sponges; and a few spray bottles filled with water (add a few drops of lemon extract to give the water a lemony scent, if desired). Place all the cleaning props in a large laundry basket in your housekeeping center.

Encourage youngsters to use the cleaning supplies to spruce up the furniture and accessories in the area. Then, when the area is sparkling clean, prepare for a few home improvements. Mount a sheet of bulletin board paper on a wall in the area. Place a bucket of paintbrushes, paint rollers, paint samples, glue, and wallpaper scraps in the area. Invite students to redecorate the area by painting the paper and then gluing wallpaper and paint samples onto the paper.

Puppy Love

Create a classroom version of a veterinary clinic. Begin by stacking some boxes along one wall of a center area and then place a stuffed animal in each box to resemble a kennel. Cover a table with a white sheet to make an examining table; then place some medical supplies—such as a stethoscope, toy thermometer, bandages, empty prescription containers, and some cotton balls—near the table. Your little veterinarians will need to write some prescriptions, so include some notepaper, pencils, and clipboards. Finally, provide some oversize white shirts for each pet doctor to wear.

Masquerade Ball

For a variation on traditional dress-up activities, invite your youngsters to attend a masquerade ball. Place a suitcase packed with a variety of interesting clothes, shoes, gloves, and hats at a center. Also include fun eyeglass frames (with the lenses removed), jewelry, false noses, and mustaches. Invite students to dress up in their choice of items. Then, when everyone has donned a disguise, play some lively instrumental music and let the dancing begin!

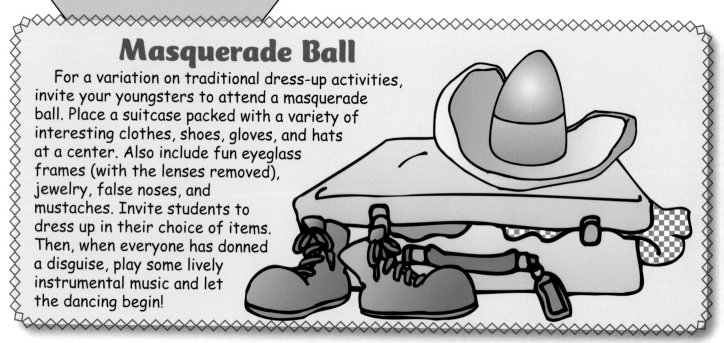

Working in the Garden

Fill a child-size wagon or small garden cart with a variety of plastic garden tools, a rake, a watering can, plastic flowerpots, a short length of garden hose, a spray nozzle, a lawn sprinkler, and a variety of artificial flowers and leaves. Place the wagon in a center along with a sensory table filled with potting soil. Add some garden garb, such as overalls, tall garden boots, gardening gloves, and a variety of gardening hats. As youngsters plant flowers and rake up leaves, you'll see sprouts of creative imagination begin to take root!

Birthday Bakery

Your little ones will whip up the best birthday cakes in town in this classroom bakery. Collect a variety of muffin cups and small tart tins. Place the pans in a center along with some play dough, plastic knives, decorative birthday plates, doilies, bits of rickrack, and birthday candles. Invite youngsters to use the materials to create a birthday feast!

Under Construction

Merge dramatic play with your block area to create a construction site. Stock the area with a variety of toy dump trucks, bulldozers, and loaders. Then break ground for some big block building by adding a collection of measuring tapes, tool belts, masking tape, flagging tape, tagboard construction-site signs, and orange safety cones. Make some orange safety vests by cutting a hole in the center of each of several orange fabric rectangles. Place the vests and some hard hats in the center. Encourage center visitors to don hard hats and get to work. Now, that's a blueprint for success!

Lights, Camera, Action!

Set the scene for dramatic play by cutting out several magazine pictures of people participating in a variety of activities. Place the pictures at your dramatic-play area along with any corresponding props. When a pair of youngsters visits the center, one child secretly chooses a picture. The other student announces, "Lights, camera, action!" to signal her partner to begin acting out the activity shown in the picture. Once her partner correctly guesses the activity, youngsters switch roles and play again.

Dig This!

Bury objects related to your current theme or unit of study in the sensory table, and watch as your little ones uncover their sorting, classifying, and problem-solving skills. For example, during a dinosaur unit, bury the pieces to a wooden dinosaur puzzle in a gravel-filled table, and encourage your little paleontologists to put together the mystery. Or for a more skill-oriented center, bury an assortment of seashells during a beach unit, and invite the children to find them and sort them by shape, kind, color, and size.

Other things to bury:

vegetables
manipulatives
dog bones
plastic worms and bugs
rocks
plastic eggs

A Work of Art

Turn your sand table into a canvas fit for a "sand-sational" nature portrait. Moisten the sand with water and pack it down evenly and firmly. Encourage a small group of students to draw a picture using sticks as drawing tools. Then encourage them to use other outdoor objects—such as leaves, nuts, grass, rocks, and twigs—for embellishing the picture.

Pour the Water Out!

Here are some super substitutions for the water or sand in your sensory table.

- **gelatin blocks**
  (Make sure you have extras for snacking!)
- **shaving cream or whipped topping**
- **crushed ice**
- **cotton balls**
- **aquarium gravel**
- **assorted pasta**
- **cereal**
- **pudding**
- **potting soil**
- **leaves**

Hidden Letters

Lots of letters are nestled in your sensory table with this center! Partially fill your sensory table with shredded paper. Then hide a supply of letter manipulatives in the paper. When a child visits the center, she reaches into the table to feel a letter without removing it. She announces what she thinks the letter is; then she removes it to check her guess. She continues in the same manner as time allows. For an added challenge, add number manipulatives to the table as well.

Plenty of Pasta

Fill your sensory table with a quantity of dyed pasta (see page 281 for a recipe) and a variety of spoons, scoops, and tubs. Encourage students to scoop, fill, and pour the pasta.

Raindrop Search

To prepare, program a supply of construction paper raindrop cutouts (patterns on page 189) with different numbers from 1 to 20. Partially fill your sensory table with cotton batting or cotton balls (clouds). Hide the raindrops in the clouds. A center visitor removes three raindrops from the clouds and places them in order from least to greatest. After confirming his order with a number line, he returns the raindrops to the table and plays again. If desired, program the raindrops with letters for alphabetical order practice.

Wacky, Wonderful Water

With just a sprinkle of this and a dash of that, you can turn your water table into a wonderful phenomenon. Simply add a few capfuls of flavoring extract to the water and just listen to the sniffs! Try lemon extract during a fruit unit or peppermint extract during the holiday season. For more visual appeal, add glitter, plastic confetti, or crayon shavings to the water. A word of caution: Avoid adding the visual stimuli to the water if you've already scented it. Little ones may be tempted to taste!

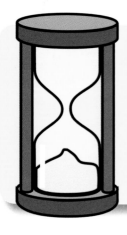

Ticktock Tower

Here's a building race that your little construction workers won't want to miss. Designate one child as the timekeeper and provide him with a timer. On his signal, instruct each of the other children in the center to build a block tower. When time is called, encourage the group to compare to see whose tower is tallest. Have the winner be the timekeeper for the next round. Get set...build!

Blocks and Blueprints

Encourage your youngsters to use these blueprints to practice visual and spatial relationship skills. To make a blueprint, trace blocks of a variety of shapes and sizes on large sheets of construction paper to create building designs. Laminate the papers for durability. Store the blueprints in the block center. As a child visits the center, challenge him to build using the blueprint of his choice. For a variation to this activity, invite each student to create his own block structure; then provide block-shaped cutouts for him to make his own blueprint for other students to follow.

Stick to the Budget

This construction budget will lead to lots of creativity and critical thinking. Explain to your little contractors what a budget is; then give each of them a budget of blocks to use in constructing a house. For example, if the budget is 12, each child can use only 12 blocks to build her structure. Write the budget numeral on a sheet of construction paper and post it in the center as a reminder. At the end of center time, have a student inspector check the houses to see whether each child stuck to her budget. Then bring in the demolition and cleanup crew!

Shapely Structures

Work on shape-recognition skills with this building plan. Assign each builder in a small group a different shape. Have her construct a building using her designated shape as its foundation. Once all buildings are complete, invite other students to visit the block center and name each building's shape.

It's CENTER Time!

8, 9, 10

YELLOW

ABC

RED

Note to the teacher: Use with "It's Center Time!" on page 171.

Bee Cards

Use with "Abuzz With Letters" on page 172.

Beehive Pattern

Use with "A Full Hive" on page 177.

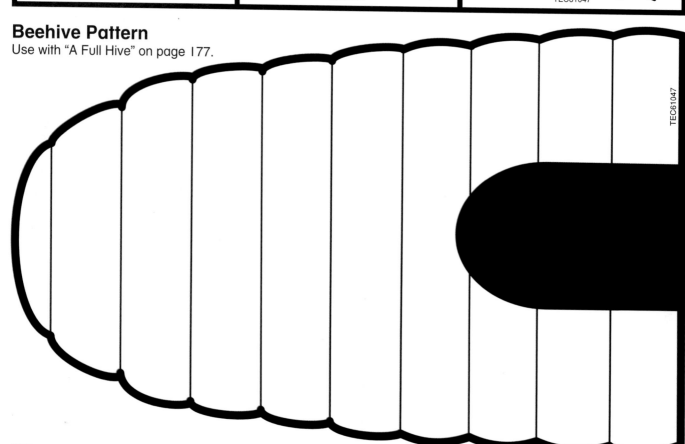

Clothing Patterns

Use with "Laundry-Day Math" on page 176 and "Clothing That Measures Up" on page 177.

TEC61047

TEC61047

TEC61047

TEC61047

Dog Cards

Use with "Seeing Spots!" on page 177.

TEC61047

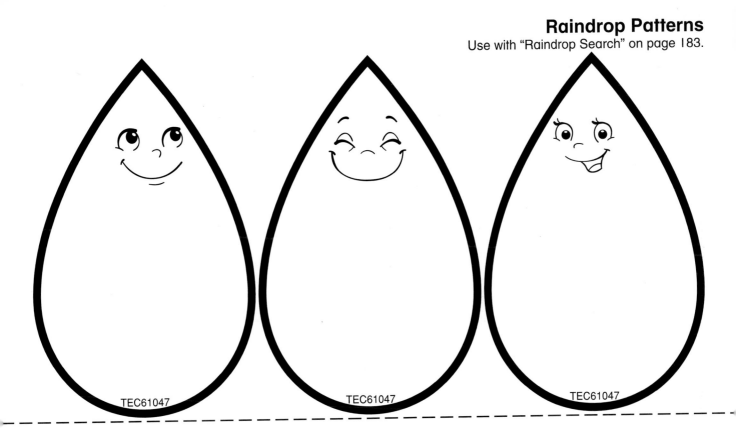

TEC61047   TEC61047   TEC61047

Name _____   Color mixing

Mix It!

Try	Guess	Color
red and blue		
yellow and blue		
red and yellow		

Note to the teacher: Use with "Mix It!" on page 179.

Circle Time & Games

Initial Sounds in Action

To begin, prepare a set of alphabet cards. During circle time, instruct each student to look and listen for the card with the letter that begins his name; then show one card at a time. When a child identifies the letter corresponding to his name, have him stand up. Then invite the standing student(s) to perform the action from the list that corresponds to the letter. When a card does not correspond to any child's name, invite the entire class to perform the named action.

Suggested Actions

A: crawl like an alligator
B: buzz like a bee
C: clap
D: dance
E: make an elephant trunk with your arm
F: make a fish face
G: gallop
H: hop
I: fly like an insect
J: jog in place
K: pretend to kick a ball
L: laugh
M: move your arms like a monkey

N: nod
O: oink
P: pat your legs
Q: pretend to shush people to be quiet
R: pretend to read a book
S: skip
T: touch your toes
U: open a pretend umbrella
V: pretend to vacuum
W: wave
X: play a pretend xylophone
Y: play with a pretend yo-yo
Z: zip a pretend coat

Cooperative Creations

Promote a spirit of creative cooperation with this circle-time illustration. Post a large sheet of bulletin board paper in your circle-time area and use a marker to draw a simple design or figure on the paper. Ask youngsters to discuss how different designs or figures might be added to the drawing to create something recognizable such as a clown or train. Then invite each child, in turn, to add her choice of designs to the illustration. As youngsters build the illustration, continue the group's discussion about what

might be created from the new additions. Does the final picture represent the group's original ideas? Label the creation with a student-generated title; then display the class illustration.

Spy Light

This spirited adaptation of I Spy will keep youngsters on the lookout for mystery objects. To play Spy Light, the spy mentally notes a specific object in the room and whispers the name and location of that object to you. Then the spy tells the class a characteristic of his chosen object such as its shape, color, or size. The other students try to guess the identity of the mystery object. The spy points a flashlight at each guessed object but does not actually turn on the light until it is pointed at the correct object. Turn on the spy light—the guess is right!

Animal Copycats

Have your students snap or clap as they chant together:

Let's be animals just for fun.
Let's copy [a monkey], that's the one.
Whatever it does, we'll do the same.
That's how we play the Copycat Game!

Then have the children stand and pretend to be monkeys. Introduce the next animal by beginning the chant again. Stop and point to a student to fill in the blank with the new animal's name.

Find the Match

Play this whole-class memory game for some practice with opposites. Color and cut out a copy of the opposite cards on pages 194 and 195. Randomly place the cards facedown in a pocket chart. Ask a volunteer to turn over a card, and help him read the word aloud. Then have another volunteer choose a different card to turn over and read aloud. Enlist students' help in deciding whether the two cards are opposites. If they are, remove the cards from the pocket chart and set them aside. If the two cards are not opposites, return them to their facedown position in the pocket chart. Continue in this manner with different students until all the opposites are matched.

Simon Does Not Say

Add a new twist to an old game by challenging little ones to do the opposite of each thing Simon says to do. Demonstrate first with a few examples, such as "Simon says frown" (smile instead of frown) or "Simon says stand up" (sit down). This may take practice, but your students will beg to play this game again and again. This is the only time students will be encouraged to do the opposite of what you say!

Presto! Change-O!

Wave your magic wand and turn your little ones into active learners. Use a variety of craft supplies to make a magic wand, or purchase an inexpensive one. Have your students sit on the floor. Show them your magic wand and introduce a game of Presto! Change-o! Wave your wand, say, "Presto! Change-o! You are now [fill in the blank]!" and invite little ones to pretend to be whatever you have said. Next, instruct them to freeze. Then, with another "Presto! Change-o!" and a wave of your wand, announce the next thing they are to become.

STORY-BOX SURPRISE

Fill a decorated box with small toys, action figures, natural objects, and other interesting small items. Seat your youngsters in a circle and pass the box around the circle. Encourage each child, in turn, to take one object from the box and use it as a prop to tell a story or act out an action.

SPIN A STORY

Have the children sit on the floor in a circle. Take a ball of yarn or string and gently wrap the loose end around your hand several times as you begin telling a story. Stop the story and roll the ball of yarn to a child, keeping the wound yarn on your hand. Invite her to wrap the yarn around her hand several times and add a few sentences to the story. Instruct her to roll the yarn to another child. The game continues until all of the children have had a turn to wrap the yarn and add to the story. Once your story ends, have each child carefully slide the yarn off her hand and lay it down on the floor. Your students will enjoy the story and the giant web that they have "spun" together!

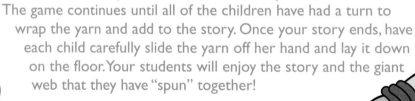

Share Time...Live!

Amplify your circle-time sharing experiences with this neat idea. Write each child's name on a separate notecard; then put the cards in a bag. Choose a volunteer to be the announcer. Have the announcer draw a card from the bag and silently read the name on the card. (Whisper the name to her if she cannot read it.) Then ask the announcer to talk into a toy microphone as she describes the person labeled on the card—without using her name. When the described child recognizes her own description, invite her to take the microphone and tell about her share topic for the day. Then have that child assume the announcer role. Continue until sharing time ends. It's share time...live!

What's Inside?

Use this language idea to help youngsters express their imaginations. Wrap a box in decorative gift-wrapping paper; then tie a ribbon around it. Have students sit in a circle during group time. Ask a volunteer to hold the wrapped box and imagine the gift he would like to find inside. Have him whisper his thought to you; then instruct him to describe his imaginary gift to the child on his right. If this child has difficulty identifying the imaginary gift, invite other class members to help him guess until it is correctly named. Then invite that child to hold the box and repeat the game, describing his imaginary gift to the child on his right. Continue around the circle in this manner so that each child has an opportunity to describe his imaginary gift. Conclude by describing your imaginary gift and asking the class to identify it.

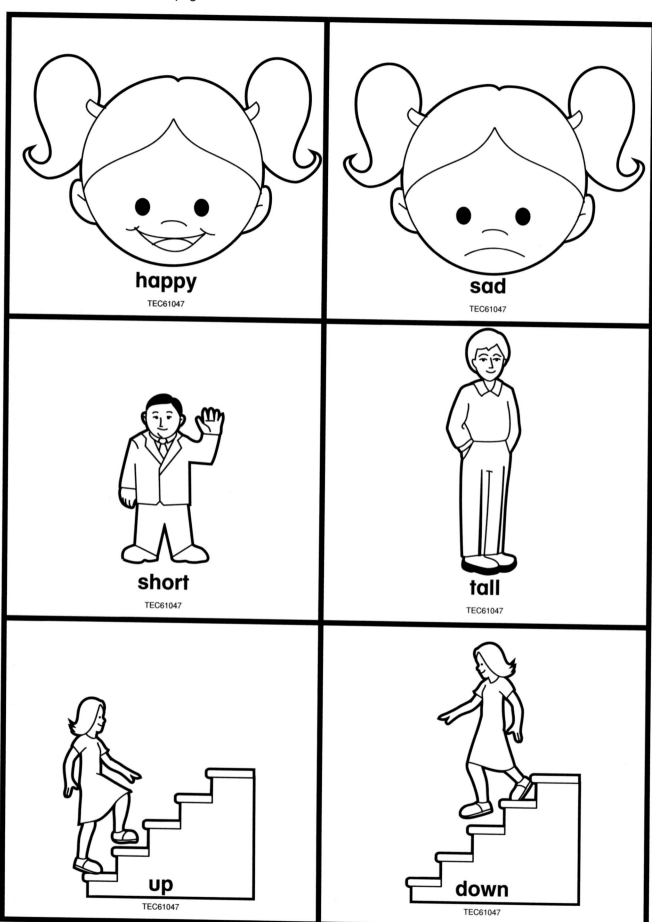

happy

TEC61047

sad

TEC61047

short

TEC61047

tall

TEC61047

up

TEC61047

down

TEC61047

little

TEC61047

big

TEC61047

dirty

TEC61047

clean

TEC61047

hot

TEC61047

cold

TEC61047

FINE-MOTOR SKILLS

Creating Confetti

Give youngsters' fine-motor skills a workout with an idea that utilizes scrap paper! After students complete various arts-and-crafts projects, place the leftover scraps of colorful construction paper in a container. When you've accumulated a large supply of scraps, place the container at a table with hole punchers (or shape punchers) and several plastic trays. Youngsters visit the table and punch holes in the paper, letting the resulting dots fall onto the trays. Use this collection of confetti for future art projects!

Soda Bottle Maracas

Both making and playing these rhythm instruments will give youngsters fine-motor practice. Collect several plastic 12- or 16-ounce soda bottles with caps. Give each child two bottles. Invite students to decorate the bottles with colorful stickers or paint pens. Then have each child remove the caps and use a funnel to partially fill each bottle with beans. Replace the caps and secure them with tape. Show the children how to shake the bottles to create rhythmic sounds.

Berry Pickin'

This center is a "berry" fun way to practice fine-motor skills. Partially fill one bucket with pom-poms to resemble berries, and provide access to a pair of tongs. Have a child use the tongs to move the berries one by one to an empty bucket.

Symmetrical Shapes

Spotlight scissor skills at this engaging center. Fold colorful pieces of paper in half; then draw half of a familiar symmetrical shape on the fold line of each piece as shown. Place the papers at a center with a supply of scissors. Then encourage youngsters to visit the center, choose a paper, and cut along the lines as they keep the paper folded. Little ones are sure to be tickled when they unfold the resulting cutout and see the entire shape. It's a shamrock!

A Padlock Puzzler

With this fun activity, you're sure to unlock a wealth of fine-motor practice! Place several different padlocks at a center. Then place each of the corresponding keys on a separate large key ring. A youngster visits the center, chooses a key, and tries the key in each padlock. When a padlock opens, he leaves the key in the lock and then repeats the process with a new key.

Cookie Wreath

Celebrate any special occasion with this festive cookie wreath. Give each child in a small group a butter-cookie ring. Have her use a plastic knife to spread frosting on top of it. Invite her to give her fine-motor skills a workout by pinching sugar sprinkles over the frosting.

Sidewalk Painting

Students will be amazed by magical masterpieces that slowly disappear! On a hot day, set out containers of water and paintbrushes in different sizes and widths—from skinny, fine-tip watercolor brushes to wide house-painting brushes. Take the class outside and invite students to water-paint on the sidewalk. Encourage them to use several different brushes to improve wrist strength and tripod grasp. When the painting's done, youngsters can watch their creations slowly evaporate.

Colored Sand

Make colored sand, then have little ones use the sand for an art project that will call on their fine-motor control. Mix together one cup of clean play sand with four teaspoons of dry tempera paint in a container. Mix several colorful batches of sand in the same way. Then place the containers of colored sand, pieces of poster board, pencils, and glue on a table. Invite each student to draw a geometric design on a piece of poster board. Next, show him how to cover a section of the drawing with a thin layer of glue and use his fingers to sprinkle on colored sand. Have him shake off the excess sand and repeat the procedure with another color. Set the finished artwork aside to dry.

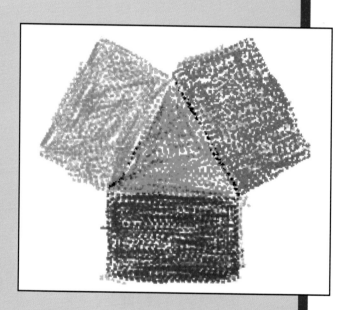

Curl and Glue

At this center, youngsters use their fine-motor skills to make open-ended art projects! Place at a center several sheets of construction paper, markers, glue, and a variety of colorful construction paper strips. A youngster curls a chosen strip around a marker. After she holds the strip in place briefly, she removes the strip and glues it to a sheet of construction paper. She continues in the same way, adding a variety of curled strips to her sheet until a desired effect is achieved.

Sock It to Me!

This activity reinforces sizing skills as it exercises a child's pincer grasp. String a clothesline in a learning center. Place a container of different-size socks and a container of clothespins in the center. Challenge students to arrange the socks by size from shortest to longest. Ask them to use the clothespins to clip the socks on the clothesline in the correct order.

Wrap-'n'-Stack Sculpture

Wrap up dexterity and creativity with this group project. Collect several cardboard tubes and small boxes with lids. Have a small group of students wrap some boxes and tubes with wrapping-paper scraps. Then have the children stack the wrapped boxes and tubes to make a cooperative sculpture. Help youngsters glue the pieces in place.

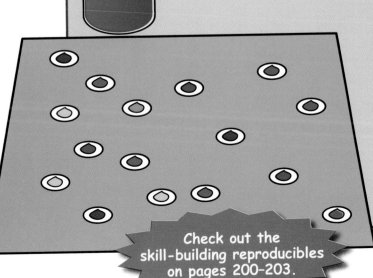

Dozens of Dots

Youngsters put the squeeze on bottles of white glue with this unique idea! Use tempera paint to tint bottles of white glue. Then place the glue at a table along with a supply of hole reinforcers and colorful paper. A child attaches several hole reinforcers to her paper. Then she grasps a glue bottle and puts a small dot of glue in the center of each reinforcer, changing glue colors as desired. This fabulous fine-motor exercise results in a nifty piece of artwork!

Check out the skill-building reproducibles on pages 200–203.

Name _____

Bad Bait

Trace.

Dancing Penguins

Trace the lines to help each penguin get to its dance partner.

Name _____

202

Bees in the Breeze

🖍 Color.

✂ Cut on the - - - lines.

Name _____

Beaver's Bake Sale

Cut.

Glue to match.

COOKIES 10¢

©The Mailbox® • Superbook® • TEC61047

Gross-Motor Skills

A Wake-Up Call

Start the day with this wake-up activity that will get your little ones pumped up for learning. Have students spread out in an open area of your classroom. Play some music that is slow at first, and then speeds up. Instruct students to mirror your actions as you move your body in different ways, beginning slowly, then moving more quickly. For example, slowly roll your head from side to side and front to back, shrug your shoulders, and stretch high and low; then gallop, slide, or jump. As students become more familiar with this activity, increase the complexity of the movements.

A-Painting We Will Go

Coat youngsters' imaginations with a fresh perspective when you take them into the world of a house painter. To begin, ask students to imagine they are house painters. Explain how a painter uses brushes and rollers to paint a house. Then talk students through the motions of painting a house (or a room in the house) as they perform the actions corresponding to your directions. For instance, you might have students reach high to brush-paint the top of a wall, then roll a paint roller down to paint the bottom of the wall. Or you might instruct your painters to make long left-to-right brush strokes across the middle of the wall or to create large circular strokes at eye level. As you direct your young painters, remind them to periodically bend to dip their brushes and rollers into the paint containers.

Ribbons With Rhythm

Encourage youngsters to work on rhythm and muscle control with this ribbon activity. To prepare a ribbon, staple a length of crepe paper to a cardboard tube for each child. Give each child a ribbon; then have her move to an area in the room where she has plenty of space for movement. On a signal, have each child move her body and ribbon to the steady rhythm of a drum. You might play the rhythm fast or slow, soft or loud, or with a simple pattern. Then, at random intervals, beat the drum using an irregular, fast, and chaotic pace. At these times, youngsters will move their bodies and ribbons as if they have lost control. Return to a rhythmic drumbeat to help students regain control of their bodies and ribbons.

Goin' Buggy

Complement a reading of Denise Fleming's *In the Tall, Tall Grass* with this version of Follow the Leader. As a group, practice moving like the animals and insects depicted in the book. Then have students form a line. Ask the child at the front of the line to demonstrate an animal or insect movement of her choice. Have the other children copy her movement and follow along. After an appropriate length of time, ask the leader to go to the end of the line and have the next child choose and demonstrate a new movement.

Unique March

Hmmm...how does a penguin march? Try this activity to find out what your students think! Play a lively marching tune. Then appoint a leader to guide a student parade around your classroom. Announce the name of an animal such as a penguin, a duck, an elephant, a monkey, or a frog. Challenge the leader to perform a march to represent that animal's marching style. Then invite the other students to imitate her actions. After a designated period of time, appoint another child to be the leader; then repeat the activity, asking the leader to create a marching style for a different animal.

Under the Big Top

Give your little ones the opportunity to perform under the big top with this movement activity. Seat your class in a circle and sing the song shown.

As each child is named in the song, have her stand and imitate a circus animal or performer. Then invite the other children to guess what animal or person she is imitating. Let the circus begin!

(sung to the tune of "Bingo")
If the circus came to town,
What would [child's name] be?
Let's watch her/him and see,
Let's watch her/him and see,
Let's watch her/him and see,
What [child's name] wants to be.

Seasonal Charades

Give your youngsters an opportunity to explore seasonal symbols in their own creative ways. Brainstorm with your youngsters a list of items relating to the current season. For example, in the fall the list might include items such as squirrels, falling leaves, and pumpkins. In the winter, it might include items such as falling snowflakes, a snowman, or a gingerbread man. Once the list is complete, draw a simple picture of each item on an index card. Invite a volunteer to choose a card and then move in a way that depicts the pictured item. Invite the remainder of the group to guess which item the child is portraying. Continue in this manner with different cards and volunteers.

Geometry in Motion

Students will become familiar with shape formation as they participate in this small-group movement activity. In advance, use masking tape to outline several different shapes on your classroom floor. Divide your class into the same number of groups as you have shapes, and ask that each group stand around the outline of a different shape. Ask one member in each group to name an action such as jump, spin, or stomp. Then have each group perform the named action as it moves along its shape's tape line. After a few moments ask a different member of each group to announce a new movement for his group to try.

Hop, Skip, and Jump a Letter

This gross-motor movement activity will have your youngsters moving in letter-perfect form. Each time you introduce a new letter, use masking tape to create a supersize version of that letter on the floor of your classroom. Invite your little ones to hop, skip, or crawl along the lines of the letter.

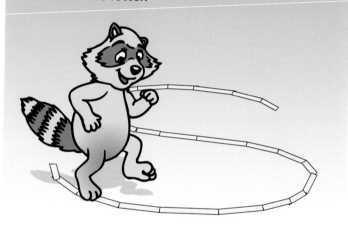

Balancing Relay

To set up the relay course, tape two lines identical in length to the floor. Divide your class into two teams. Assign each team a line; then position half of each team at one end of its line and the other half at the opposite end. Explain that the line represents a high wire similar to one seen at a circus. On a signal, the first team member uses his balance to walk the high wire to the opposite side. He then tags his awaiting team member. That student walks the high wire back to his team at the opposite end. When he arrives, he tags the next team member. Encourage each team to continue in this manner until every member has a turn. If desired, play circus music while the teams compete.

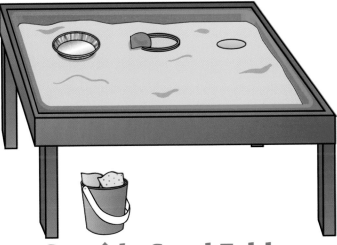

Musical Squares

This musical game will have youngsters walking—or hopping or tiptoeing—in circles. To prepare, collect a class set of carpet squares and arrange them in a circle. Invite students to stand in a circle surrounding the carpet squares. To play, name an action for youngsters to perform such as walk, hop on one foot, or tiptoe; then play a selection of lively music. Instruct youngsters to perform the action to the music as they circle around the carpet squares. After a short period of time, stop the music. Have each student step onto the nearest square so that each child is standing on a separate square. Then choose a child to name the action to be performed for the next round.

Seaside Sand Table

Turn your sand table into a gross-motor game space, and your youngsters will feel like they're playing at the beach. Gather several beanbags and place them in a child's sand pail. Then lay the following three targets out on the sand: bury a wide cup so that its rim is level with the sand's surface, lay a plastic lid or an embroidery hoop on the sand, and set a round sand sieve or pie pan on top of the sand so that its rim is above the sand's surface. Ask youngsters to take turns tossing the beanbags onto the sand table, attempting to hit the targets.

Pass the Beanbag, Please

Give youngsters' throwing and catching skills a workout with this activity. Instruct each child to select a partner; then give each partner a sturdy paper plate. Also give each student pair a beanbag. Explain that the partners will pass the beanbag back and forth to each other using their plates to catch and toss the bag. Encourage each pair to count the number of successful catches before one of the partners misses the beanbag. Then have the pair repeat the game, trying to improve the number of catches made. Increase the challenge by having the partners stand a little farther away from each other each time the game is repeated.

Differentiation Tips

Keeping Track

This versatile chart helps monitor the progress of youngsters within different instructional groups! For each group, program a copy of the chart on page 210 with the group name, date, and student names. Then write a different skill or goal at the top of each column. Keep this chart handy when working with small groups and make notes on it as needed.

Guided Reading Group 2 Checklist Date October 3-7				
Name / Skill	Tracks text from left to right	Tracks text from top to bottom	Turns pages to follow along	
Daniel	✓	most of the time	✓	
Gillian	often	✓	needs prompts	
Alec	✓	Rarely needs prompts.	✓	
Latoya	✓	✓	✓	
Veronica	Needed a lot of support.	✓	✓	

Personalized Info

Try this tip to help you organize each student's word lists, reading goals, math goals, and more! Program a copy of page 211 with the date and then make a class supply. Personalize each page and then write any relevant information in each section. Hole-punch the papers and store them in a three-ring binder for easy access. If desired, send home a copy of each child's chart for parents to view. Repeat the process to update goals as needed.

Individual Reading Collections

With these book boxes, youngsters have a selection of books aimed at their own interests or reading levels. Obtain a class supply of empty cereal boxes. Remove the tops and then trim the boxes as shown. After each student decorates his box, label it with his name. Store the boxes in an easily accessible area. In each child's box, place books that are at his independent-reading level or, if the child is not reading independently, books that reflect the child's interests. Periodically rotate the books to keep interest high. If desired, invite each student to help you select appropriate books for his box.

Practice in a Box

Here's a simple way to provide each student with just-right skill practice! To prepare, write each child's name on a separate blank card. Obtain a class supply of shoe boxes or small tubs. In each box, place materials for students to practice a desired skill. Consider items such as file-folder games, matching cards, or patterning cards. Attach the hook side of a Velcro fastener to one side of each box; then attach the loop side of a Velcro fastener to the back of each name card. Each week, attach the name cards to the boxes to provide each student with the practice she needs.

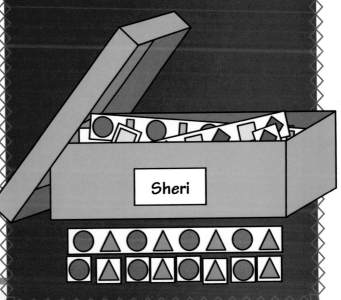

Center Selections

To make sure students choose center activities that are at their individual levels, try this idea! Laminate a personalized card for each student. Establish a color-coding system for the varying levels of your center activities. Place a colored dot sticker on each center activity. Use a wipe-off marker to color a dot on each name card to correspond with the level of center you would like each student to visit. Store the cards in an easily accessible location. During center time, direct youngsters to take their cards with them to choose activities that match their cards. As students progress to different levels, simply wipe off the dot and replace it with a different color.

Checklist

Name _____ Skill _____ Date _____

210

Note to the teacher: Use with "Keeping Track" on page 208.

Name_____ Date _____

Week of: _____

Literacy

Math

Science/Social Studies

Additional Comments:

_____

_____

_____

_____

Note to the teacher: Use with "Personalized Info" on page 208.

ENGLISH LANGUAGE LEARNERS

Sort It!

Your English language learners sort pictures of common words with this activity! Cut out a copy of the picture cards on page 215 and store them in a resealable plastic bag. Label individual sheets of tagboard with the following categories: school, clothes, food. Post the prepared sheets within students' reach. Invite a child to remove a card, name the pictured item, and attach it under the corresponding category (provide assistance as necessary). After all of the cards are sorted, lead youngsters in reviewing each resulting poster for more vocabulary practice.

Picture-Perfect Routine

Instead of just telling students what activity is next, show them! To prepare this schedule idea, take photos of students during routine activities and each special subject, such as art or music. Or, color and cut out an enlarged copy of the schedule cards on page 216. Each morning, post the day's schedule as desired. Then display selected photos or schedule cards beside the corresponding times. Since students will know what to expect, they're sure to feel comfortable in your classroom!

8:15 Morning Work	
8:30 Calendar	
9:00 Reading	
10:00 Snack	

Pack a Picnic

This class activity stretches students' oral language skills. Cut out a class supply of pictures of familiar food items from magazines or grocery store circulars. Mount each picture on a tagboard square; then place the resulting cards in a basket. To begin, seat students in a circle and hand the basket to a child. Have the student remove a card and insert the item name and a descriptive word into the following sentence: "I am taking [descriptive word] [food item] on a picnic." Then direct the remaining students to repeat the sentence, changing *I am* to *he* or *she is*. Set the card aside and direct the youngster to pass the basket to the next student. Continue the activity in the same manner until each child has had a turn.

> I am taking crunchy cookies on a picnic.

> She is taking crunchy cookies on a picnic.

Valuable Storytimes

When it comes to developing vocabulary and language skills, read-alouds are some of the best teaching tools. Use these storytime suggestions and the recommended titles to reinforce a variety of skills.

- **Alphabet Books:** Use grade-appropriate selections to introduce chosen words. Then guide youngsters to use the words in sentences.

- **Predictable Books:** Promote oral expression by inviting youngsters to join in the reading. Then encourage students to revisit the books on their own.

- **Wordless Books:** Introduce key words as you discuss the pictures with students. Then write student-generated phrases or sentences that tell about the pictures.

Alphabet Books
Eating the Alphabet: Fruits & Vegetables From A to Z by Lois Ehlert
Alphabet Under Construction by Denise Fleming
26 Letters and 99 Cents by Tana Hoban
Action Alphabet by Shelly Rotner

Predictable Books
I Was Walking Down the Road by Sarah E. Barchas
The Very Hungry Caterpillar by Eric Carle
Have You Seen My Cat? by Eric Carle
The Chick and the Duckling by Mirra Ginsburg
The Doorbell Rang by Pat Hutchins
Jump Frog, Jump! by Robert Kalan
Brown Bear, Brown Bear, What Do You See?
    by Bill Martin Jr. and Eric Carle
It Looked Like Spilt Milk by Charles G. Shaw

Wordless Books
The Snowman by Raymond Biggs
Pancakes for Breakfast by Tomie dePaola
Rosie's Walk by Pat Hutchins
Frog Goes to Dinner by Mercer Mayer

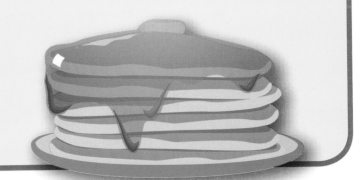

Songs and Chants

What better way to promote oral language than with repetitive songs and chants? After all, they provide plenty of opportunities for modeling and every student can successfully participate. Incorporate actions or props to enhance students' understanding.

Let's Play!

Before taking little ones outside for recess, lead them in singing this toe-tapping tune. Then encourage students to share what they enjoy doing during outdoor play.

(sung to the tune of "If You're Happy and You Know It")

We are going out to play. What will you do?
We are going out to play. What will you do?
Will you run or jump or slide before we go inside?
We are going out to play. What will you do?

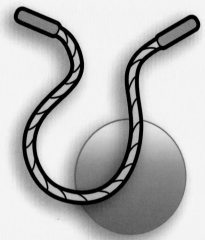

Color Clues

Give students meaningful practice with color words with this song! Lead students in the song shown. At the end of the verse, encourage youngsters to identify the corresponding color. Repeat the song several times, inserting a different colored object each time.

(sung to the tune of "I'm a Little Teapot")

I'm a little crayon, bold and bright.
I think my color is just right!
I'm the color of a [frog], you see.
Just what color can I be?

Lunchtime Review

Review food-related vocabulary after lunch with this savory chant! After students recite the chant, encourage them to discuss what they ate.

What did you eat today?
Did you eat vegetables?
Did you eat meat?
Did you eat fruit
Or something sweet?
What did you eat today?

TEC61047

TEC61047

TEC61047

TEC61047

TEC61047

TEC61047

TEC61047

TEC61047

TEC61047

TEC61047

TEC61047

TEC61047

TEC61047

TEC61047

TEC61047

Schedule Cards

Use with "Picture-Perfect Routine" on page 212.

TEC61047

TEC61047

TEC61047

TEC61047

TEC61047

TEC61047

TEC61047

TEC61047

TEC61047

TEC61047

TEC61047

TEC61047

TEC61047

TEC61047

TEC61047

TEC61047

Assessment

Write On!

Monitor youngsters' writing progress with this handy assessment. To prepare, program the writing assessment on page 219 with the date you plan to give the assessment and then copy to make a class supply. Ask each student to write her name and a sentence or two about herself on a copy of the assessment. Then have each child draw a self-portrait in the box. After collecting and evaluating the papers, file them for future reference. Repeat this process several times throughout the year. Periodically compare the completed assessments to monitor students' progress over time.

Organized Notebook

Prepare this notebook at the beginning of the year to keep assessments at your fingertips. Divide a three-ring binder into a desired number of sections, such as one for each quarter or month of the year. Make one copy of each assessment you plan to use during the school year. Slip each assessment in a page protector and place it in the corresponding section of the notebook. At the beginning of each quarter or month, simply open the notebook to the appropriate section and copy the assessment pages as needed.

Easy Evaluations

Try this idea to help keep anecdotal notes organized. Label a manila file folder with a desired skill. Write each student's name on a separate index card and tape the cards to the inside of the folder as shown. When a student is working on the featured skill, record observations on his index card. If desired, make a folder in this manner for each skill you want to assess. Refer to these handy folders when completing progress reports or report cards.

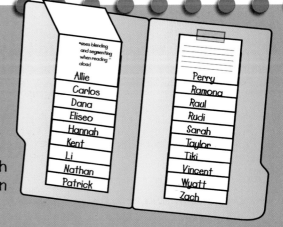

Anytime Assessment

You choose the skill with this versatile assessment idea. To prepare, make a copy of page 220. Label the page with the skill and program the gumballs with corresponding items. Copy the programmed sheet to make a class supply. Then, individually assess each student on the featured items. When a student has mastered an item, have him color the corresponding gumball(s) on his paper. When he has colored each gumball, invite him to color the rest of the picture. If desired, program a new copy of the page to assess a different skill.

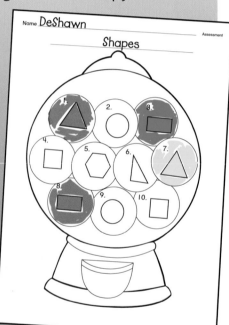

Color-Coded Year

If you give the same assessment at different times during the year, try this idea to keep them organized. Choose a different-colored paper for each time of year you wish to give the assessment. Then copy the assessment to make a class supply. After completing an assessment, file it in the corresponding student's record. When the assessments are complete, you will have an easy way to evaluate students' progress throughout the school year.

Handy Labels

Keeping track of student progress is easy with this assessment method. To prepare, write each student's name on a manila file folder. Each week program a sheet of mailing labels by writing the date and a different student's name on each label. As you monitor students, keep the labels handy to record student behaviors, work habits, and skill mastery. At the end of the week attach each label to the inside of the corresponding student's folder. These labels are a quick reference to enable you to better meet your students' needs.

Name _____

Date _____

ALL ABOUT ME

_____
_____
_____
_____
_____
_____
_____

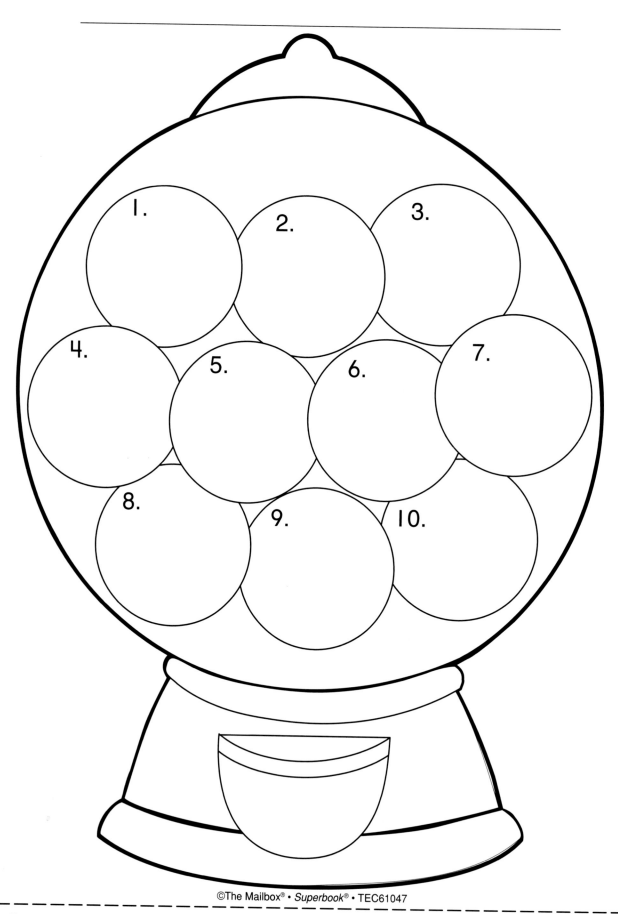

Classroom Management

Supply Storage

Try this idea to help students store their own supplies. For each child, cut off the top of a two-liter soda bottle. Cover the bottle bottom with solid-colored Con-Tact paper, paying particular attention to the cut edge. Use a wide, permanent marker to clearly label each container with a child's name. Have each child fill his bin with his crayons, scissors, pencils, glue, or any other items he'll need on a daily basis.

Creative Cubbies

If storage space is lacking, create your own crate cubby system to accommodate your little ones' classroom supplies or personal items. Purchase a supply of plastic milk crates. (It's best to use only one brand so they will interlock correctly.) Stack the crates next to and on top of each other to make a storage wall. Reinforce the interlocked structure by using twist ties to fasten the crates together.

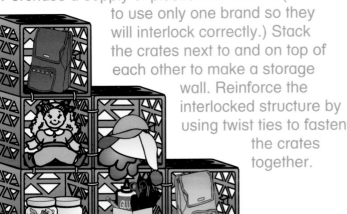

Toy Storage

This idea will end your search for a place to store large toys and manipulatives. Purchase a few large outdoor trash cans. Use a wide permanent marker to label each container. Store items such as large toy trucks, blocks, jump ropes, and playground balls in the corresponding containers.

Attendance Graph

Quickly see which youngsters are absent with this interactive chart. Make a poster board chart similar to the one shown and post it within student reach. Laminate a paper strip and post it above the chart. Each day use a wipe-off marker to write a different yes/no question on the strip. Personalize a class supply of clothespins and place it in a container near the chart. Each day a student reads the question (provide assistance as necessary) and indicates her answer by clipping her clothespin on the appropriate side of the chart. A quick glance at the container of clothespins will let you know who's absent.

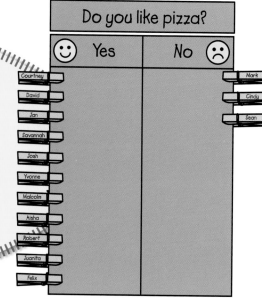

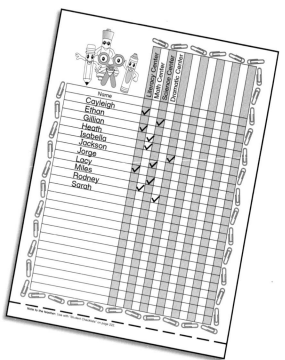

Student Checklists

A class list of names can be used to save time in a variety of ways! Label the checklist on page 230 with student names and copy a supply to keep on hand. Use a copy of the checklist to keep track of which students still need to turn in forms and important paperwork. Or use it to let you know which students have completed an assignment or visited a center. Checklists can also be used to keep anecdotal notes about each student. The possibilities are endless!

Workspace Dividers

Help students stay within their own workspaces when doing an assignment. Attach strips of thin, colored tape to your tables to create individual sections. These visual lines will remind your youngsters of their boundaries during work time.

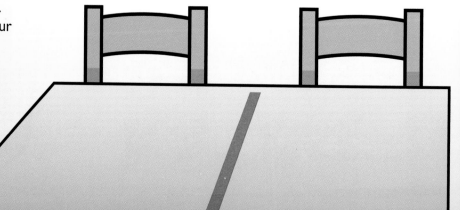

Helping Hand

Do you get interrupted when working with individuals and small groups of children? If so, try this handy suggestion. In advance, cut out several hand shapes from tagboard. Write "I need a helping hand!" on each one and laminate if desired. When a child needs your help, have him place the cutout on his workspace until you are able to help him.

Circle-Time Seating

This helpful tip allows your little ones to practice matching skills as they search for their circle time seats. For each child, attach a different sticker to a separate index card. Use cards of a different color to make a second set of cards with stickers that match the first set. After laminating the cards for durability, separate the two sets and place one set in a basket. Before group time, arrange the cards from the other set in the style best suited for your upcoming activity. Then have each child choose a card from the basket and sit down on the spot with the matching card. Any seating arrangement you desire can be achieved in a snap!

Tidy Tables

If you need a quick and easy solution to messy tables, then give this neat idea a try. Purchase a plastic sand pail for each table in your classroom. Place a pail on each table. Throughout the day, have your youngsters discard paper scraps and trash in the pails. At the end of the day, designate one child from each table to empty the pail into the trash can.

Choosing Helpers

Try this simple idea to be fair when choosing student helpers. Collect a class supply of craft sticks and label one end of each stick with a different student's name. Place a ministicker on the other end of each stick. Gather the sticks in a cup with the sticker side up. When you need a helper, randomly pull out a stick and call on that child. Return the stick to the cup name side up. When all the names are pointing upward and every child has been chosen, turn the sticks upside down and begin again.

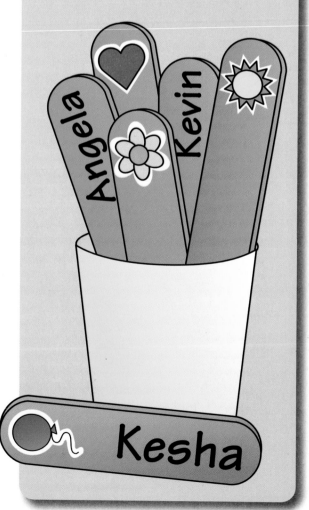

Art "Online"

A clothesline is the perfect place for gluey or painted papers to dry. Hang a clothesline in an area that your youngsters can easily reach and that will be a safe spot for drip-drying. Lay a shower curtain underneath to catch excess paint and glue. Use a permanent marker to write each child's name on a clothespin. Arrange the clothespins on the line alphabetically by first name. As a student finishes a project, he clips it to the clothesline to dry. You can also quickly tell who has and who has not completed the activity.

Week in a Wink

You can easily keep track of daily details with this handy system. Purchase five stackable letter trays and label each one with a day of the school week. Stack your daily trays on or near your desk. As you plan activities for the week, put all of the activity notes, lesson plans, and reproducibles you need in the letter tray for the corresponding day. By planning ahead, all of your materials will be within easy reach when you need them.

Note Tote

This organizational tip will help you keep up with notes from parents. Label a gift bag "Note Tote" and then mount the bag near your desk. When a student hands you a note, read it and immediately place it in the Note Tote. Later, you'll know right where to find it and be able to respond if necessary. Empty the tote at the end of the day and file the notes as desired.

Note Tote

Get-Well Greetings

Send this get-well greeting to a youngster who has been sick and absent from school for several days. Program the outside of a paper grocery bag with a get-well greeting. Then have each child in your class sign the outside of the bag. Place any projects the child has missed while sick, stickers, and perhaps a few treats in the bag, and take it to the child. What a nice way to show her that she's missed!

A Full Bag

Use a tote bag or a small suitcase to help remind students on which day they are scheduled to share for show-and-tell. In advance, label a tote bag or small suitcase "Show-and-Tell" and decorate the bag. Inside the bag, place a note telling parents about the bag and how it will be used during the year. The day before a designated child is scheduled for show-and-tell, give her the bag to take home. Encourage her to place her show-and-tell items in the bag to bring to school with her the next day.

Birthday Sundaes

Here's the scoop on a mouth-watering birthday display. Prepare 12 construction paper ice-cream dishes (pattern on page 231). Label an ice-cream dish for each month of the year and post them on a wall or bulletin board. Personalize construction paper scoops of ice cream with each child's name and birthdate; then attach each scoop to the appropriate dish. Top off each dish with a cherry cutout. If desired, give each child a personalized copy of the birthday card on page 232 on his birthday.

Greg 27
Paul 16
Emily 6
January

The Birthday Song

Students will quickly tune in to their birthdates with this little ditty sung to the tune of "The More We Get Together."

Class:
What day is your birthday,
Your birthday, your birthday?
What day is your birthday?

Student's response:
It's _____.

Field Trip Clothing

On the day of a field trip, have everyone wear coordinated clothing. Choose a common article of clothing, such as a red T-shirt or a school sweatshirt, for youngsters and chaperones to wear so that members of your group are easily recognizable.

Once you've divided your class into chaperoned groups, assign each group a different color. Then make each group's nametags in its designated color with colored paper, markers, or colored sticky dots. Each chaperone will be able to see quickly who belongs in her group. Be sure to make a master list of the colored groupings so that you can sort out any stragglers.

Field Trip Packs

Help your chaperones be prepared by assembling these handy travel packs. Collect several fanny packs and stock each one with baby wipes, bandages, an instant cold pack, spare change, a pen, safety pins, emergency first-aid information, and the phone number of the school. Each chaperone will have supplies that are readily accessible and convenient. After the trip, collect the packs and restock them as necessary.

Substitute Survival Kit

Transform a portable file box into a substitute teacher's treasure chest. Appropriately label the box and fill it with the items listed below. Keep the box near your desk so that it will be easy to find and ready to use upon your replacement's arrival.

- **a schedule**—Outline the basics of your daily schedule and procedures, leaving spaces to insert details of lesson plans. Laminate the schedule; then when the need arises, use a wipe-off marker to add additional information specific to the day you'll be absent.

- **a class roster**—Arrange copies of students' pictures on a sheet of paper; then label each picture with the student's name.

- **nametags**—Make a class supply of laminated nametags. If desired, provide the teacher with small stickers to attach to the nametags as rewards throughout the day.

- **dismissal information**—On a bus-shaped cutout, list the bus numbers and riders. Similarly, list car riders on a car-shaped cutout and walkers on a sneaker-shaped cutout.

- **a list of students' special needs**—such as medication, physical limitations, or custody restrictions

- **emergency procedures and a map of your school**

- **discipline policy**

- **parents' phone numbers**

BUS RIDERS

Alice Jeremy Peter

Daily Schedule

8:30
9:30
11:30
1:30
2:30

Substitute Read-Alouds

Reading aloud a class favorite is always a great way for your substitute and class to spend time together. Leave a list of favorite read-aloud titles for your substitute. Also include a list of story extensions that are appropriate for any of the stories.

Story Extensions

- As a group, list and describe the characters.
- Ask each child to draw a favorite scene from the story.
- Together, make a timeline of the story's events.
- Ask each child to draw a poster recommending the book.

And There's More

Be sure to check out the teacher-resource reproducibles on pages 230 and 232-235. You'll find a student checklist, a birthday card, parent notes, a variety of nametags, and a classroom newsletter.

Musical Management

Use this collection of songs to help you manage your youngsters throughout the day.

Morning Rap

Start the day in a cool sort of way with this lively rap.

Say, "Hi! Hi! Hi!
Hello! Hello!
What a great day
For school, you know!"

Say, "Hi! Hi! Hi!
Hello! Hello!
Time to get started.
Let's go, go, go!"

Listen Closely

Sing this song with youngsters to call the attention of all ears and eyes to the teacher.

(sung to the tune of "I've Been Working on the Railroad")

Listen closely to the teacher.
Listen as (s)he speaks.
Listen closely to the teacher.
No grunts, no growls, no squeaks.
Everyone is oh so quiet
And looking the teacher's way.
Everyone is still and ready
To hear what (s)he has to say.

Wiggle-Time Rhyme

Encourage students to manage their wiggles by singing this little ditty.

(sung to the tune of "Twinkle, Twinkle, Little Star")

Wiggle your toes and bend your legs;
Sway your hips and nod your head.
Shake your shoulders, blink your eyes;
Stretch your arms up to the sky!
Cross your legs; sit on the floor.
Wiggles are gone—we have no more!

Line Up, Children

Here's a snappy tune that will prepare youngsters for a trek down the hall.

(sung to the tune of "Head and Shoulders")

Line up, children.
Line up one. Line up all.
Quiet children.
Quiet one. Quiet all.
Let's walk softly down the hall.
Line up, children.
Line up one. Line up all.

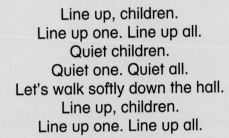

It's Time to Pick Up

Make cleanup time quick and breezy with this bouncy tune.

(sung to the tune of "She'll Be Comin' Round the Mountain")

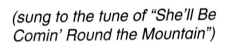

Oh, it's time to pick up all our things right now.
Yes, it's time to pick up all our things right now.
When we work together, it's easy—
Cleanup time is quick and breezy.
Oh, it's time to pick up all our things right now!

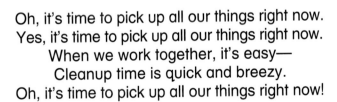

A-cleaning We Will Go

Everyone will want to join in the cleanup fun when you sing this song.

(sung to the tune of "A-hunting We Will Go")

A-cleaning we will go!
A-cleaning we will go!
We'll pick up toys and blocks and books
And put them where they go!

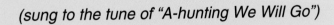

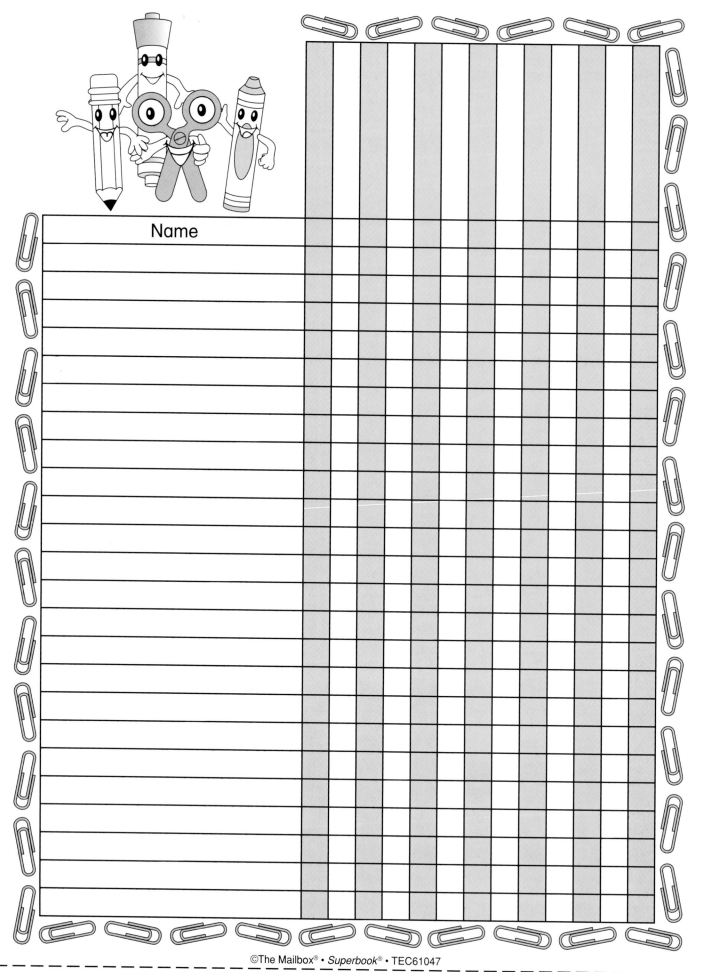

Name									

Note to the teacher: Use with "Student Checklists" on page 222.

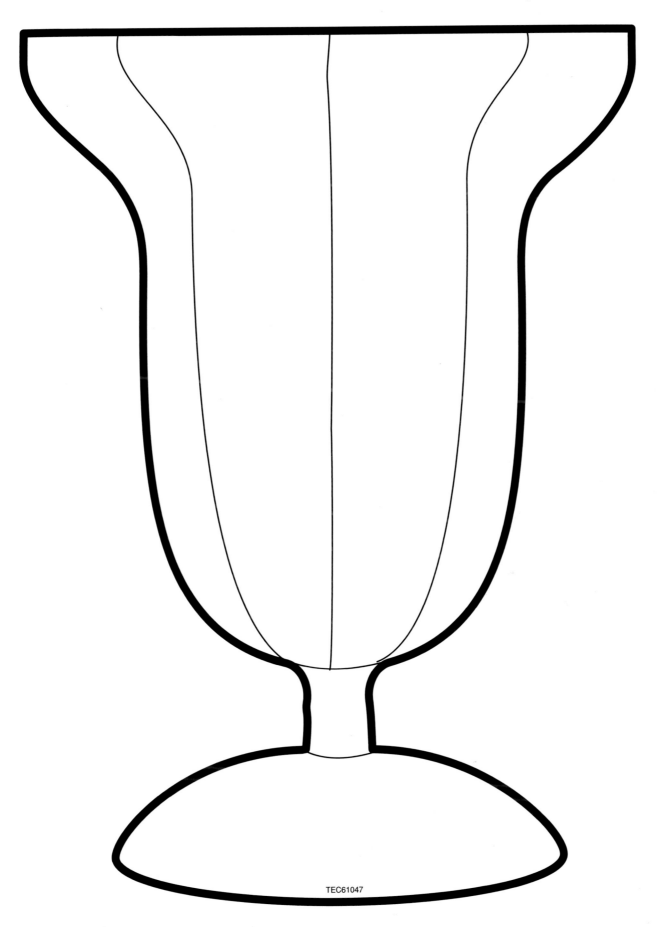

TEC61047

Birthday Card

HAPPY BIRTHDAY,

_____ !

Teacher Notes

PLEASE CALL

A NOTE TO LET YOU KNOW...

Nametags

CLASSROOM NEWS

Teacher: _____

Date: _____

What We're Learning

★ Superstars ★

Special Thanks

Please Remember

Help Wanted

Transitions & Time Fillers

Tidy-Up Transition

Bubbles help make the transition to cleanup time a breeze! To begin, blow bubbles in the areas of the classroom that need to be tidied up. Your youngsters will be drawn to these areas in need of attention by the fun of following and popping the bubbles. Once the bubbles are all popped, have each youngster straighten up the area he is in. Your classroom will be neat and organized in no time!

All Aboard

Students will chug right along to the next destination on the Classroom Express. Choose a child to be the engineer. When he calls, "All aboard!" have the other children get in line behind him. Direct each child to put his hands on the shoulders of the person in front of him to make a train. Then it's chug, chug, chug—on to the next stop in your school day!

On another day, invite your class to move like a caterpillar by putting their hands on one another's waists. Encourage students to think of other creative ways they can move together.

Ticket to Ride (or Read, or Play)

Try this transition tip after a messy art session and your classroom will be clean in a snap. Tell students that to join you for the next activity, they'll each need a ticket. The ticket is one scrap of paper from the floor. (On really messy days, request two or more tickets.) Have them bring the scraps to the next activity and place them in a wastebasket. What a tidy transition!

STEP BY STEP

Use extra minutes throughout the day to sneak in a little estimation practice. Have a small group of students estimate and then figure out the distance between two objects or places. Ask them to guess the number of footsteps from your classroom door to the bathroom door, from the water fountain to the swings, from the windows to the bookshelf, or from your classroom to the gym. Then invite student volunteers to do the measuring and compare the results with students' predictions.

Tranquil Transitions

Ensure calm youngsters when they move from one activity to another by making a transition song tape. Record a song or instrumental piece a few times onto a cassette tape. When it is time for children to change activities, play the tape and instruct children to hop, skip, "swim," walk, or "skate" to the next activity. When the tape ends, students should be ready for the next activity. In no time at all, your students will be cooperatively moving to the next activity.

Let's Get Shakin'!

Round up your youngsters to shake, stamp, snap, and clap to transition to group time.

(sung to the tune of "The Wheels on the Bus")

It's time to shake
And shake and shake.
Stamp and stamp.
Snap and clap.

It's time to shake
And shake and shake.
Now everyone sit down!

Colorful Chairs

This time-filling activity helps color practice become a variation on Musical Chairs. Ask each student to sit in a chair. Scan the room to determine the most popular colors of students' clothing. Tell children you are going to clap your hands and say a color. If they are wearing that color, they should get up and find a new seat. Clap and call out colors as time permits. Every so often clap and call, "All colors." Your little ones will love this game of chair-changing fun.

Roll 'Em

This quick and easy counting game will help little ones get the wiggles out. Make a pair of jumbo foam dice by cutting a giant car wash sponge in half. Place the appropriate number of dot stickers on each side of each die. To play, have students take turns rolling one die or both dice. When the dice have been rolled, have the child announce the number of dots showing on top of the dice. Ask the child to pick an activity for the whole class to repeat that number of times. For example, if seven is rolled, students might do seven jumping jacks, toe touches, sit-ups, or hand claps.

One-Minute Challenge

When you've got a few minutes to spare, have some fun with the classroom clock or a stopwatch. Ask students to see how many times they can write their names in one minute. Start and stop the challenge with the help of students who will take turns being the timekeeper. Other one-minute challenges could include counting how many times students can jump up and down, how many blocks they can stack, or how many times they can clap their hands.

An elephant is the largest animal that lives on land.

All About Animals

Invite youngsters to share their knowledge of different animals when they participate in this quick activity. To prepare, place an assortment of plastic animals in a bag. Then invite a child to choose an animal from the bag. Encourage him to tell the class what he knows about the selected animal.

Double Simon

Here's a variation on a favorite time-filler game. Have children sit at a table or on the floor. Offer children instructions with two variables. For example:

—Simon says, "People with sneakers and turtlenecks, stand up."

—Simon says, "People with sneakers and turtlenecks, sit down."

—Simon says, "People wearing white socks and zippers, jog in place."

— Simon says, "People wearing white socks and zippers, sit down."

Once the rules are familiar, invite a student to be the leader of this fun, new game.

Animal Antics

Students will love this time-filling game. Invite three or four volunteers to stand in front of the class. Secretly show the standing group a plastic animal. In turn, direct each child standing to act out the actions of the suggested animal. When each child has had a turn, ask the remainder of the class to guess the name of the depicted animal. When the animal has been named, or after several guesses, ask each standing child to choose a new person to be an actor.

SOMETHING'S DIFFERENT

Play this nifty memory game to easily fill spare minutes. Ask one student to stand in front of the class where everyone can see her. Tell the class to carefully study the student's appearance and remember as many details as possible. Then, while your little ones cover their eyes, quickly change one aspect of the student's appearance, such as taking off a sock, cuffing one pant leg, or untucking her shirt. Challenge the class to guess what's different about its classmate.

Book-Buddy Basket

Here's a cozy way to settle students down for quiet time. Fill a large basket with small stuffed animals, puppets, books, and magazines. Encourage each child to select a buddy (a stuffed animal or puppet) and a book or magazine to read with that buddy. Shhh…we're reading!

Motivation & Positive Discipline

Seasonal Sticker Strips

Prevent students from turning in carelessly completed work with this splendid idea. Personalize a sentence strip for each student as shown; then mount the strips vertically on a bulletin board or classroom wall. Each time a child completes a paper that represents his best work, give him a sticker to add to his strip. When a student earns a predetermined number of stickers, he redeems the strip for a special privilege or treat.

Add a Link

At the end of the school day, gather youngsters around and encourage them to share ways that their classmates have been kind that day. Write each act of kindness mentioned on a paper strip. Then have students help you transform the strips into a paper chain. Continue in the same way each day, adding links to the original chain. Youngsters will be tickled to watch this chain grow and grow!

I CAN

- draw
- run
- swim
- kick a ball
- make my lunch
- ride a bike

Yes, I Can

Adopt a "Yes, I Can!" attitude in your classroom with this character-building activity. To begin, read aloud *The Little Engine That Could* by Watty Piper. After reading the story aloud, ask students to tell about tasks they mastered after trying again and again. Responses might include learning to ride a bike, learning to swim, or learning the alphabet. Provide each student with a copy of one of the engine patterns on page 243. First, instruct the student to draw himself in the window as the engineer. Next, help him write "I CAN" on the front of the pattern and then list some of his accomplishments on the back of the pattern.

Mascot Monitor

No doubt students will be motivated to be on their best behavior with this fun idea! Each morning, place the class mascot (a small stuffed animal) on the desk of one child who demonstrated exceptional behavior the previous school day. During your morning routine, spotlight the child's behavior and congratulate her on being the keeper of the class mascot for the day.

School of Kindness

To prepare for this idea, attach a length of blue bulletin board paper to your wall. Then add the title shown. Cut out several copies of the treasure chest pattern on page 244. Write on each chest a different way to be kind to someone; then color the chests and attach them to the paper. Embellish the scene with other details as desired. Place a supply of simple fish cutouts nearby. When you notice a child being kind, have her label a fish with her name and then attach it to the display.

Pleasant Postcards

Your little ones will anxiously await the mail if they know they'll be receiving postcards of praise. Periodically record on a postcard positive behavior you've observed and mail the card to the child's home to inform his parents of his actions. Now, that's first-class mail!

Pleasing Pearls

Recognize youngsters' hard work with these underwater wonders! For each child, cut an oyster shape from a folded sheet of construction paper as shown. Label it with the child's name and draw a happy face on the front. Attach a folded oyster to each child's desk or work area. When a child exhibits a desired behavior or completes a certain task, open his oyster and place a sticky dot (pearl) inside. This way the youngster's successes are kept private. After he has a predetermined number of pearls, reward him with a small prize or special privilege.

The "Berry" Best!

Harvest a bunch of positive lunchroom behavior with this plan! Display a green construction paper bush cutout with the title shown. Make a desired number of blueberry cutouts. Then attach corresponding pieces of Velcro fasteners to the cutouts and the bush. Each time the class receives a good report from lunchroom monitors, attach a blueberry to the bush. When the bush is filled with ripe blueberries, reward youngsters with a special treat, such as a batch of blueberry muffins!

The "Berry" Best Lunch Bunch!

AWARDS WHEEL

This award-winning wheel will keep your youngsters spinning with good behavior. Divide a tagboard circle into sections; then laminate it. Use a wipe-off marker to program each section with a simple activity or class privilege, such as singing a favorite song or performing a quick-movement activity. To use the wheel, the teacher uses a pencil to hold a paper clip spinner in place. Then a child spins the paper clip to determine the privilege. The students then earn the privilege with good behavior. With this management help, goals for good behavior are just a spin away!

Play a favorite game.

Bubbles at center time.

Have a special snack.

Extra ten minutes on the playground.

TEC61047

TEC61047

Treasure Chest Pattern

Use with "School of Kindness" on page 241.

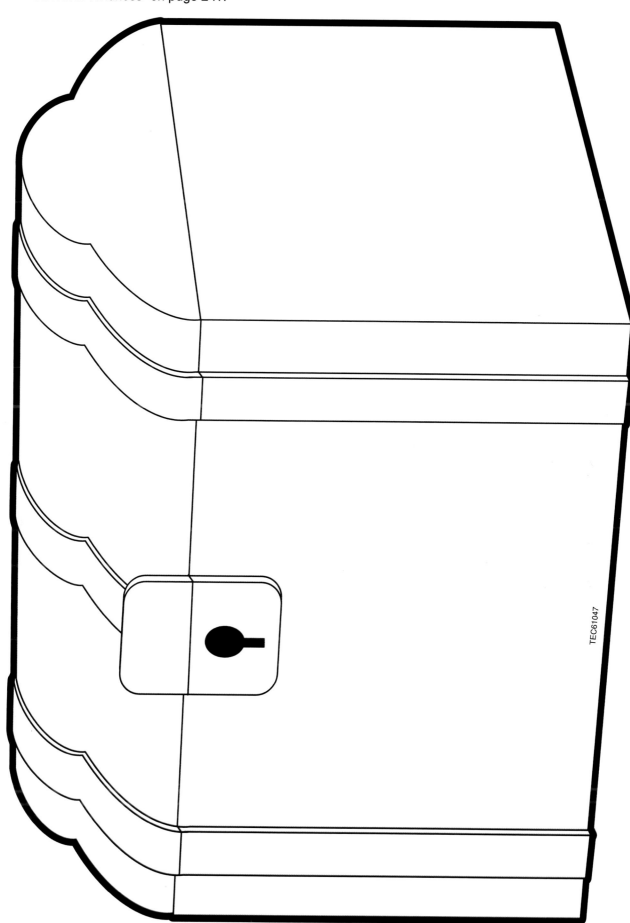

TEC61047

Home & School Connection

What's the Scoop?

Help parents get the scoop on upcoming classroom events as well as classmates' acts of kindness with this weekly newsletter. Each week program a copy of the newsletter on page 250 with relevant information such as the week's activities, upcoming events, or requests for supplies. Also include anecdotes praising students who performed outstanding acts of kindness during the previous week. Then make a class supply of the prepared newsletter and send a copy home with each child. No doubt parents will be grateful for this weekly scoop!

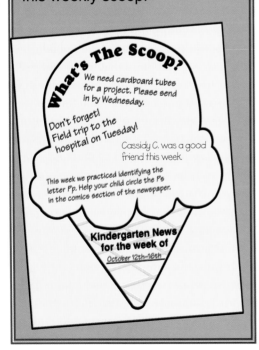

What's The Scoop?

We need cardboard tubes for a project. Please send in by Wednesday.

Don't forget! Field trip to the hospital on Tuesday!

Cassidy C. was a good friend this week.

This week we practiced identifying the letter Pp. Help your child circle the Ps in the comics section of the newspaper.

Kindergarten News for the week of
October 12th–16th

Friday on My Mind

To make sharing the school week with parents part of your students' regular routine, try preparing Friday Files for your students. Purchase a class supply of 10" x 13" manila envelopes. Decorate the envelopes and label each one with a different student's name. Laminate the envelopes with the flaps open and use an X-acto knife to carefully slit through the laminate at the envelope opening. If desired, apply Velcro closures to the envelopes for easier opening and closing. During the week, fill the envelopes with students' work as well as important notes and information for parents. On Friday, students can take home their packets for weekend reviews. Make youngsters responsible for returning their envelopes on Monday with any appropriate at-home activities or notes from parents.

Icebreakers, Smile Makers

Here's an idea that's sure to break the ice with parents and bring smiles to their kindergartners' faces. Prepare a simple questionnaire asking parents to describe particular events from their own kindergarten experiences, such as their first day of school or special times with a kindergarten friend. Send a copy of the questionnaire home to each parent and ask her to return it to school by a specified date. After each questionnaire is returned to school, read each parent's memories during a group time. Invite students to try to identify to which classmate each parent belongs. Then display the completed pages with a title, such as "When I Was a Kindergartner…".

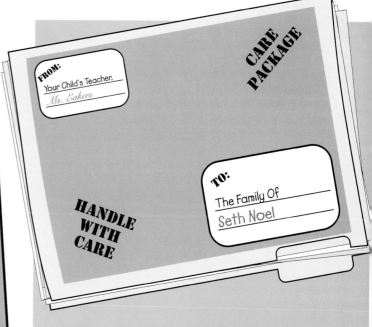

Brown-Bag It

Take the opportunity to become better acquainted with your kindergarten parents during a special lunchtime. In advance, send each parent an invitation to bring a lunch for herself and her child on an appointed day. During lunch, ask parents to share interesting information about themselves and their families. Then share a few things about yourself with your guests. Conclude the lunch activities with a summary of the upcoming happenings in your classroom.

Handle With Care

A few times throughout the school year, prepare a care package for each family. To do this, make a class supply of the cover sheet on page 251 on tan construction paper. For each child, glue a cover sheet to the front of a file folder. Fill each folder with artwork and other creations made by the student, as well as work assignments. "Address" each care package and send it home to each family.

Classroom Photo Gallery

Here's a picture-perfect way to share classroom events with your students' parents. Each month, take pictures of special events and classroom happenings. Mount the pictures on a wall or bulletin board with a brief description of each event near the corresponding photograph. Title the board "Our Classroom Gallery." Invite parents and youngsters to check out the gallery each month.

Sing-Alongs at Home

These personalized kindergarten sing-along tapes will quickly become home-school language links. Ask each parent to send a blank cassette labeled with her child's name to school. Prepare to have some extras on hand. Then, when the class sings favorite songs or recites popular rhymes and chants, tape its performances. After a significant number of items have been recorded, make multiple copies of the cassette using the tapes sent by your students. Send each child's tape home with a note inviting family members to join in as they listen to it together.

Mrs. Riley's Kindergarten Class

Thanks "bear-y" much for your help!

A "Bear-y" Nice Gift

If you're looking for a way to say thanks to parents who have been helpful in your classroom, give this sweet idea a try. Cut out a brown construction paper copy of the bear on page 252 and attach it to a resealable bag filled with honey-flavored candy. Then add a note to the bear that reads, "Thanks 'bear-y' much for your help!"

Parent Appreciation Certificates

After special class events or activities that require parental input or support, present each involved parent with a personalized, programmed copy of the parent certificate on page 252. With the help of this simple and appreciative means of acknowledgement, your parents will be pleased to participate in upcoming events.

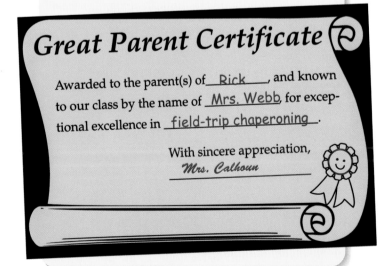

Great Parent Certificate

Awarded to the parent(s) of __Rick__, and known to our class by the name of __Mrs. Webb__, for exceptional excellence in __field-trip chaperoning__.

With sincere appreciation,
Mrs. Calhoun

Wanted: Parents to Attend Conferences

This invitation is sure to create enthusiasm for parent conferences. Make a copy of the invitation on page 253. List available conference times on the invitation; then make a class supply. Personalize each invitation; then ask each child to draw a picture of his parent(s) on the corresponding invitation. Send home the invitations. When each parent returns an invitation with his conference choices listed, assign the parent a conference time. Record the assigned time on your personal calendar before sending the invitation home once more with the assigned time noted.

WANTED:

The Parent(s) Of ___Jimmy T.___ To Attend
        (child's name)
A Parent-Teacher Conference

Please choose three conference times.
   Oct. 19: 3:00, 3:30, 4:00, 5:30
   Oct. 20: 3:30, 4:30, 6:00

1st choice: _____

2nd choice: _____

3rd choice: _____

Homework for Parents!

Here's a great way to let your students' parents know that you value their input and that you are eager to address their concerns. For each parent, duplicate the parent homework assignment on page 253; and send them home several days prior to your conferences. When each assignment is returned, review it and make a note of comments and concerns to discuss with each parent.

Next on the Agenda...

Preparing agendas in advance and using them during conferences will help you make the most of conference times. For each conference, complete a copy of the agenda on page 254 by listing a different topic or portion of the conference in each of the train's boxcars. At the beginning of the conference, review the agenda with the parent(s); then refer to it as you continue your discussion. Finally, send home the agenda with the visiting parent so that he will have a reference of your discussion for future use.

Conference Agenda

John's strengths · Current Assessments · Explanation of our goals this year · Parents' Questions

A Pleasant Wait

Since most parents arrive prior to their assigned conference times, make their wait time informative and insightful. Set a table and chairs in the hall just outside your door. Try the following ideas to enhance your waiting area:

- Post your conference schedule on your door along with a note requesting that the parent knock to let you know she has arrived. When you hear the knock, you'll know it's time to finish your conversation so that you can move to the next conference in a timely manner.

- Place a basket of student-created books on the table.

- Give parents a chance to learn about your life outside the classroom by arranging pictures and brief descriptions on the table.

- Place goodies on the table with a note inviting parents to eat before you meet.

- Make copies of parenting- or education-related articles. Display a note encouraging parents to take copies of articles that interest them.

- Provide an album filled with pictures of students involved in school activities.

- Since it's often necessary for young children to accompany parents to conferences, consider providing age-appropriate toys and books.

Friendly Reminders

Here's a friendly list of tips that make conferences run smoothly:

 Invite parents to sit beside you rather than in front of you.

 Keep blank paper and pens handy for writing reminders and taking notes.

 Always begin a conference by discussing the child's unique strengths and qualities.

 Empower parents by asking for their input.

 Be prepared to suggest ways that a parent can work with her child at home.

 Suggest goals for the child to work toward.

A Fun Follow-Up

Follow up each conference by sending a small bag of goodies to that parent. Attach a note to let him know that you appreciate him taking time to visit and that you are available should he have additional questions.

Glad we could meet— Enjoy this treat!

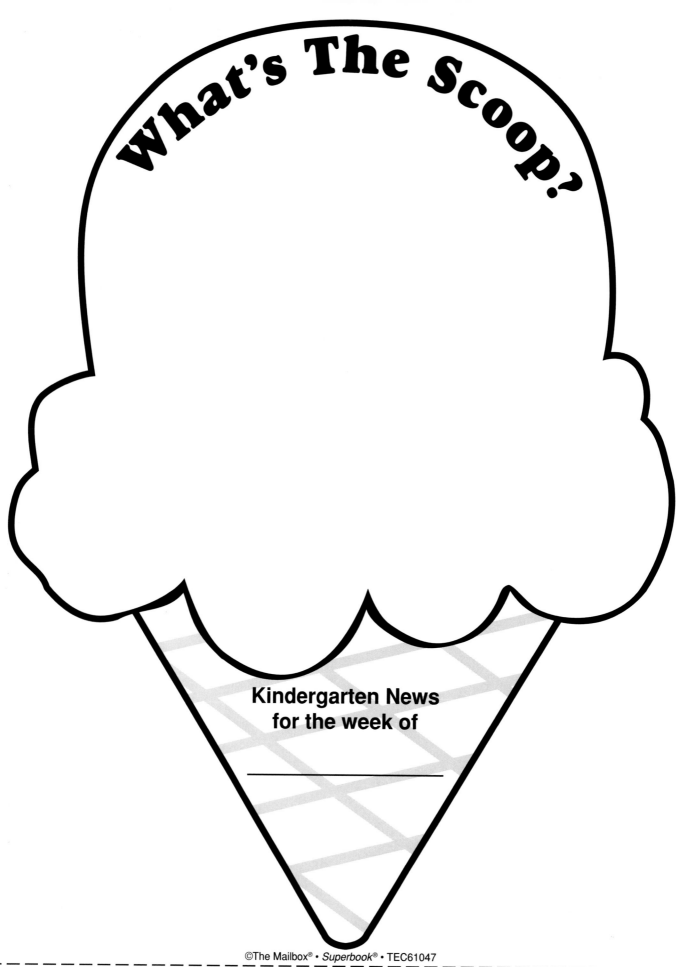

What's The Scoop?

Kindergarten News
for the week of

_____

Note to the teacher: Use with "What's the Scoop?" on page 245.

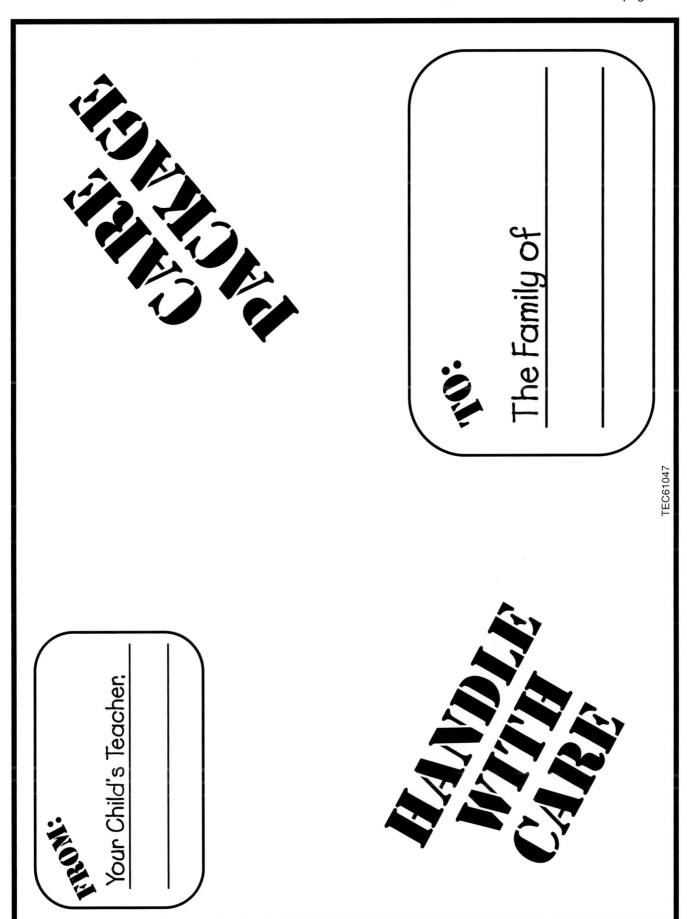

CARE PACKAGE

TO:
The Family of _____

FROM:
Your Child's Teacher, _____

HANDLE WITH CARE

TEC61047

Parent Certificate

Use with "Parent Appreciation Certificates" on page 247.

Great Parent Certificate

Awarded to the parent(s) of _____, and known
(child)

to our class by the name of _____, for excep-
(parent)

tional excellence in _____.

With sincere appreciation,

_____
(teacher)

©The Mailbox® • Superbook® • TEC61047

Bear Pattern

Use with "A 'Bear-y' Nice Gift" on page 247.

TEC61047

©The Mailbox® • Superbook® • TEC61047

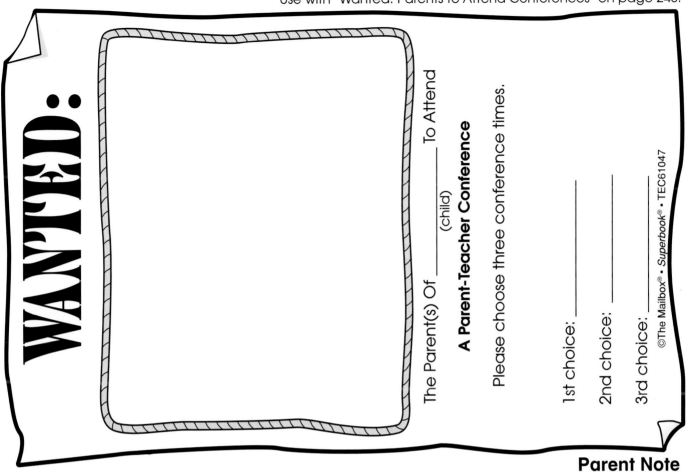

WANTED:

The Parent(s) Of _____ To Attend

(child)

A Parent-Teacher Conference

Please choose three conference times.

1st choice: _____

2nd choice: _____

3rd choice: _____

©The Mailbox® • *Superbook*® • TEC61047

Parent Note
Use with "Homework for Parents!" on page 248.

Homework for Parents

To help prepare for our upcoming conference, please jot down your questions and concerns. Return the form by _____.

(date)

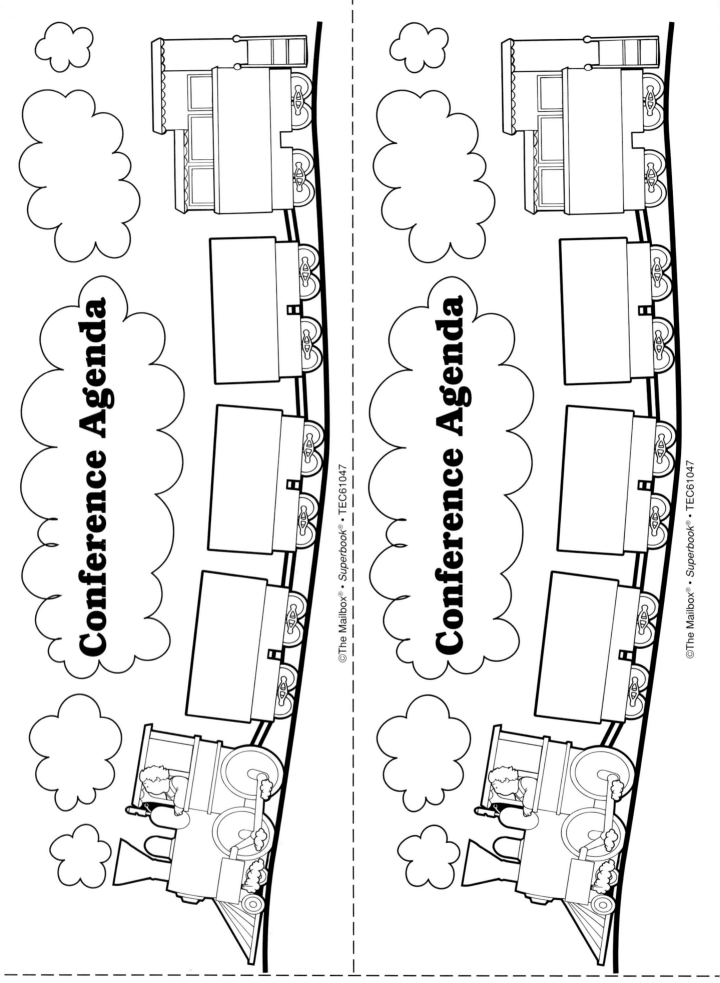

Conference Agenda

©The Mailbox® • Superbook® • TEC61047

Conference Agenda

©The Mailbox® • Superbook® • TEC61047

Bulletin Boards

A New Crop!

Showcase your new crop of kindergartners with this "a-peel-ing" display! Give each child a construction paper apple cutout to personalize. Trim a sheet of bulletin board paper to resemble a bushel; then label it with your name. Mount the bushel on a wall with the student apples and a title.

For this Open House display, give each child a paper towel that you have folded into a square. Arrange containers of water tinted with food coloring. Invite each child to dip each side of his towel into different colors of water. Then have him open it up and set it aside to dry. Next, help him trim his towel into a shirt shape and glue it to a sheet of construction paper. Encourage him to incorporate the shirt in a picture of himself. Display the completed projects with the title shown.

Fall Is All Around Us

Have each child brush a coffee filter with water and then squeeze a few drops of red and yellow food coloring onto the filter. Provide tagboard leaf templates. Have each child trace a leaf onto her dried filter and then cut it out. Arrange the leaves as a border and add student-drawn fall pictures and a title to your display.

Sizing Up Pumpkins

Big

Little

On opposite ends of a bulletin board, post two paper signs labeled "Big" and "Little." Then add a scarecrow character (enlarge and color the pattern on page 265) and the title, as shown. Have each child cut out a pumpkin shape from orange construction paper. Encourage him to add details with markers and construction paper scraps. In turn, help each youngster attach his pumpkin to the appropriate side of the display.

Have each child make a gorgeous gobbler for this Thanksgiving display. To make one, staple together two 5-inch circles cut from a brown paper bag, stuffing shredded newspaper between the layers before stapling around them completely. Cut a red head and orange beak and feet from construction paper, add eyes, and then glue them in place. Trace one hand onto four different colors of construction paper; then cut out the hand shapes. Glue the hand cutouts onto the turkey's body. Attach all the turkeys and the title to the bulletin board.

To make a winter scene, give each child a sheet of dark blue construction paper and a white colored pencil or crayon. Help him write a sentence on the paper telling what he likes to do in the snow. Then invite him to use the white pencil to draw a matching scene. After he adds crayon details, direct him to glue his paper to a slightly larger piece of aluminum foil. Display the completed projects on a board decorated like the one shown.

Celebrate Hanukkah with this festive bulletin board. To create the menorah, wrap tubes from paper towels or wrapping paper in shiny paper or cellophane. Staple the tubes to the board in the shape of a menorah (as shown). Use construction paper and glitter to make the flames. "Light" the middle candle first; then add one flame to the bulletin board for each of the eight nights of Hanukkah. Invite students to draw pictures of Hanukkah celebrations; then display their artwork around the menorah.

Ask students to give you a hand with Christmas decorating. Trace each child's two hands and help him cut out the shapes. Place the pairs of hands so that one hand slightly overlaps the other; then glue them in place. Have each child use construction paper, glue, and glitter to make a star for the top and a brown trunk for the bottom of his tree. Have students use different colors of ink pads to make fingerprint ornaments for their trees. Display these "hand-y" trees with a Christmas-lights border.

A Penny for Your Hearts

Everyone will love this sweet Valentine's Day bulletin board. Provide each child with a large white circle, a small white square, a red trapezoid, and several small hearts cut from construction paper. Have each student decorate her hearts with glitter and then glue them onto her circle. Have her glue the square to the trapezoid (as shown) and then glue the trapezoid below the circle to resemble the base of a gumball machine. Use hot glue to attach a real penny and a candy conversation heart as shown. Mount the designs and title on a bulletin board for a delicious display!

What's at the End of a Rainbow?

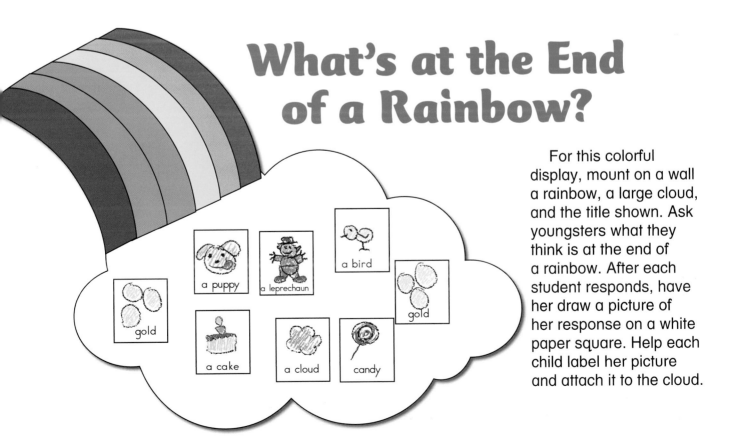

For this colorful display, mount on a wall a rainbow, a large cloud, and the title shown. Ask youngsters what they think is at the end of a rainbow. After each student responds, have her draw a picture of her response on a white paper square. Help each child label her picture and attach it to the cloud.

Invite youngsters to create springtime crafts for this display. To create a butterfly, paint a coffee filter with watercolors. Pinch the center with a clothespin and add pipe cleaner antennae. To make a bee, add gold-glitter stripes, a pipe cleaner stinger, waxed paper wings, and eye stickers to a black construction paper circle. To make a kite, decorate a construction paper diamond with glitter; then add a yarn-and-ribbon tail. Look…up in the air…it's spring!

This interactive display is grade A! Have each child decorate a construction paper egg cutout and then puzzle-cut it in half. Mount on a board the bottom half of each egg and the title shown. Store the other egg halves in a bag and place the bag near the display. Invite students to use Sticky-Tac to attach each egg half to its match.

Love is in bloom with this special Mother's Day bulletin board. Ask each child to bring in a picture of herself with her mother. Then have her create a flower by making ten loops from 12-inch strips of construction paper. Have her glue the loops around a six-inch construction paper circle and then add a green stem and loop leaf. Invite her to glue her special photo to the center of her flower. Display the finished flowers and title where moms can see them, and watch their smiles blossom!

Show off your youngsters' sunny smiles with this sunflower display. Provide each child with a six-inch brown circle and several yellow triangles cut from construction paper. Have each student glue his triangles around his circle. Have him add a personalized green stem and a leaf; then have him glue a photo of himself to the center of his flower. Invite him to glue on some construction paper seeds to complete his project. Display the flowers and title, and enjoy your little ones' gorgeous grins!

Keep alphabet skills on the right track with this display. Mount an engine, similar to the one shown, on a wall. Add a title and a labeled construction paper car for each letter of the alphabet. As each letter is being studied, have children cut out magazine pictures of items that begin with that letter and then glue them onto the corresponding car.

Help your children take a bite out of counting! Prepare ten cookie jar cutouts. Label each jar with a different numeral from one to ten. Mount the jars and title on a wall. Copy and cut out a large supply of construction paper cookies (patterns on page 268). Store the cookie cutouts and a supply of Sticky-Tac near your display; then invite a student to place the correct number of cookies on each jar.

To keep track of helpers, copy and cut out a desired number of construction paper honey pots (page 266). Label each pot with a classroom job. Personalize a bear for each child (pattern on page 266). Stack and pin the bears inside a brown paper cave. Staple the honey pots on the board and assign classroom helpers by pinning a child's bear next to the appropriate honey pot.

This display will have students grinning from ear to ear! Enlarge and color the tooth character on page 267. Mount it on one side of a background. Add a rope border and a title as shown. Then make additional copies of the tooth character and cut them out. Each time a child loses a tooth, write his name and the date on the hat of a cutout. Have the child color the cutout and blacken in the missing tooth before adding it to the display.

Birthdays are sweet with this display. Cut one edge on each of 12 half-sheets of construction paper to resemble a paper bag. Decorate the bags as desired. Label each bag with a different month; then glue each bag onto a separate sheet of construction paper, leaving the top edge free. Personalize a separate candy shape (patterns on page 268) with each child's name and birthdate. Mount the bags and title on a bulletin board; then staple the candies to the tops of the appropriate bags.

Your little ones will shine with pride over this display. Brush glue on top of a large star shape; then sprinkle it with glitter. Draw facial features on the star; then laminate it. Mount the star on a bulletin board with the bullte title "Shining Star." Use a dry-erase marker to personalize the star with a different child's name each week. Encourage your little shining star to bring in pictures of himself, his family, and a few of his favorite things. Display the items on the board.

TEC61047

Bear and Honey Pot Patterns

Use with "Honey Helpers" on page 263.

TEC61047

TEC61047

TEC61047

Cookie Patterns

Use with "Cookie Counters" on page 262.

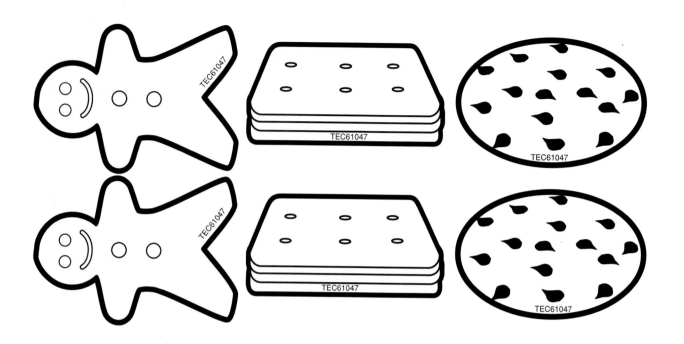

Candy Patterns

Use with "Sweet Celebrations" on page 264.

Seasonal ARTS & CRAFTS

Blowin' in the Wind

Take youngsters on a nature walk to collect some fall leaves; then head back to the classroom to make these windsocks. To make one, place a leaf vein side up under a sheet of construction paper. Rub the paper with the side of an unwrapped crayon. Repeat this process, overlapping the leaves and using different crayon colors and different leaves. Then cut fall-colored crepe paper into 14-inch strips. Glue a few construction paper leaves onto each strip; then glue the strips to the bottom edge of the paper. Roll the paper into a cylinder and staple it in place. Punch holes near the top; then lace a length of yarn through the holes and tie the ends together. Suspend the windsocks in your classroom for a fabulous fall display.

Apple Wreaths

Apple prints are the inspiration for these student-made wreaths. To make a wreath, repeatedly press an apple half into thinned tempera paint and then onto a sheet of paper. When the paint is dry, add brown stems with a thin marker and then cut around the apple prints. Cut out the center from a paper plate; then glue the apple-print cutouts onto the remaining rim of the plate. Glue a school photo to another apple-print cutout; then use yarn and tape to suspend this apple from the rim of the plate so that it hangs in the center opening. Add a bow to complete the wreath.

Handy Pumpkin

To make a pumpkin, cover a white construction paper pumpkin cutout with overlapping tissue paper squares. While the glue is drying, trace your hand twice on green construction paper; then cut out the tracings. To complete the project, glue the hand cutouts to the top of the pumpkin to resemble leaves.

I am thankful for
my dog.

I am thankful for
my mom.

I am thankful for
good food.

I am thankful for
toys.

A Grand Gobbler

This turkey makes a perfect centerpiece for a Thanksgiving feast! To make a turkey, copy the four feather patterns from page 284 onto colorful construction paper. Cut out each feather and write a different thankful thought on each one. Next, use glue to cover a six-inch length of a cardboard tube with brown tissue paper strips. When dry, arrange the feathers as shown and staple them together. Then glue the feathers to the back of the tube. Use construction paper scraps to add a turkey face to the front of the tube.

Snowflake Ornament

Use a pencil to sketch a simple snowflake shape on a sheet of waxed paper. Trace over the pencil lines with thick streams of glue. Then shake a small amount of glitter over the glue. Leave the shape to dry overnight. When the shape is firm, peel it off the waxed paper, punch a hole near one tip, and thread a yarn length through the hole. Tie the ends of the yarn to create an ornament.

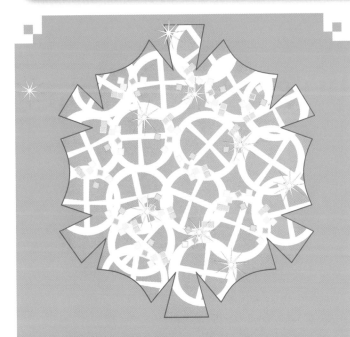

Spoolin' Around With Snowflakes

Create a blizzard of excitement with these icy wonders! To make a snowflake, cut out a blue construction paper copy of the snowflake pattern on page 285. Repeatedly press one end of a spool into paint and onto the snowflake. While the paint is still wet, sprinkle the entire snowflake with glitter and set aside to dry. If desired, hot-glue a tagboard ring to the back of the snowflake so that it's ready to top a holiday tree.

Gingerbread Hanger

These delightful gingerbread pals will fill your classroom with a delicious aroma. To make one, paint a tagboard gingerbread pal cutout (patterns on page 286) with brown tempera paint; then sprinkle the wet paint with pumpkin-pie spice or cinnamon. When the paint is dry, decorate the cutout with a variety of craft supplies such as glitter, ribbon, fabric scraps, and stickers. Punch a hole at the top and attach a ribbon hanger.

Frosty Snowpal

This cute little snowpal is sure to warm hearts. Cut out a tagboard copy of the snowpal pattern on page 284. Decorate the snowpal with felt scraps, ribbon, and other craft supplies. Cut two slits in the center of the snowpal where indicated; then insert a peppermint or cinnamon stick through the slits to create arms. Personalize each snowpal; then punch a hole in the top. Thread a length of ribbon through the hole and tie the ends together.

Madison

Sparkling Menorahs

Light up the Hanukkah season with this dazzling menorah!

Materials for each student:
paper plate
two 8" pieces of aluminum foil
12" x 18" sheet of black construction paper
eight ¾" x 5" strips of blue construction paper
¾" x 6" strip of blue construction paper
nine 1" squares of yellow construction paper
glue
scissors

Steps:

1. Fold the paper plate in half; then open it up and cut it in half on the crease.

2. Cover the base of each paper-plate half with aluminum foil.

3. To create the base of the menorah, glue the covered paper-plate halves onto the black paper so the curved edges meet as shown.

4. Glue the blue construction paper strips to the black paper to create candles as shown.

5. Cut a flame from each yellow square.

6. Glue a flame to the end of each candle.

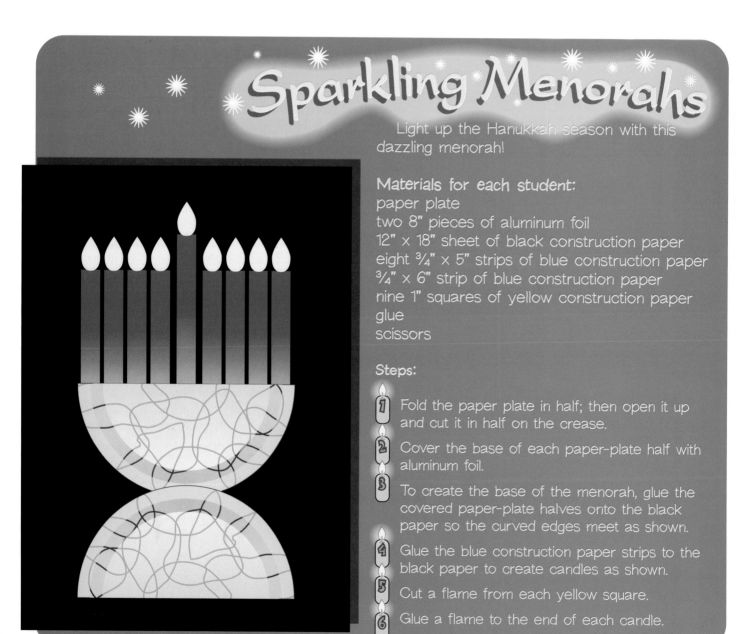

Radiant Rainbow

To make a rainbow, place drops of paint in rainbow colors along the left side of a sheet of paper. Then use one edge of a jumbo craft stick or ruler to pull the paint along the paper to resemble a rainbow. When the paint is dry, draw desired details and glue on cotton-ball clouds.

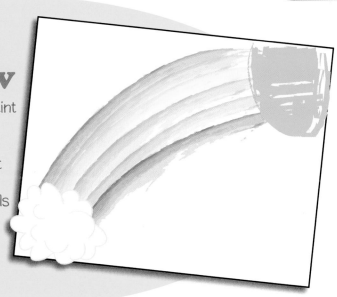

Heart Critters

If your students are wild about animals, February is the perfect time to create a bunch of wild-and-crazy critters. Provide students with various colors of construction paper, several sizes of heart-shaped templates, glue, crayons, and scissors. Have each student decide on an animal to make out of hearts; then have her trace and cut out construction paper hearts. Have each student glue the hearts together and use crayons to convert the hearts into a critter.

Shy Sheep

This shy sheep is a "shear" delight! To make one, glue cotton balls onto a paper doily, making sure the frilly edge remains exposed. Glue two 1" x 2" black construction paper strips to the lower edge of the doily to resemble legs. Make a face by folding down two points of a three-inch black construction paper triangle as shown. Glue the face to the center of the sheep's body. Add eyes, a cotton-ball tuft of hair, and a pink pom-pom nose to the sheep's face.

Bunny Puppet

Your little ones will be hopping down the bunny trail with this sweet puppet. Cover a length of a cardboard tube with white construction paper. Cut a pink pipe cleaner in half; then bend each piece into a loop to resemble a bunny ear. Glue the ears to the inside of one end of the tube. Make a face by gluing paper eyes, string whiskers, and a pink pom-pom nose onto the tube. Complete the bunny by drawing a mouth and gluing on a cotton-ball tail. To use the puppet, insert two fingers inside the tube and make the bunny hop!

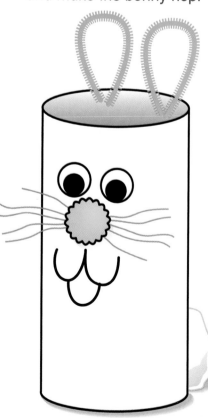

Monarch Magnets

Each child's handprints will make this butterfly magnet an extra special gift for Mother's Day or Father's Day. Invite a child to press his hand into paint and then onto a sheet of tagboard twice. When the paint is dry, cut out the two handprints. Have the child embellish the handprints with glitter and sequins. To assemble the butterfly, have the child glue the handprints to either side of a clothespin body to resemble wings. Then direct him to add eyes and glue pipe cleaner antennae to the clothespin. To complete the butterfly, attach a magnet to the back of the clothespin. If desired, ask each student to clip a greeting to the butterfly.

Happy Mother's Day!

Mr. Frog

To make a frog, paint the back of a red paper plate green. When the paint is dry, fold the plate in half so that the green side is facing out. Glue paper eyes to the top of two large green pom-poms; then glue the pom-poms to the plate. Create back legs by accordion-folding two 2" x 12" green construction paper strips. Glue the strips to the back of the plate as shown. Accordion-fold two 2" x 6" green construction paper strips; then glue them in place to create front legs. Trim all the legs at the ends as shown. To complete the frog, roll a narrow strip of red construction paper around a pencil; unroll it and then glue it to the inside rim to create a tongue.

Thumb Bugs in a Jar

Got the springtime bug? If so, then this project will get you buzzin'! For each child, outline a simple jar shape on a sheet of white construction paper. Have a child repeatedly press a thumb into paint and then onto her paper. When the paint is dry, have her use a marker to add wings, eyes, legs, and other bug features to each thumbprint. If desired, use the completed picture as a page in a number book or as a booklet cover. Bugs near, bugs far—how many bugs are in your bug jar?

Sunny Suncatchers

Fill your classroom with the warm glow of summer colors when you hang these "sun-sational" catchers in your windows. To make one, press a variety of craft materials—such as foil pieces, tissue paper scraps, and glitter—onto the adhesive side of a piece of clear Con-Tact covering. Cover the collage with another sheet of Con-Tact covering so that the adhesive sides are together. Trim the edges; then tape the collage into a black construction paper frame. Tape the suncatchers to your classroom window to create a stained-glass effect.

Exploratory ART

Glove Painting

Little ones will get a new feel for fingerpainting with this activity. Gather a variety of gloves: rubber gloves, old leather gloves, garden gloves, dress gloves, loofah mitts, or surgical gloves. (Ask for donations from parents or check out your local thrift shop.) Invite youngsters to wear different pairs of gloves as they fingerpaint. Have them observe the differences in the feel of the paint, and in the strokes and textures created on the paper or tabletop.

Padded Prints

Visit the foot-care aisle of the drugstore for some unique painting materials. Purchase a few packs of bunion or corn pads. Attach the self-adhesive pads to the fingers of a rubber dishwashing glove to create a random pattern of circles and ovals. Invite a child to put on the glove, use a paintbrush to apply tempera paint to the pads, and then press his gloved hand onto his paper. Help him reapply the paint as necessary.

Prepare several gloves (some left-handed and some right-handed) with different patterns, as well as trays of different paint colors. Invite several children to paint at once, trading gloves as they desire.

Salty Squeeze Paint

Create a mixture that is one part flour, one part salt, and two parts water. Stir the ingredients together thoroughly to remove lumps; then divide the mixture and add a different shade of food coloring to each portion. Pour each color of paint into a separate squeeze bottle. The mixture will be fairly thin, so provide thick drawing paper and have little ones squeeze designs onto their papers. Set the papers aside to dry thoroughly. Then check out the sparkly results!

Fingerpainting Fever!

Your youngsters will catch fingerpainting fever when you provide some unusual surfaces on which to paint. Try any or all of the following:

aluminum foil
plastic picture or poster frames
waxed paper
a shower curtain
large mirrors
cafeteria trays
vinyl tile samples
cookie sheets
grocery bags

Paint Prints—Neat!

If you've ever invited children to dip a printing item, such as a cookie cutter or a cut vegetable, into a container of paint, you know how messy the results can be. Try this tip for neater printing: Place a wet sponge in a disposable pie plate, sprinkle dry tempera paint on it, and then have children press the printing object onto the sponge to take on the color. Add water as necessary to keep the sponge wet.

Broom Painting

You may have considered your sidewalk as a canvas for chalk art, but have you considered a broom as a paintbrush? Why not? Gather several small brooms (like those from your housekeeping center) and a few buckets. Fill the buckets with water and invite youngsters to broom-paint water designs on the sidewalk. As a variation, spread long lengths of white bulletin board paper on the sidewalk. Add some food coloring to the water, and have children broom-paint colored designs on the paper. (Caution: The food coloring may permanently discolor the broom bristles, so consider this before you proceed.) This art activity is sure to be a sweeping success!

Combing Through Creativity

While you're feeling adventurous about painting tools, try using combs. Give the paint some texture for combing by thickening it with flour. Simply pour the thickened paint into squeeze bottles; then invite children to squeeze out paint onto their papers and run combs through the paint to create designs. Try combs of various sizes with teeth of different sizes and spacing.

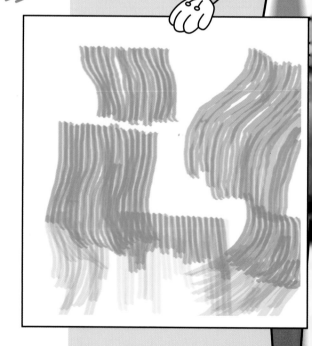

Scrubber Scribbles

For yet another paintbrush alternative, purchase (or ask parents to donate) a few nylon dish-scrubbing puffs. Clip each one to a spring-type clothespin. Provide a different color of tempera paint for each scrubber. Encourage a youngster to hold the clothespin handle and dip a scrubber into a shallow tray of paint, then press the scrubber on her paper to create a design. Have her continue with other colors as she desires.

Drip-Drop Painting

What do you get when you mix partners, pie plates, and paper? Drip-drop painting! To prepare, simply poke a few small holes in the bottoms of several aluminum pie plates. Pour a different color of thinned tempera paint into each of several small containers. Give a pie plate, a container, and a sheet of paper to a pair of children. Have one child slowly pour the thinned paint into the pie plate as his partner holds the pie plate over the paper. Have the child holding the pie plate rock it slowly as the children watch the paint drip through the holes. Invite them to add drips of different colors of paint to their creation if they desire.

Leaf Glitter

When autumn leaves fall, head outdoors to collect them and make some leaf glitter. Invite youngsters to crush some dry, crinkly leaves into small bits and chunks. Sprinkle the leaf glitter over spread glue (as you would glitter) or add it to tempera paint in fall colors for a lumpy, leafy texture. If desired, add some regular glitter to the leaf glitter for a special sparkle.

Dry/Wet Paintings

Usually paintings start out wet, then get dry. Reverse that process with this painting technique. Provide dry tempera paint in several colors, cotton balls, and paper. Encourage each youngster to dip a cotton ball into a paint color and brush it onto his paper. Have him continue this dry painting with as many colors as he desires. Then provide a container of water and some eyedroppers. Invite each artist to use an eyedropper to place drops of water onto his paper. Or have him dip his fingertips into the water and sprinkle water over the dry tempera, watching the colors move and meld. Then set the paintings aside to dry. A light coating of unscented hair-spray will provide a finishing coat.

Drive 'n' Draw

If your students love miniature cars, then they'll love this drawing activity! Use masking tape to securely attach a crayon (tip down) to the back of a toy car. Test the position of the crayon by "driving" the car over a piece of scrap paper. Adjust the position, if necessary, so that the crayon draws a line as the car moves. Prepare several car crayons in this manner, get out the paper, and steer your youngsters into a whole new art experience!

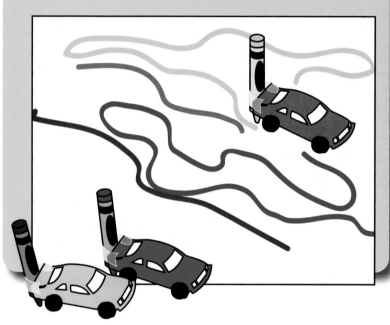

Foil Fun

Go beyond a construction paper picture when you provide aluminum foil instead. Give each artist a one-foot section of aluminum foil and a pair of scissors. Youngsters can strengthen cutting skills as they trim the foil into various shapes and forms of their choice. Have each child glue her foil pieces to a sheet of construction paper (black is especially striking). When the glue is dry, display the pictures. Then turn out the lights and have children take turns shining a flashlight on the pictures to observe their shiny creations.

Noodle Art

Create spaghetti art using overcooked spaghetti. Provide each child with a bowl of sticky spaghetti. Invite her to arrange the spaghetti onto a sheet of construction paper to create a design. When the spaghetti dries, it will stick to the paper.

RECIPES

For Arts and Crafts

Baking Dough

2 cups flour
1 cup salt
water

Mix the dry ingredients; then add enough water to create a workable dough. Invite children to sculpt figures or roll and cut the dough with cookie cutters. Bake the dough at 300°F for 1 to 1½ hours (depending on the thickness of each figure). Finished products can be painted.

Milk Paint

evaporated milk
food coloring

Divide one or more cans of evaporated milk evenly among several containers. Add a few drops of a different color of food coloring to each container and mix until the desired shades are achieved. Have youngsters paint with this mixture on construction paper to create a creamy, pastel look.

Magic Crystals

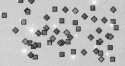

2 cups water
2 cups Epsom salts
food coloring (optional)

In a saucepan, combine the water and Epsom salts and bring to a boil. Stir the mixture and allow it to cool. If desired, add a few drops of food coloring. Have students paint with this mixture on construction paper. The paint will dry to create clear or colored crystals.

Decorative Dye

1 tablespoon rubbing alcohol
food coloring
rice or pasta

In a small, tightly lidded container, put one tablespoon of rubbing alcohol and a few drops of food coloring. Place rice or pasta into the mixture and seal the lid. Shake the container gently for one minute. Spread out the dyed objects on paper towels or newspaper until dry.

Teacher-Made Play Dough

1 cup flour
½ cup salt
2 teaspoons cream of tartar
1 cup water
1 teaspoon vegetable oil
food coloring

Mix the dry ingredients together. Then add the remaining ingredients and stir. In a heavy skillet, cook the mixture for two to three minutes, stirring frequently. Turn the dough onto a lightly floured surface and knead it until it becomes soft and smooth. Mix up a separate batch of dough for each color desired. Store the dough in an airtight container.

Colored Glue

food coloring
white glue

Add a few drops of a different color of food coloring to each of several empty squeeze bottles. Gradually add glue, using a drinking straw to stir the glue until it's evenly tinted.

Extra-Bright Tempera Paint

2 cups dry tempera paint
1 cup liquid soap (clear or white works best)
1 cup liquid starch

Mix the paint and soap; then add starch and stir. If the mixture becomes too thick, add more liquid soap. Store the paint in a coffee can with a plastic lid.

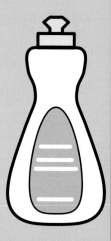

Bubble Mixture

¼ cup dishwashing liquid
½ cup water
1 teaspoon sugar
food coloring (optional)

Mix the dishwashing liquid, water, and sugar together in a container. If color is desired, mix in a few drops of food coloring.

Corn Syrup Paint

light corn syrup
food coloring

Divide one or more bottles of corn syrup evenly among several containers. Add a few drops of a different color of food coloring to each container and mix until the desired shades are achieved. This paint requires a few days of drying time.

Kool-Aid Dough

2½–3 cups flour
½ cup salt
1 package unsweetened Kool-Aid
1 tablespoon alum
2 cups boiling water
3 tablespoons corn oil
1 cup additional flour

Mix the first six ingredients into a dough. Using some or all of the additional flour, knead the dough until it reaches the desired consistency. Store the dough in an airtight container.

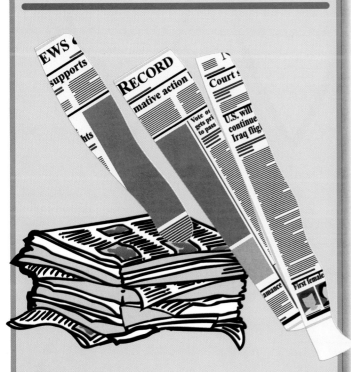

Easy Papier-Mâché

liquid starch
cold water
newspaper torn into strips

Mix equal parts of liquid starch and cold water. Dip the newspaper strips into the mixture before applying to a form of chicken wire or rolled newspaper.

Salt Paint

2 teaspoons salt
1 teaspoon liquid starch
a few drops of tempera paint

Mix the ingredients together. The salt gives a frosted appearance to the paint.

Colored Grits

liquid tempera paint
grits

In a large bowl, mix the ingredients, being careful not to let the grits get too wet. Spread the mixture onto cookie sheets to dry for a day or two, stirring occasionally. Use as you would colored sand.

Shiny Paint

1 part white liquid glue
1 part liquid tempera paint

Mix the ingredients. This paint will retain a wet look after it has dried.

Feather Patterns

Use with "A Grand Gobbler" on page 270.

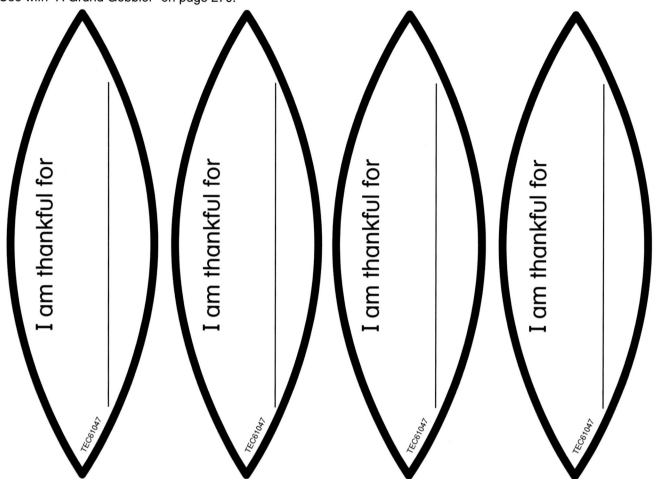

Snowpal Pattern

Use with "Frosty Snowpal" on page 272.

TEC61047

Gingerbread Pal Patterns
Use with "Gingerbread Hanger" on page 271.

TEC61047

TEC61047

TEC61047

TEC61047

IT'S FALL!

Welcome fall with a poem that reviews the five senses.

Fall is all around you.
Yes, it's time for fall.
Feel fall with your senses—
Five senses in all.

See fall with your two eyes,
In the leaves so bright.
Red and orange and brown leaves,
Such a pretty sight.

Hear fall with your two ears
As the birds fly by.
Squawking, honking, loud geese,
Calling way up high.

Smell fall with your nose,
In the chilly air.
Cool and damp and wet rain,
Falling everywhere.

Feel fall with your two hands,
On the clothes you wear.
Warm and snuggly, soft coat,
Like a fuzzy bear.

Taste fall with your tongue now,
In an apple sweet.
Juicy, crunchy apple—
What a yummy treat!

Fall is all around you.
Yes, it's time for fall.
Feel fall with your senses—
Five senses in all.

Johnny Appleseed Headbands

Your youngsters will love wearing these headbands for Johnny Appleseed's birthday (September 26). To make one, staple two 6" x 12" black construction paper strips end to end and glue an apple cutout to the center. Staple the resulting band to fit a child's head. Then round one end of a 3" x 9" construction paper rectangle to resemble a pot handle. Use a round or apple-shaped hole puncher to punch a hole in the rounded end of the handle. Fold the opposite end of the handle to create a tab for gluing. Then glue the handle to the headband as shown.

Exploring Apples

Here's a tasty way to help students compare and contrast. Ask volunteers to donate a class supply of four-ounce applesauce containers, plastic spoons, and a supply of apples cut into wedges. (If desired, sprinkle apple wedges with lemon juice to prevent browning.) On a large sheet of paper, draw an apple-themed Venn diagram similar to the one shown and add section titles. Display the resulting poster in your group area.

To begin, show students an apple and ask them to observe details about how the apple looks. Give each child an apple wedge and invite her to touch, taste, and smell it. Then give each youngster a container of applesauce and a spoon and have her explore the applesauce in the same manner. Guide students to use their observations and prior knowledge to compare and contrast the apple and the applesauce. Write each comment in the appropriate section of the diagram. To conclude, invite each youngster to finish eating her apple and applesauce.

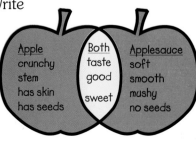

Apple	Both	Applesauce
crunchy	taste	soft
stem	good	smooth
has skin		mushy
has seeds	sweet	no seeds

The Leaves in the Trees

Rustle up a lesson on fall leaves with this lively movement exercise.

The leaves up in the top of trees
   (Hold hands above head; stand on toes.)
Sway from left to right.
   (Sway from left to right.)
Rustling softly in the breeze,
   (Slowly rub hands together.)
They swish throughout the night.
   (Swish arms to left and then right.)

A strong wind comes and shakes the trees.
   (Shake arms above head.)
They rattle in the wind.
   (Shake arms vigorously.)
Swaying wildly to and fro,
   (Sway arms above head.)
The branches bend and bend!
   (Bend from side to side.)

The strong wind blows the leaves all off!
   (Drop arms to sides.)
They flitter to the ground.
   (Wiggle fingers from over head to floor.)
Swirling, twirling, silently,
   (Twirl.)
They fall without a sound.
   (Touch floor.)

The leaves now crunch beneath my feet.
   (Step in place.)
I listen with a grin.
   (Smile broadly.)
I rake them in a great big pile.
   (Pretend to rake.)
And then I jump right in!
   (Sit on the floor.)

Leave It to Autumn

Youngsters discover their classmates favorite fall colors with this group graphing activity. Make a large graph, as shown, with drawings of leaves in each of the following colors: yellow, red, orange, and brown. Cut construction paper squares in the same four colors. Ask each child to choose the leaf color she likes best and write her name on a construction paper square of that color. Then have her attach her square to the graph beside the appropriate leaf. Have students count the squares in each row and determine which leaf color is the class favorite.

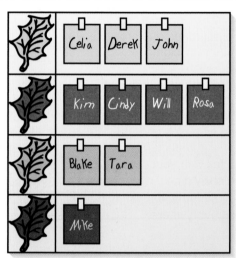

Leaf Look-Alikes

Spark students' imaginations with fall foliage! In advance collect a class supply of a variety of leaves. Invite each youngster to choose a leaf. Have him place a sheet of white paper on top of the leaf and firmly rub an unwrapped crayon over it to make a leaf rubbing. Next, ask him to add desired details to his leaf rubbing to make the leaf part of a drawing. Then ask him to write or dictate a sentence to describe what the leaf represents in his illustration.

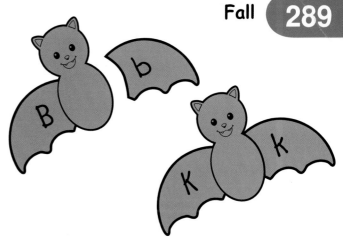

Seed Sets

Get ready for plenty of math practice in this pumpkin patch center! To prepare, make ten white seed cutouts and ten orange pumpkin cutouts. Program each pumpkin with a different number from 1 to 10. Make the center self-checking by drawing the corresponding number of seeds on the back of each pumpkin. Store the pumpkins and seeds in a basket at a center. A child visits the center and chooses a pumpkin. He counts out the corresponding number of seeds and places them near the pumpkin. Then he checks his work by flipping the pumpkin over. He continues in this manner for each remaining pumpkin.

Missing Wings

This matching center can be programmed for practice with a wide variety of skills! To prepare, make several construction paper copies of the bat patterns on page 291. Choose a skill, such as uppercase and lowercase letters, and for each bat write corresponding items on each of the wings. Then cut out the pieces and store them in a large envelope at a center. A child visits the center and finds the corresponding wing to match each bat.

Hungry Jack

Little ones will be hungry for knowledge when you add this activity to your fall circle time. To prepare, cut a simple jack-o'-lantern shape from orange poster board and cut an opening for the mouth. Attach the cutout to a large shoebox so the box sits below the mouth opening. Then program a set of index cards for a basic skill you'd like to reinforce, such as letters, numerals, or shapes.

Each day during circle time, bring out the cards and introduce the jack-o'-lantern as Hungry Jack. Present a card and ask a volunteer to identify the symbol shown. If the child is correct, he may "feed" the card to Hungry Jack. Continue as time permits and add cards for other skills as desired.

Turkeys on Top!

Unique patterns will abound when your youngsters make these adorable hats! To make a hat, each youngster paints a cone-shaped birthday hat brown. After the paint is dry, he adds details—such as eyes, a beak, and a wattle—to his turkey. Then he uses colorful feather cutouts to make a pattern. When he is satisfied with his work, he glues the feathers to his hat as shown.

I am thankful for my family.

I am thankful for my dog.

I am thankful for food to eat.

I am thankful for my teacher.

A Thankful Quilt

Showcase students' thankfulness on this delightful display. Program a sheet of paper with the phrase "I am thankful for…" and copy a class supply on colorful construction paper. Give one to each child and ask her to write and illustrate something she is thankful for. When each child is finished, assemble the completed pieces to resemble a quilt. Embellish the quilt as desired and display the finished product with an appropriate title.

The Turkey Lurkey

Your youngsters will be struttin' their stuff when they sing this plucky version of "The Hokey-Pokey."

(sung to the tune of "The Hokey-Pokey")

You put your wing in. You put your wing out.
You put your wing in, and you flap it all about.
You do the Turkey Lurkey, and you turn
    yourself around.
That's what it's all about! Gobble, gobble!
You put your drumstick in…
You put your wattle in…
You put your tail feathers in…
You put your whole turkey in…

Check out the skill-building reproducibles on pages 292 and 293.

TEC61047

Name_____

Beginning Sounds: /b/, /m/, /t/

Falling Leaves

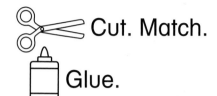 Cut. Match.

Glue.

Bb **Mm** **Tt**

©The Mailbox® • Superbook® • TEC61047

Name_____

Plenty of Pumpkin Seeds

 Count.

Write.

Programming Suggestions: Use a copy of this page for a newsletter, a parent note, a booklist, or a student's creative writing.

Programming Suggestions: Use a copy of this page for a newsletter, a parent note, a booklist, or a student's creative writing.

©The Mailbox® • *Superbook*® • TEC61047

Programming Suggestions: Use a copy of this page for a newsletter, a parent note, a booklist, or a student's creative writing.

Flurry of Numbers

Youngsters will have a ball practicing number writing at this center! Place a supply of cotton balls (snowballs) and a class supply of a recording sheet, similar to the one shown, at a center. A child visits the center and arranges the snowballs in the shape of a number of her choosing. When she is pleased with her number, she writes it on her recording sheet. She repeats the process for each box on the sheet by forming and writing a different number each time.

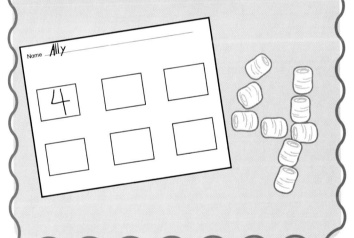

Frosty Friends

To make a snowpal, each youngster glues two or three white construction paper circles to a sheet of colorful construction paper. Then he uses a variety of craft supplies to add desired details. When he is satisfied with his snowpal, he writes or dictates a sentence to describe it.

My snowpal has colorful hair.

Five Little Snowpals

Youngsters practice counting to five as they recite this chilly chant. If desired, make snowpal puppets and invite a different group of five children to use the puppets to act out the poem for each reading.

Five little snowpals shivering in the ice.
The first one said, "This isn't very nice."
The second one said, "I can hardly wait for spring."
The third one said, "Then birds will sing!"
The fourth one said, "Here comes the bright, warm sun!"
The fifth one said, "This is our last day of fun!"
"Aah," said the snow as warm breezes blew.
Five little snowpals know winter is through.

A Bright Idea

Here's an idea that will light up your classroom. In advance, hang a strand of colorful lights out of student reach. To begin, lead children in counting the number of bulbs there are on the strand. Then ask a different student volunteer to name the color of each bulb. Guide students in counting how many bulbs there are of each color and in finding the pattern made by the placement of each bulb. To repeat the activity, change the color and position of each bulb as desired.

The ABC Tree

The alphabet becomes a holiday decoration in this small-group game. To prepare, cut a large Christmas tree from a piece of green tagboard. Select several letters you'd like to review with your students. Prepare uppercase and lowercase cutouts of these letters or plan to use letter manipulatives. To begin, decorate the tree with the uppercase letters. Then distribute the lowercase letters to children in the group. Ask each child, in turn, to replace the correct uppercase letter with her lowercase version. If time permits, try the reverse: have students replace lowercase letters with uppercase ones.

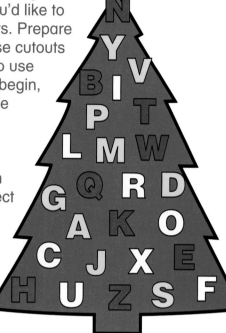

Hanukkah Candles

Brighten a celebration of Hanukkah by singing this catchy tune.

(sung to the tune of "This Little Light of Mine")

These little candles bright,
Are such a pretty sight.
These little candles bright,
Are such a pretty sight.
These little candles bright,
Are such a pretty sight.
Let them shine!
Let them shine!
Let them shine!

Colorful Kwanzaa

Explain to students that Kwanzaa is traditionally represented by three colors—black, red, and green. Black represents the African-American people, red symbolizes their struggles, and green stands for a happy future. In honor of this cultural celebration, place a supply of various sizes of red, green, and black pom-poms in a basket at a center. Invite a child to visit the center and sort the pom-poms by color. Then have him sort the pom-poms again using a different attribute, such as size. If desired, challenge him to sort the pom-poms another time using both attributes.

Resolution Roundup

To begin this circle-time activity, discuss with youngsters the tradition of making a New Year's resolution. Invite students to think of a resolution they would like to make. Then give a noisemaker or party hat to a child and ask her to share her chosen resolution with the group. After she has shared, have her pass the prop to the child seated beside her. Continue in this manner until each student has had a chance to share her resolution.

Cheer for the New Year

Sing this festive song to welcome the new year into your classroom.

(sung to the tune of "Row, Row, Row Your Boat")

Cheer, cheer, let's all cheer.
January's here!
Hip, hip, hooray! The very first day
Of a brand new year.

100th-Day Fingerplay

Lead youngsters in chanting this rhyme to celebrate the 100th day and also to practice skip-counting by tens.

(chanted to the rhythm of "Bubble Gum, Bubble Gum")

We deserve, we deserve a lot of praise.
We've been at school one hundred days!
10, 20, 30, 40, 50, 60, 70, 80, 90, 100.
Hooray, hooray, hooray!

Dr. King's Dream

Invite youngsters to share their dreams as they make this class book. To begin, remind youngsters of Martin Luther King's famous "I Have a Dream" speech. Explain that Dr. King's dream was not a dream he had when he was sleeping. Instead, it was his hope or wish for the future. Invite students to share their dreams for the future. Then ask each youngster to draw a picture of his dream and write or dictate a sentence to describe it. When each child has completed his page, fasten all the pages between two construction paper covers and add a title such as "Our Class Dreams."

Pepl wl b nis to ech oter.

Hearty Numbers

To prepare for this partner game, number a construction paper grid like the one shown for every two students. Then give each twosome a grid, a pair of jumbo dice, and a container of small, colorful heart cutouts. To begin, Player 1 rolls the dice, determines the sum of the numbers he rolled, and places a heart cutout on the corresponding box on the grid. If that number is already covered, his turn is over. Player 2 takes a turn in the same manner. Alternate play continues until the entire grid is filled. To extend the activity, challenge students to roll the dice to remove the corresponding heart cutouts from their grids in the same manner.

2	3	4	5	6	7	8	9	10	11	12

Presidential Coin Sort

Invite youngsters to cash in their sorting skills at this hands-on center. Make a few copies of page 301. Cut the patterns apart and store each set in a separate resealable plastic bag. Then place the bags at a center. A child visits the center, takes a bag, and places the coins and presidential cards faceup on his workspace. After studying the presidential sorting mats, he chooses a coin and sorts it onto the appropriate mat. He repeats this process until all of his coins are sorted correctly.

Abraham Lincoln is on the penny.

George Washington is on the quarter.

A Valentine Is...

Spread a little love and cheer with this seasonal song.

(sung to the tune of "My Bonnie Lies Over the Ocean")

A valentine is very special.
A valentine is very sweet.
A valentine is very friendly.
A true valentine can't be beat.

Will you, will you,
Oh, will you be my valentine? Be mine!
Will you, will you,
Oh, will you be my valentine?

Check out the skill-building reproducibles on pages 302 and 303.

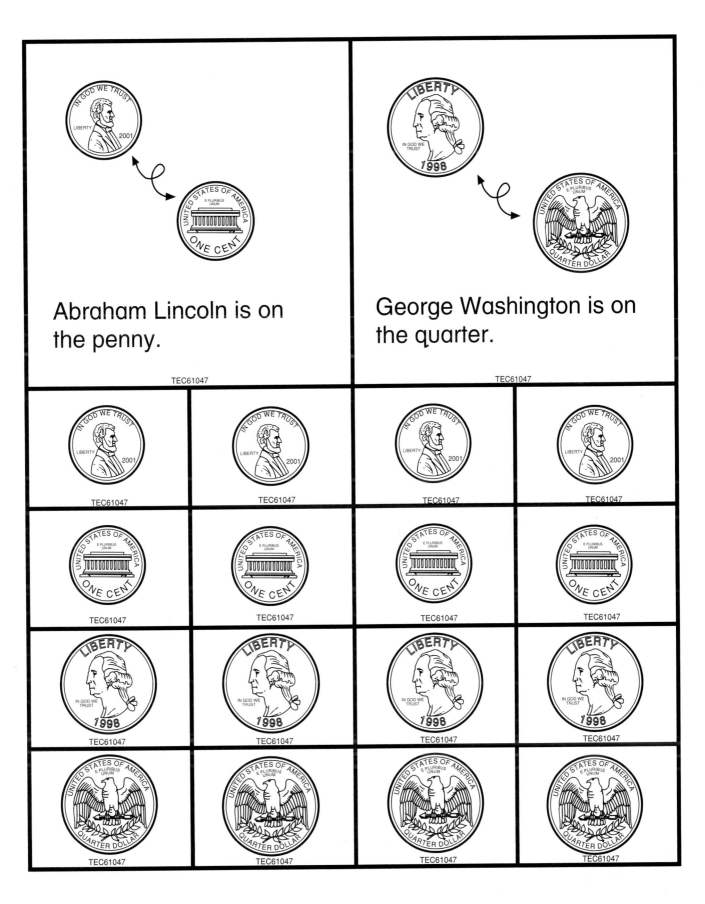

Abraham Lincoln is on the penny.

TEC61047

George Washington is on the quarter.

TEC61047

Sweet Treats

Color the cookies that are divided into equal parts.

Special Delivery

Cut.
Glue to match.

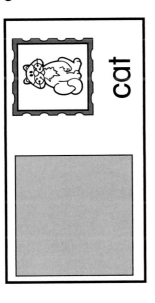

cat	

dog	

king	

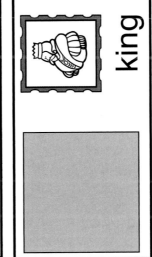

man

rug	

pear	

 bat

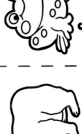 frog

 bear

 bug

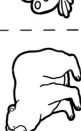 ring

 can

©The Mailbox® • Superbook® • TEC61047

303

Programming Suggestions: Use a copy of this page for a newsletter, a parent note, a booklist, or a student's creative writing.

Programming Suggestions: Use a copy of this page for a newsletter, a parent note, a booklist, or a student's creative writing.

Programming Suggestions: Use a copy of this page for a newsletter, a parent note, a booklist, or a student's creative writing.

Spring Is Here!

Take your youngsters outside to breathe the fresh spring air and feel the warm sun. Then use this poem as a springboard for discussing and anticipating lots of spring fun.

Spring is here! Let's all cheer!
Time for bikes and nature hikes.
Time for skates and picnic dates.
Time for the park and games at dark.
Time for friends and tent weekends.
Time to cheer—new life is here!

It's a Breeze

A warm and breezy spring day is the perfect setting for a lesson on air power. Place several small objects—such as a feather, a key, a cotton ball, a piece of paper, a wood block, a toy car, and a Ping-Pong ball—on a table. Ask your students to help you sort the items according to which are easy to move with air and which are not. Then take students outside and place the items on the ground. Watch what happens as the wind blows. Ask students if their predictions were correct.

If the weather is not cooperative, have your children provide the wind power. Invite a child to blow through a drinking straw to create a "gust" of wind directed at each object. Ask students to compare their predictions with what really happened.

A Windy Day

Once youngsters are familiar with this song, encourage each child to substitute the boldfaced word with something else that the wind blows.

*(sung to the tune of
"Row, Row, Row Your Boat")*

What does the March wind blow
On a windy day?
Tumbling, tumbling, **paper** is tumbling.
Watch it blow away!

What does the March wind blow
On a windy day?
Tumbling, tumbling, **leaves** are tumbling.
Watch them blow away!

Lots of Luck

Spark students' imaginations with a lucky charm! To begin, have each student make four heart-shaped cutouts from green construction paper. Ask him to glue the hearts together to resemble a four-leaf clover as shown. Then have him add a stem and label the bottom of the clover with his name. Next, help him write on a blank card a reason he feels lucky and glue his card to his clover. Display the finished projects with a title such as, "We Feel Lucky!"

I am luKy to hav a good famly. Tha ar nis.

JaRed

Sorting Bows

Students count syllables at this high-flying center. To prepare, number three construction paper kite cutouts and tape a length of string to each. Copy and cut out the bow cards on page 311 and place them in a container. Set the container at a center along with the kite cutouts. A child visits the center and lays out each numbered kite. Then she chooses a bow and names the picture. She counts the number of syllables in the pictured word (clapping quietly if desired) and places the bow card onto the corresponding kite string. She sorts the remaining bows in the same manner.

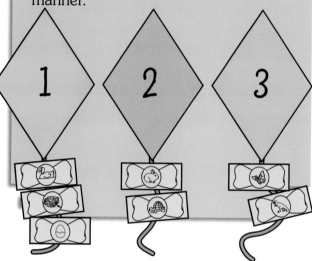

BEAUTIFUL SPRING

With this action rhyme, youngsters demonstrate how April showers bring May flowers!

Here's April rain that drizzles down.
(Hold arms up and wiggle fingers as arms lower.)
Here is the sun that warms the ground.
(Form circle above head with arms.)
Here is the seed, so very small.
(Press thumb and pointer finger together.)
Here is the plant, so strong and tall.
(Hold arms up straight, above head.)
Here is the bud that blooms one day.
(Clasp hands together, above head.)
Here's the pretty flower. It must be May!
(Open hands and spread fingers wide to form a flower.)

How Many Eggs?

Students will be "eggs-pert" counters after visiting this center. In advance, label each of several baskets with a different number from 1 to 10. For each basket, gather a matching number of plastic eggs. Place all of the eggs in a container. Then set the container at a center along with the labeled baskets. A child visits the center and chooses a basket. She reads the number on the basket and places the corresponding number of eggs inside. She continues in this manner until each basket holds the appropriate number of eggs.

BOPPIN' BUNNY HOP

Reinforce left and right concepts when you teach your little ones this bunny hop. To make a bunny-ear headband for each child in your class, staple a construction paper bunny-ear shape to each side of a construction paper band. Staple the ends of the strip together; then glue a cotton ball to the back. Give each child a headband to wear.

Have students make a line, and direct each child to place her hands on the shoulders of the child in front of her. Instruct students in the following steps for this modified version of the bunny hop: feet together, right heel out, feet together, left heel out, feet together, jump forward three times. Hop, hop, hop!

Alphabet Egg Hunt

To prepare, place a different letter manipulative inside each of 26 plastic eggs. Then hide the eggs in your classroom. Invite a small group of children to find the eggs. Ask them to open the eggs and identify the letters they find inside. Challenge students to place the letters in alphabetical order. They'll know that they've located all the eggs when the alphabet is complete. Finally, ask youngsters to replace the letters in the eggs and hide them for the next group of children.

Flower Petals

Make counting skills blossom at this small-group center! Cut four one-inch circles from yellow construction paper and 32 petal shapes from red construction paper. Place the flower pieces and a jumbo die in a large resealable plastic bag at your math center. Invite four children to visit the center. Each child takes a yellow circle (a flower center). Instruct the players to take turns rolling the die and adding the corresponding number of petals to their flowers. Play continues until each player has eight petals on his flower. Then have players roll the die and remove the corresponding number of petals, replacing them in the plastic bag.

Bugs in a Box

Students will go buggy over this small-group guessing game. To prepare, collect several small shoeboxes with lids. Put a different number of plastic bugs in each box. Invite each child in the group to shake one box and estimate the number of bugs inside. Record all the guesses on a sheet of chart paper. Then open the box and count together the actual number of plastic bugs to determine whose guess was closest to the actual number. Repeat the activity with the remaining boxes.

I liked when we went to the pmpkn pach.

Jared
Tommy   Will
Emily   Michael
            Ryan
    Eric   Pam
Sandra   Matt
        A.J.

Up, Up, and Away

Try this idea to give students a memorable keepsake of the school year! Use colorful construction paper to make a large, balloon-shaped cutout for each child. Then have each youngster draw a picture of her favorite memory from the school year on her balloon and write or dictate a sentence to describe it. Attach a length of yarn to each balloon as shown. Invite students to collect their classmates' signatures on the back of their balloons before taking them home.

Check out the skill-building reproducibles on pages 312 and 313.

Bow Patterns

Use with "Sorting Bows" on page 308.

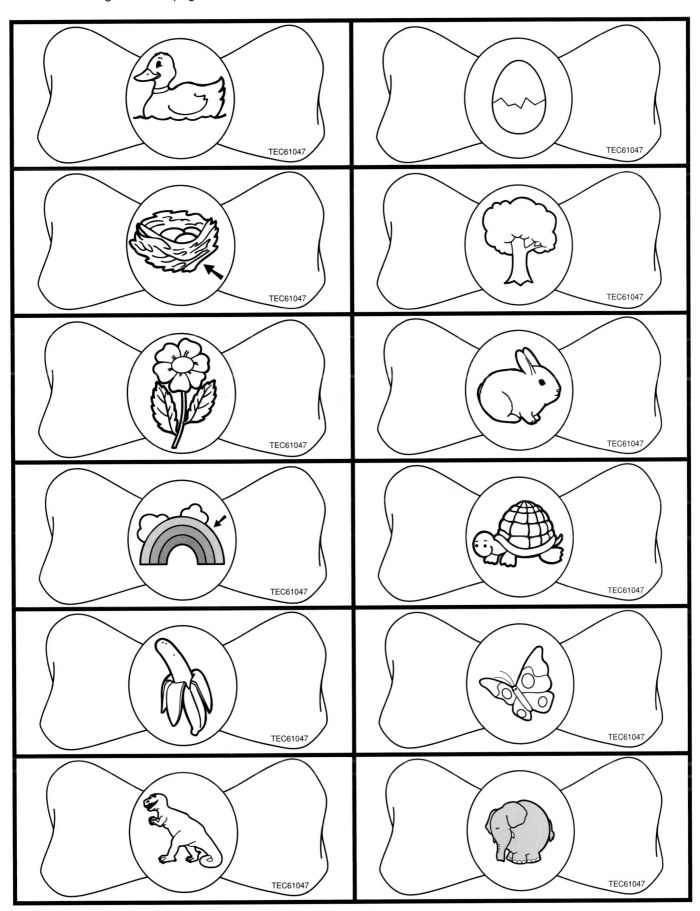

A Rainy Day

Count.

Write how many are in each set.

Add.

____ + ____ = ____

____ + ____ = ____

____ + ____ = ____

____ + ____ = ____

____ + ____ = ____

____ + ____ = ____

____ + ____ = ____

____ + ____ = ____

Name _____

Spring Chicks

Name each picture.
Write each word.

-an

-at

©The Mailbox® • Superbook® • TEC61047

Programming Suggestions: Use a copy of this page for a newsletter, a parent note, a booklist, or a student's creative writing.

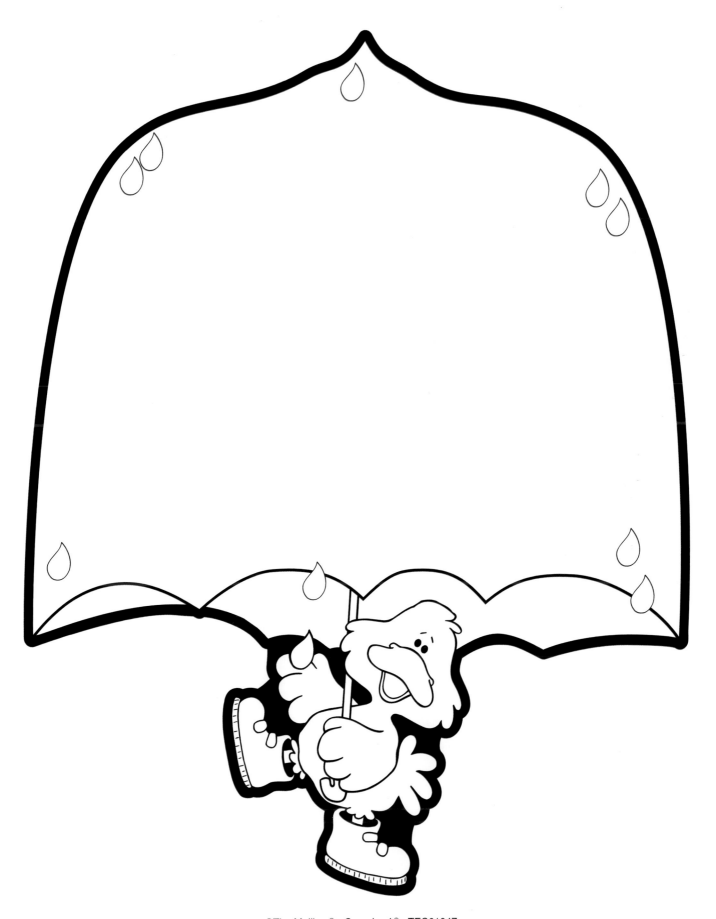

Programming Suggestions: Use a copy of this page for a newsletter, a parent note, a booklist, or a student's creative writing.

Programming Suggestions: Use a copy of this page for a newsletter, a parent note, a booklist, or a student's creative writing.

Index